To Improve the Academy

To Improve the Academy

Resources for Faculty, Instructional, and Organizational Development

Volume 18

Matthew Kaplan, Editor
University of Michigan

Devorah Lieberman, Associate Editor
Portland State University

ANKER PUBLISHING COMPANY, INC.

Bolton, Massachusetts

To Improve the Academy
Resources for Faculty, Instructional, and Organizational Development

Volume 18

ISBN 1-882982-31-2

Composition by Sherican Books, Inc.
Cover design by Boynton Hue Studio

Anker Publishing Company, Inc.
176 Ballville Road
P.O. Box 249
Bolton, MA 01740-0249

www.ankerpub.com

To Improve the Academy

To Improve the Academy is published annually by the Professional and Organizational Development Network in Higher Education (POD) through Anker Publishing Company, and is abstracted in ERIC documents and in Higher Education Abstracts.

ORDERING INFORMATION

The annual volume of *To Improve the Academy* is distributed to members at the POD conference in the autumn of each year. To order or to obtain ordering information, contact:

Anker Publishing Company, Inc.
P.O. Box 249
Bolton, MA 01740-0249
voice (978) 779-6190
fax (978) 779-6366
email ankerpub@aol.com
web www.ankerpub.com

PERMISSION TO COPY

INSTRUCTIONS TO CONTRIBUTORS FOR THE NEXT VOLUME

Anyone interested in the issues related to instructional, faculty, and organizational development in higher education may submit manuscripts. Manuscripts are submitted to the current editors in December of each year and sent through a blind review process. Correspondence, including requests for information about guidelines and submission of manuscripts for Volume 19, should be directed to:

Devorah Lieberman
Center for Academic Excellence
Portland State University
Portland, OR 97207-0751
(503) 725-5642 voice
(503) 725-5262 fax
liebermand@pdx.edu

Professional and Organizational Development Network in Higher Education (POD)

Mission Statement

Approved by the Core Committee on March 24, 1991:

The Professional and Organizational Development Network in Higher Education (POD) fosters human development in higher education through faculty, instructional, and organizational development.

POD believes that people have value, as individuals and as members of groups. The development of students is a fundamental purpose of higher education and requires for its success effective advising, teaching, leadership, and management. Central to POD's philosophy is lifelong, holistic, personal, and professional learning growth, and change for the higher education community.

The three purposes of POD are:

1) To provide support and services for its members through publications, conferences, consulting, and networking.

2) To offer services and resources to others interested in faculty development.

3) To fulfill an advocacy role, nationally, seeking to inform and persuade educational leaders of the value of faculty, instructional, and organizational development in institutions of higher education.

Membership, Conference, and Programs Information

For information contact:

David Graf
POD Network
Center for the Advancement of Teaching and Learning
Valdosta State University / 1115A Slater
Valdosta, GA 31698
(912) 293-6065

Table of Contents

Preface

The theme of the 1998 POD conference, Collaboration, Connections, and Community, is reflected in this year's edition of *To Improve the Academy*, both in terms of product and process. The product contains three sections. Section I contains articles on organizational development, an inherently cooperative undertaking; Section II deals explicitly with programs that involve connections between individuals or units to improve teaching and learning; and the articles in Section III examine assumptions about various members of the teaching and learning community including educational developers, faculty, and students.

The process of putting together this volume of *To Improve the Academy* involved the collaborative effort of many individuals, beginning with the authors who submitted manuscripts this year and the reviewers whose careful reading and commentary formed the basis for the current volume. Educational developers tend to work at or over capacity much of the year, collaborating with instructors and administrators on their campuses to improve the climate for student learning. It takes a special dedication to work beyond the walls of one's own institution by setting aside time to share insights about current practice in the field.

In particular, I wish to thank Devorah Lieberman, the Associate Editor. Devorah took on a number of roles this year. She served as a reviewer and worked with the keynote speakers on their articles; acted as a liaison with members of the publications committee as we made the transition to a new publisher; and offered her advice and support all along the way. *TIA* could not be in better hands for the next two years.

I also wish to acknowledge the work of three of my University of Michigan colleagues. Lisa Mets, the Associate Director of the Center for Research on Learning and Teaching (CRLT), filled in for one of the reviewers at the last minute. Jennifer Sinor spent long hours doing careful work as an editorial assistant. And Connie Cook, Director of CRLT, was, once again, supportive and encouraging of my work with POD.

This year marks a transition for *To Improve the Academy*, as we work with Anker Publishing Company for the first time. Jim Anker has been both thoughtful and patient in helping us adjust to a new system. And Susan Anker provided much needed advice as we did final preparation of the manuscript. We look forward to a successful and productive collaboration in the future between Anker and POD.

Matthew Kaplan
University of Michigan
Ann Arbor, Michigan
July 1999

Introduction

The articles brought together in this volume of *To Improve the Academy* reflect both the 1998 POD conference theme—Collaborations, Connections and Community—and the changing priorities within faculty development. The shift to organizational issues and long-term collaborations and away from individual services and one-time events has been underway for several years now, and approximately two-thirds of the articles in the current volume focus on that trend. Authors of the remaining articles explore more traditional faculty and instructional development topics, but they do so by examining how long-held assumptions may no longer be valid. Significantly, this reexamination is not restricted to the academy and the constituents with whom POD members work; it also involves a careful look at POD as an organization, our priorities, values, and our vision for the future.

Section I: Organizational Change in the Academy and in POD begins with three articles that undertake this self-reflective approach to organizational development within POD. As we approach this topic, we need to place ourselves in the roles of learners and realize that, while the development of critical thinking skills is a necessary part of higher learning, it can also be an uncomfortable process for learners since it entails a questioning of fundamental values and assumptions. POD members experienced some moments of great discomfort at last year's conference when a speaker at a plenary session made remarks many of us found to be racist and offensive. As an organization and as individuals, we have the opportunity to learn from that experience if we expend the necessary effort to reflect on and think critically about what happened. By documenting the events of last year, examining their significance, and putting them into historical context, the first three pieces of Section I help us begin this task. At the same time these articles still represent only four perspectives. Hopefully, we can find venues to broaden the conversation and involve a larger and more diverse group in this important dialogue.

Lewis and Gillespie each address the critical incident in a personal essay but from different perspectives. Lewis writes as a faculty member of color new to POD but with considerable experience in faculty development, especially as it relates to the needs of faculty of color. She documents her reactions to the POD conference, the plenary incident, and the organization's response to it. She then moves on to a discussion of her experiences at a conference on recruiting and retaining faculty of color. From that latter conference Lewis offers research and personal evidence of the importance of effective faculty development efforts to address the needs of faculty from under-represented groups. Gillespie writes from a different perspective, as a white faculty developer in a predominantly white organization and as the immediate Past-President and an early member of POD. She goes back to the POD mission to reiterate some of our central values and then looks at how these values were challenged by the critical incident. She goes on to explore the reactions to that incident as a reassertion of POD's basic values. She suggests that this type of response is necessary (both in POD and in the academy at large) to assure that our institutions live up to our ideals. The self-reflective part of Section I ends with an article by Stanley and Ouellet, two long-time advocates of diversity within POD. They review the history of efforts to make POD a more multicultural organization, not only in terms of membership, but also with regards to mission, policies, programming, etc. Using the literature on multicultural organizational development, they trace POD's history in incorporating diversity and chart a path for how we might create a truly inclusive, multicultural organization in the future.

The final three articles in Section I explore the topic of organizational change in the academy. Laycock offers a perspective from an institution in the UK where change has been mandated from outside the academy. On the one hand he explores the background for the mistrust that can sometimes characterize the relationship between higher education and society as a whole (often represented by ill-conceived attempts at regulation). On the other hand he describes a process for self-examination developed within his institution that responds to needs for accountability but also empowers faculty to set the agenda for change and for their own development. Middendorf addresses the question of how educational developers can help to foster change on their campuses by seeking out and working with key members of the faculty. These change agents include opinion leaders and some early adapters, and she describes ways to identify these individuals and collaborate with them most effectively to achieve change. Finally, Cambridge describes the efforts underway at the national level to use Boyer's concept of the scholarship of teaching as a lever to effect change in the academy. She describes programs sponsored by Carnegie, Pew, AAHE, and others to bring together faculty working on their teaching as scholarly projects. She examines the potential for these efforts to alter the value system of higher education.

The conference theme takes center stage in the six articles in *Section II: Collaboration and Partnerships*. In each article, the programs described are strengthened and made more effective by the collaborative efforts of those involved. Cox and Sorenson discuss a specific method by which educational developers can promote the shift from a teaching to a learning paradigm by involving students in their activities for faculty. The authors provide several examples of ways that teaching centers on their campuses and others have incorporated students into their programs. These include the use of students as consultants and observers, participants with faculty in discussions at workshops, and members of a learning community with faculty. In addition to offering guidelines for working with undergraduates, Cox and Sorenson raise the larger issue of how this type of collaboration has the potential to place students in the role of change agents on a campus. Osborne, Browne, Shapiro, and Wagor describe how a group of faculty members in psychology completely revised the introductory survey course. The authors began by undertaking institutional research through which they discovered that the course was not addressing students' real needs. They then developed exit competencies and reworked the course to include a critical thinking lab, undergraduate teaching assistants, and a common final exam. The end product was a course for which the whole team of faculty felt ownership and responsibility for student success.

The remainder of the pieces in Section II explore initiatives that draw on cooperative efforts between educational developers and others, including a coordinator of teaching technology, faculty members, and the assessment office. Shih and Sorcinelli describe an ongoing project that brings together the expertise of the teaching center director and the coordinator of teaching technology to create programs integrating the new technology with principles of good teaching and learning. They describe the process used to identify faculty needs and examine in depth a program that brought together senior faculty who wanted to develop technology-related projects for their teaching. Cottell, Hansen, and Ronald report on a cooperative effort between writing specialists and faculty in the disciplines aimed at helping faculty teach writing more effectively. The writing specialist works closely with the faculty member, learning about the course and the discipline. Together they identify student difficulties and develop strategies to make more explicit the writing conventions of the discipline that otherwise remain "transparent." By learning the language of the discipline, students not only improve their writing skills, but they also come away with a deeper understanding of the content.

The reality of scarce resources always influences the scope of work possible for educational developers. Wilhite, Lunde, and Latta discuss how their center expanded its offerings by using faculty associates to lead campus-wide discussion groups. In the process, the faculty associates become advocates for issues of teaching and learning and draw in colleagues from their own units who might not otherwise attend center events. This strategy of using a small set of faculty to affect a wider audience is also the basis for the program described by Ross, Schwaller, and Helmin. The directors of the teaching center and the campus assessment office worked together to meet a common goal: increasing the use of formative assessment and classroom research in classes across campus. Their strategy was to have departments nominate faculty who would participate in an extensive training and support program and then disseminate their learning about classroom assessment and research to colleagues in their unit.

The authors in *Section III: Examining Assumptions About Teaching and Faculty Development* ask us to think critically about our work as instructors and developers. Kreber and Cranton take issue with a central feature of the faculty career trajectory, the need to integrate teaching, research, and service throughout one's career. Based on the literature around expertise, they claim that integration is a long-term project that can best be fostered by allowing faculty to develop their expertise in one area initially. That in-depth experience will then allow them to turn to the other two areas and create a truly integrated, rather than fragmented, professional identity. Brookfield and Preskill take on another very basic issue for developers, the understanding and uses of classroom discussion. They focus on misplaced assumptions by both developers and faculty and how those misunderstandings can prevent faculty from adopting the discussion method and using it successfully. They offer both concrete suggestions for ways to realistically address faculty concerns and strategies to recalibrate instructor and student expectations for what a good discussion should look and feel like.

The need to consider both faculty and students is the basis for Stassen's article. Using a qualitative approach based on extensive interviewing, she explores the question of how faculty "develop" by teaching in a program designed to acculturate first-year students to the university. While most studies have focused on how these programs affect students, Stassen finds that they also make an impact on faculty and their understanding of student culture and preparedness and even the nature of good teaching. Just as faculty might experience "culture shock" working closely with first-year students, developers often experience similar feelings when they consult in unfamiliar disciplines. Lee explores these difficulties from a conceptual perspective and then uses the hard sciences as a case study of what developers need to know and do to be effective when working beyond their disciplinary expertise. The nature of the environment in which we do our work is the topic for Wright's article. She reports on the results of a survey of teaching centers at Research I and Research II universities. The questions she explores include the size and budget of centers, the backgrounds and classifications of both directors and staff, and vision for new initiatives in the future.

The articles in this year's *To Improve the Academy* reflect a field that has internalized certain changes and is still grappling with others. Taken together, the information they report and the ways in which they challenge us to think carefully about how and why we work as we do should help us as we turn to next year's conference topic, "New Pathways Through the Field."

Matthew Kaplan
University of Michigan
Ann Arbor, Michigan
July 1999

Section I:

Organizational Change in the Academy and in POD

1

Diversity and Its Discontents: Rays of Light in the Faculty Development Movement for Faculty of Color

Edith A. Lewis
University of Michigan

Two faculty development conferences held within a six-day period during October 1998 yielded important experiences and lessons for faculty and professionals interested in working with faculty of color. This paper, written from the standpoint of a faculty member of color, outlines the strengths and challenges of working on these issues in higher education institutions.

Introduction

Journal entry, Saturday, October 18, 1998, 6:45 p.m. EST. I am on a flight between Salt Lake City, Utah, and Minneapolis, Minnesota, moving between two conferences focusing on faculty development issues. The first conference is sponsored by the professional organization of faculty development personnel, while the second conference is dedicated to the retention and recruitment of faculty of color in higher educational institutions. In many ways this flight is a tangible expression of the differences in the two cities and, I expect, the two conferences.

I had originally been seated with a family with small children and was having a bit of difficulty concentrating on some writing I intended to complete before we landed in Minneapolis. In mid-flight, one of the passengers, who also attended the first conference in Salt Lake City, passed through the cabin and informed me that the flight had a number of empty seats in its rear, and that I might have a more pleasant ride if I chose a different part of the airplane. After checking with the flight attendant, I moved to change my seat and give the family some additional space.

A quick glance around the plane yields the bonanza of a full bank of seats in an exit row of the airplane, with plenty of legroom. This part of the plane is also virtually empty, with the exception of a couple sitting across the aisle in another exit row, and the family seated behind them. As soon as I choose a vacant row in the exit aisle across from the couple, the silence in the area I have chosen changes dramatically. The woman across the aisle (who had been resting her head on her male companion's shoulder until I sat down) hops out of her seat, begins muttering something to the man she is seated with and points at me. I'm a bit tired of negative confrontations after the first three days of this trip and choose to simply ignore her. Eventually she gathers her things and, in an extremely agitated state, moves, apparently, to another seat. The man just stays and continues to sleep. Approximately 30 minutes later, however, the woman returns and wakes him up. She again points to me and then to other vacant seats near the galley of the airplane. By now, the woman is visibly angry and loudly says something about my interfering with her ability to stay in this aisle and her assigned seat. After a moment, the man shrugs his shoulders, collects his belongings, and moves with her to another place on the airplane.

Accustomed to this type of response over the past three days, I go through the inventory to make certain that my perceptions of why this woman moved were accurate. I had bathed that morning; I hadn't had a drink of alcohol in over 25 years so I'm not drunk; I'm not playing loud music; and I'm not flirting with her male partner. I am dressed as the university professor that I am and am working on a quiet laptop computer. Still my presence is repugnant and odious. I view the experience as my "racial slight of the day" and move on. Later, when the flight attendant comes with the food cart, I ask her what reason the couple had given her for changing seats. Her response was that the children in the seats behind the couple were kicking her seat and made her uncomfortable. Why, then was she pointing at me? Is this healthy cultural paranoia?

In some ways, this flight might as well have been between two worlds, rather than two cities, as it bridges two distinct perspectives on the importance of doing faculty development work with faculty of color across the country. At one end of the bridge are those who believe that faculty of color have the exact experiences of white faculty and that there is no need for attention to issues of diversity or multiculturalism within the faculty development field. In fact, at one of the conferences, findings from a national study of faculty developers place issues of diversity at the bottom of the list of priorities for faculty developers (Wright, 1998). The "no difference, no need" perspective extends beyond issues of race and ethnicity to include similar mindsets on class and sexual orientation. At the other side of the bridge is the perspective that the most important issue for retaining faculty of color is the existence of faculty development programs geared directly to their needs (Myers, 1998). This perspective might otherwise be termed "important difference, critical need."

Thus, this is a story about the bridge of diversity for faculty of color in higher education and my six-day experience of moving across it at a unique time period when two conferences on faculty development were being held within the same week. While the experience is generally related in its chronological order, it also attempts an analysis of the week in relation to some of the literature on individual and organizational change. This is a story about how difficult the experience of the "no difference, no need" perspective can be for faculty of color, even when they have experienced, and the scholarship supports, the likelihood of reactance by faculty colleagues and administrators in higher education when issues of diversity are raised. It is also a story about how vital it is for faculty of color to have programs and places in which the "important difference, critical need" experiences may be addressed.

Most importantly, however, it is a story of the moments of transformation that make it possible for those interested in diversity issues to continue to do our work. Transformation can occur in many forms, and this paper provides two examples in very different contexts—one geared toward the "general population" faculty developers and the other focusing directly on the faculty development needs of faculty of color. It is those transformative "rays of light" that, in touching even one mind, have ripple effects on the ways organizations, programs, and educational institutions operate (Gutiérrez & Lewis, 1999).

The POD Conference and the Challenge of Placing Diversity at the Forefront of the Agenda

The Opening Plenary: Preaching Without the Choir

There is an old phrase used in my community of origin, "preaching to the choir." It refers to making presentations or disseminating material to an audience that has some familiarity with it. While the phrase "preaching to the choir" suggests that the recipient group or audience is somewhat supportive of what they are hearing, it by no means requires complete and total agreement with the speaker, as any minister waiting for an "amen" from their congregation can testify.

Those doing diversity work often experience preaching without a choir. As we enter new situations, it is helpful but not always possible to have an in-depth understanding of the set of interactions we are about to join. This is true in organizational as well as interpersonal contexts. My entrance into the Professional and Organization Development Network in Higher Education was to be more of an experience of preaching without a choir than I had seen in over a decade.

The Professional and Organizational Development Network in Higher Education (POD) is an organization that comprises faculty development specialists from across North America. POD members meet annually to share information across their programs about what they hope are the most exciting innovations in faculty development work. This includes the findings from programs as well as research on teaching, student assessment, classroom climate, and faculty recruitment and retention. POD also annually publishes a resource volume entitled *To Improve the Academy*, which offers valuable assistance to anyone interested in faculty development at higher educational institutions.

POD's mission statement, adopted in 1991, includes the following:

> POD believes that people have value, as individuals and as members of groups. The development of students is a fundamental purpose of higher education and requires for its success effective advising, teaching, leadership, and management. Central to POD's philosophy is lifelong, holistic, personal and professional learning, growth, and change for the higher education community (see p. vi, this volume).

While this is the organization's 23rd year, I have only recently learned of its existence. My connection with POD has been stimulated by my work as the Multicultural Faculty Associate in the University of Michigan's Center for Research on Learning and Teaching (CRLT). Staff from this well-respected unit have been active in POD for many years and have made significant contributions to the development of the organization. In fact, I have become interested in the POD network precisely because of the leadership its founders and current staff have had in the organization.

During the summer of 1997, while working with CRLT colleagues on their first Summer Multicultural Institute, I met trainers and administrators from other faculty development programs across the country who provided more information about POD. One of these individuals invited me to participate on a plenary panel she was organizing for the 1998 conference. The conference theme for 1998, "Collaborations, Connections, and Community," intrigued me. It focused on the linkages between diversity and community in higher educational institutions. Coincidentally, my CRLT colleagues asked me to participate in a workshop they had organized on using Intergroup Dialogue (Zúñiga & Nagda, 1993) as one method for addressing issues of difference in the classroom.

One of the concerns expressed by the POD members who invited me to attend the conference is the lack of attention to issues of "diversity" among the membership. I had interpreted this concern to refer to a wide range of diversity issues including the social group memberships of race and ethnicity, sexual orientation, and gender. Furthermore, the social group membership of economic class is almost entirely omitted from discussions of diversity but continues to present an issue for those members of higher educational institutions who are from working class or more impoverished backgrounds (Lewis, 1993). Literature in this area suggests that it is far easier to discuss gender diversity than racial/ethnic or sexual orientation diversity in organizations (Adams, 1992; Figueira-McDonough, 1998; Icard, Jones, & Wahab, 1999; Schoem, Frankel, Zúñiga, & Lewis, 1993). As research on social group memberships has now embraced the development of measurement tools for the construct of "intersectionality"—that is, the simultaneous embodiment of several "different" social group memberships (e.g., being a lesbian woman of color from an upper-income family background)—knowing "what to do" as a faculty member also becomes increasingly complex (Adams, 1992; Bell, Washington, Weinstein, & Love, 1997; Icard, Jones, & Wahab, 1999). My personal experience as a trainer in this area for over 20 years also supports these findings. Moreover, my experience as a faculty member working with other faculty members on several campuses has helped me to understand that what the behavioral sociologists, social workers, and psychologists have documented about "diversity discomfort" is not restricted to those outside of the academy (Davis, 1998). When I accepted the invitation to participate in the conference to discuss the linkages between faculty development and diversity, I assumed that the discomfort with various types of diversity would continue to be the case at this conference.

In fairness, some POD members have joined the choir in their home institutions through the years. There are, for example, individual POD members who have worked tirelessly to bring the discussion of diversity to POD meetings and literature. The organization also has a Diversity Commission, and the group has been quite busy developing an outstanding program on the conference theme. In addition to addressing the issue of diversity through conference presentations, several faculty of color involved with faculty development work on their own campuses had been invited to the 1998 meeting and asked to consider joining POD. These efforts, and the discomfort of some POD members about the issues of diversity being discussed at the conference, formed the two ends of the bridge framing the 1998 annual conference.

The panel I had been asked to participate in was the opening plenary held after dinner on the first evening of the conference. The five panel members had been meeting via electronic mail and telephone during several months before the conference to plan our session. We represented institutions from all regions of the US, different disciplines, and diverse social group memberships. We also represented vastly different philosophical positions with regard to our subject matter, and our discussions had been quite lively. Using a prepared set of questions, we decided to share the discussions we had been having with the audience of 497 registered participants. The decision allowed us to model for the audience the utility of dialogue about the delicate topics included in a discussion of diversity issues. How, for example, is unity possible with a focus on diversity? How do different definitions of community influence our behavior in working on college and university campuses? What have we learned from our experiences in helping to shape diversity agendas on our respective campuses? What findings could we share with our colleagues about "best practices" in this work?

One of the phrases I often use in teaching is "where you stand determines what you see." Having had little prior exposure to POD, I believed that the plenary had generally been well received and provided several provocative questions that could be addressed throughout the remainder of the conference. I learned later that approximately one-third of the participants left the room immediately after completing their dinner and did not stay for the plenary session. Even more ominous was the warning a colleague on the panel gave me as we prepared to leave the ballroom stage: "There will be a backlash from this."

Those working on faculty development issues that address the particular experiences of diverse populations should always be on the lookout for what I often term "the backlash" from non-choir members (Gutiérrez & Lewis, 1997). Rooney (1992), in fact, suggests that this reaction is to be expected from individuals placed in involuntary situations. Recognizing as normal the feelings and behaviors of those encountering new information about racial, ethnic, gender, sexual orientation, and class diversity allows faculty developers (and faculty in the classroom) to continue their work while the process of learning takes place (Lewis, 1993). After the plenary, lacking a former standing place to serve as a baseline, I was unable to "see" in advance how intense the backlash would be.

The Backlash

The conference's second plenary session was held after lunch the next day and was titled Student Evaluation of Teaching for Summative Purposes: What Collaborative Roles Can Developers Play? This session, I had been told, was my opportunity to hear several of the founders of the faculty development movement in higher education speak. I also looked forward to the event because I would have a chance to hear a colleague with whom I had a more personal relationship speak for the first time in many years.

My pleasure at attending the session was short-lived. The first speaker began his comments by linking criminal behavior with African-Americans. When this first happened, I thought I had surely misunderstood what he had said. As he continued with this racist (in the classic definition of individual racism) analogy, I began to look at others at my table for some type of guidance. At last, one of the people at my table leaned over and whispered, "He comes from one of the most conservative schools in California." This saddened me deeply, as I had hoped that the person was not using the analogy as a weapon. After the comment, I knew that a weapon was being wielded against anyone who cared about a recognition of "important difference, critical need" in higher education. I also wondered how such a recognized scholar in the area of measurement could have misapplied one of the first rules of interpreting statistical analyses: correlation does not equal causation.

More to my horror, no one on the panel or in the audience interrupted the first speaker's diatribe. He simply went on with his analogy until the end of his presentation and sat down. The next speaker was introduced as though nothing out of the ordinary had happened during the session. My eye contact with other persons of color seated around the room was my only clue that something quite painful to many of us had actually occurred (Johnsrud & Sadao, 1998). My reaction (now more fleeting after years of developing scar tissue to cover the wounds) was, "Is doing this work really worth it?" (Comás-Díaz & Greene, 1994; Rains, 1998).

I was not completely dismayed, however. My colleague was introduced to speak next, and I was certain that he would address this issue. I was mistaken. The colleague provided a counterpoint to the first speaker's position but slipped into the same analogy to develop his argument.

I left before the third speaker began her remarks because I knew that I could no longer stay in the room without stopping the session (or being ejected from it). The reality was that it was not my role to stop a process considered perfectly respectable to the majority of POD members. To paraphrase an African proverb, "I was a guest in your house." It also became quite clear to me that this organization, in the aggregate, was still in the "Old Boy's Club" stage of organizational development in terms of diversity issues (Katz & Miller, 1993). As that stage is usually the first of eight stages of multicultural organizational development, I realized that POD as an entity would need to participate in some very serious organization-wide discussions for diversity to be fully addressed. The question of "Where were my allies?" kept coming to mind as I left the plenary hall surrounded by several other individuals of color who had also left the session because they had also been offended by the first speaker's remarks.

Later, I learned that a brave soul in the audience had stood up at the end of the session and raised a question about the appropriateness of the first speaker's analogy. By that time, however, I was staring out of the window of my hotel room, looking at the mountains, and engaging in a forgiveness exercise in hopes that I could return to the conference and participate in the next workshop session with my CRLT colleagues.

On Forgiving

Research on persons of color in professional positions has yielded a great deal of information about the physical, emotional, and psychological toll of working within, and interacting with the wider society (Comás-Díaz & Greene, 1994; Hurtado, 1996; Jordan, 1997). Having focused my scholarship on women of color, I have learned a great deal about how holding rage rather than engaging in forgiveness negatively impacts one's ability to work effectively in the wider society (hooks, 1994; Hurtado, 1996; Jordan, 1997; Lewis, 1999). With the guidance and support of a very distinguished teacher and friend, I have developed a three-part forgiveness ritual that I use when it is appropriate to do so. First I forgive myself for ways in which I may have hurt myself in thought, word, deed, action, or reaction. I then forgive those who have hurt me in any of the same ways. Finally, I ask the forgiveness of those whom I have hurt.

While looking at the mountains, then, I forgave myself for the intensity of my reaction to the plenary speaker's provocations because I had encountered this type of behavior all of my life, beginning with segregated buses as a young child in the South. Next, I forgave the speaker for his need to destroy others out of his own fear of change. Finally, I asked the forgiveness of my ancestors for once again spending time working outside of my community when there is still so much to be done within it. After completing the acts of forgiveness, I realized that it was time to go to the CRLT workshop and help to model an intergroup dialogue.

Where Were My Allies?

Our CRLT-sponsored workshop following the luncheon session was titled "You Say 'Multicultural,' I say . . ." The room I entered was full and, as the session began, became quite crowded, with standing room only. Among the framing questions those of us who had organized this workshop had offered was, "In what ways do we feel committed to, ambivalent about, or adverse to a multicultural approach in our work?" As we began the session with a brief closed fishbowl demonstration, each of us struggled aloud with how we had responded internally and externally to the preceding session. I raised aloud the "Where were my allies?" question that had left the room with me earlier in the afternoon. Others participating in the fishbowl spoke candidly of not knowing how to respond to the incident, feeling distressed about the ways in which the incident was affecting their colleagues and themselves, and wondering how the incident would impact on POD's ability to become a more diverse organization.

The workshop came at the appropriate point in the program, as many individuals wished to speak in the open fishbowl about their experience of the previous two hours. CRLT staff facilitated the discussion and made it possible for a large group of individuals to think collectively about what had happened and what it meant professionally and personally to each person.

Faculty attempting to manage emotionally volatile or stressful situations in the classroom can also use this technique of stopping to process the preceding statement, discussion, or incident with the class membership as a way of addressing rather than avoiding conflict about the topic. It requires faculty members to think ahead about the potential sources of conflict in the learning situation and to prepare themselves for them as well as help facilitate discussions so that they serve as learning experiences for the students. While, as noted earlier, I have been trained to do this work, I had such little knowledge of the actual situation that my emotional response to it would have been problematic had it not been for my skilled colleagues who could shape the afternoon into a valuable lesson for all of us.

Ray of Light One: Interpersonal Relationships and Diversity

Immediately following the workshop, I asked the colleague who had served on the panel if I might speak with him. He immediately agreed, although my reaction to his behavior on the panel had been shared with him after the plenary. He said that he hadn't recognized the impact of the first speaker's words, as he was trying to address the fallacies in that speaker's analysis. I told him that the first speaker's inappropriate behavior was less of a concern to me than his non-response to it. During our discussion, my colleague noted that the first speaker's remark had gone over his head. This led to my summation of the literature on the outcomes of being unconscious about racism—when things go over one's head.

Acts of overt and covert discrimination negatively affect interactions between members of target and agent groups (Zúñiga & Nagda, 1993). Acts of covert discrimination can be particularly problematic in that exclusionary behaviors, policies, and procedures woven into daily interactions faced by the target group are ignored by members of the agent group (Bell, 1997; Figueira-McDonough, 1998; Icard, Jones, & Wahab, 1999; Lubiano, 1996). Membership in one target group does not automatically permit an understanding of all target groups (Frankenberg, 1993). Those interested in supporting the inclusion of faculty of color in academia need to be aware of the daily experiences with overt racism and the ways in which these contribute to the turnover in some educational institutions (Antonio, 1998; hooks, 1994; Chan & Hune, 1998). The development of a critical consciousness is required of those who desire to work toward inclusion of populations of color in the classroom, workplace, and wider society (Gutiérrez & Lewis, 1999; Reed, Newman, Súarez, & Lewis, 1997).

While my colleague was beginning to understand the impact of the incident on our interpersonal relationship, the full impact of the situation became clear to him when I began to tell him about several young people of color from our community whom he remembered as bright and generous children who were now in trouble with the law or had dropped out of school. My colleague appeared both horrified and deflated as he apologized profusely because he then fully "got it." In hindsight, I realized that until my colleague "got it," I was unable to "get over it" and stop mourning the incident. Sometimes people just need to be heard and have their experience validated.

Ray of Light Two: Moving Diversity from the Margins . . . [1]

Organizational leadership has an important role to play in the support of the retention of faculty from diverse backgrounds. Family leave policies, stopping tenure clocks after the birth of a new child, and providing writing leaves for those who are disproportionately called upon to work with diverse student groups or to represent diverse viewpoints in faculty governance situations are all mechanisms developed within educational institutions to recognize the unique experiences of diverse faculty members (Patchen, 1999; Project on Campus Community and Diversity, 1994; Statham, Richardson, & Cook, 1991).

In addition to long-term strategies to foster diversity, there are short-term and more immediate activities that can be undertaken by professional, organizational leadership in higher education. Recognizing that sometimes "teachable moments" present themselves in ways not included in the agenda of a meeting or conference, organizational leaders can embrace those moments as ways to build the organization's awareness and strengthen its membership base. The POD leadership took a courageous stance for a group unaccustomed to struggling organizationally with diversity issues in their activities during the second evening of the conference.

At the end of the dinner, POD's President announced to all assembled that instead of the scheduled talent show, the participants would undertake a "difficult dialogue," necessary because of the events of the afternoon. She noted that she would provide a ten-minute break between the end of the dinner and the beginning of the discussion so that those interested in leaving might do so.

By 8:00 p.m., approximately 40% of the participants who had attended the dinner left the room so as not to have to participate in the "difficult dialogue." Rather than viewing this as a "glass half empty," the POD leadership committed to fostering diversity within the organization could be cheered that 60% of those attending the event thought it important to attend and participate in the dialogue. This number was operationally, if not statistically, significant in that the number remaining in the room was more than enough to mount and sustain a diversity movement within the organization.

During the public commentary (held after small group discussions at individual tables in the dining room), my long-time colleague with whom I'd had the conversation earlier in the afternoon stood up and apologized to the audience for not speaking up during the panel discussion. This apology was extremely significant for several first-time participants—especially for a South African scholar attending his first conference in the US after helping to develop educational programming in South Africa and the UK, and a group of feminist researchers who were also at POD for the first time. These individuals had sought out one another (and me) to discuss the events of the day and frame our responses to our continued involvement with the organization. Some of the first-time participants who had been working on issues of diversity for some time on their home campuses and in other professional organizations also noted that the evening's activity had brought a light to what had otherwise been a very disheartening week in terms of diversity issues on college campuses. Matthew Shepard, an undergraduate student member of the Gay/Lesbian Alliance at the University of Wyoming, had very recently been brutally beaten, tied to a fence, and left to die by two men in a heterosexist hate crime. Matthew, after struggling to live for three days, had died earlier that afternoon. The lyrics "You have to be carefully taught" reverberated for some of us, both in terms of the despair of losing another student from a diverse background as well as the hope of being involved with an organization making first steps toward recognizing the importance of that diversity for both the organization and those academic community members it served.

Ray of Light Three: The Allies Find Their Voices

Following the incident, the Conference's Chairperson located the plenary speaker who had stimulated the controversy. She pointed out the inappropriate nature of his actions and requested that an apology be made in writing to the membership. The individual promised to submit a letter and it was included in the conference's newsletter the next day.

The reprinted letter did not apologize; rather it simply stated the point (which wasn't done at the conference presentation) that "The analogy between racism and pedagogical stereotyping upset some people. Perhaps that's the best way to get people thinking about it. . . . We have duties we must perform. There are many ways to do that, and our style is our chosen way to do it. Don't judge us by appeal to style generalizations, that's stereotyping."[2]

Cognizant of the tone of the speaker's letter and of the importance of taking a public stance on diversity within POD, the Program Chair placed a note at the bottom of the plenary speaker's letter: "The use of an analogy—especially when charged with highly emotional content and when the transfer to a different context is not elaborated and made explicit—can produce hurt and severe misunderstandings. I believe that [the speakers]'s argument (above) strongly supports the position that the use of racial identity in personnel decisions is not only inappropriate but highly unethical."

Also included in the following day's POD conference newsletter, distributed at the final luncheon session, was a letter from two POD members. I was gratified to note that they were from my academic institution. They commented:

> This newsletter contains a response from [the speaker] who was asked by POD to respond to the offensive example he made in his address. However, we as POD members need to ask all of us to respond as well. This situation comes up in classrooms all the time, and we counsel faculty that it is their responsibility to respond—that inaction is action. Yet we all sat through the remainder of the address, taking no action ourselves. Why? We know the consequences on individuals, on the collective, as well as on the learning process—although many of us stayed in the room, we were not really able to engage in the rest of this program. How can we talk about this? How can we hold ourselves and our organization to the same standards we hold faculty and our institutions? Especially those of us who are white. Too often our strategy is to let people of color (or whoever is being victimized in a situation) take the lead and bear the responsibility. We too often think we can afford to wait and just do something different later, the next time . . . But we can't. Thank you to Ann for her courage. But all of us, especially white people, need to know our own responsibility to have addressed [this issue] even sooner and to find our own courage.

Within two days the POD organization had, through its conference and committed membership, moved the topic of organizational diversity from a non-existent, "false peace" stance to one where those holding different opinions had begun to struggle with the implications of recognizing and including topics of diversity for the organization and its membership. It moved, using the Katz and Miller (1993) conceptual framework, from an "Old Boy's Club" to the beginnings of a multicultural organization, skipping several stages along the way. While it would have been tempting to think that the group had "crossed the bridge" to "important issues," organizational change does not occur that easily. POD members will have to revisit some of those less enjoyable stages in the process with the 40% of the membership who left the dialogue during the second night and others like them. Nonetheless, individual and organizational transformations had begun to take place.

Ray of Light Four: External Support of an Organizational Transformation

All allies supporting organizational transformation do not have to be found within the boundaries of the organization itself. When given the opportunity to reflect on the utility of incorporating issues of diversity into the activities of an organization or educational institution, surprising external allies sometimes emerge.

The keynote speaker for the final plenary of the conference on its last morning was Margaret Wheatley, author of the well regarded text *Leadership and the New Science: Learning About Organization from an Orderly Universe* (1992). POD had apparently been attempting to arrange for Wheatley to speak for several years, and some had remarked that the conference site was chosen with her in mind. From the program: "In part because Snowbird is in Wheatley's 'backyard,' we are able at this POD conference to engage one of the decade's brightest, most creative thinkers about purposeful organizations and their renewal and change. Meg Wheatley's keynote address and conversation group at the conference are ones you won't want to miss."

Unknown to many of us, Wheatley had attended and participated in some of the conference proceedings (including the dialogue facilitated by my colleagues from CRLT) and had been affected by the events of the preceding two days. Rather than giving her originally scheduled speech, she changed her presentation to address the experiences of the preceding two days as possibilities for growth and transformation. Her presentation provided additional information for those POD members who had committed themselves to fostering diversity within the organization and at their home institutions. It was also new information to that 40% of the audience who had not participated in the "difficult dialogue" but had yearned to hear her speak. Her speech demonstrated that diversity was not a marginal issue but one central to those of us who are committed to building communities reflective of our "different" life experiences. What a wonderful way to end this conference!

As I boarded the airplane bound for Minneapolis I wondered whether POD could hold onto the momentum that the conference experience had generated. Would those who had begun to recognize "a need" to address forms of diversity be supported by the organization in their moves from a "no difference" stance? Could the organization identify ways to make difference a central issue to be addressed in all aspects of its work and not a marginal one? Could fledgling bridges built between the new POD members of racial and ethnic groups of color be strengthened? Could those POD members who remained firm in their "no difference, no need" stances maintain their participation in the organization? Would it be possible to move the issue of diversity from the bottom of the priorities list for faculty developers?

In doing organizational development work around the issue of diversity, I generally recommend that a small group of individuals be constituted, representing all levels off the organizational membership and divergent viewpoints on the topic of diversity in the context of the organization. That group would be charged with the movement of the diversity agenda (as operationally defined by the organization) for the organization. Acting as a core team, the group would be responsible for developing a set of actions expected of the organization's mission, its administrative leadership, and its membership. The same core team would monitor the organization's progress on its diversity initiative and would report outcome data to its membership and to the larger society through the development of papers for publication and dissemination.

"Saving our Faculties" or the Role of Faculty Development Programs for People of Color

Saturday, October 18, 1998—Joining the Choir

There is something interesting about coming back home to the places that shaped one's career trajectory in diversity work. Minneapolis/St. Paul is one of those places for me. My first faculty development seminar presentation was in November 1972, when I was sent by the administration of the university to meet with teachers (not all faculty) in northern Minnesota to speak on diversity issues. The reception was typical for the times in that the predominantly male audience spent their hour with me staring out of the window, placing their feet on the seats in front of them, and generally ignoring the materials we were working through. At the time, those wishing to fulfill their credentialing process needed simply to attend rather than participate in diversity training seminars. I remember wondering what young people this group of teachers was likely to influence and knowing how little I would value being in their classrooms.

The Twin Cities also gave me a number of role models for excellence in faculty development programs pertaining to diversity issues. One of those individuals was Professor Josie Johnson who, at the time, was a faculty member in the new department of Afro-American studies. Within minutes of arriving at the Saving Our Faculties conference, I was in a conversation with a woman who looked familiar to me (and I to her). It wasn't until we exchanged names that I realized I was speaking to the same Professor Johnson, former University Vice President and former Regent, now retired but still working tirelessly for faculty and students on the University of Minnesota campus. Others from my faculty development "home" had also gone on to prestigious positions within the system of higher education institutions in the state including two former classmates—a Dean of the General College at the University and his wife, Vice President of the Minneapolis Community and Technical College System. We were, in some respects, a significant reason faculty of color remained in higher education 30 years before, and as we became reacquainted, realized that we were serving that same function for faculty and students of color in our respective institutions. The mentors who were our allies had prepared us to become allies for the next generation of faculty and staff. As a first-generation college student myself, mentorship from human beings who shared similar historical and political, if not social, backgrounds was particularly significant to me. Returning to Minnesota for this conference was an opportunity to surround myself with allies and have opportunities to discuss rather than explain.

Ray of Light Five: Participants—When the Marginal Are the Center

At a conference on the recruitment and retention of faculty of color in higher education held in October in Minnesota, one might expect heavy representation from local institutions. Interestingly enough, this conference truly had national representation from colleges and universities and from national educational organizations. Faculty and administrators from 92 institutions of higher education attended—from as far away as the University of Hawaii. Organizations monitoring the activities of higher education such as the American Association of University Professors, South Carolina Commission on Higher Education, the Association of American Colleges and Universities, the Council on Asian Pacific

Minorities, and the Michigan Department of Education were also represented.

With 92 institutions represented, this faculty development conference attracted some of the more prominent faculty of color interested and engaged in diversity work. The conference offered an opportunity to meet and talk with Professors Gloria Holguín Cuádraz (featured in the video *Shattering the Silences*) and Samuel Myers, Jr. (whose early research in economics on the underrepresentation of Black women in past censuses challenged the conventional wisdom about actual and modeled poverty data). The conference also drew Frances Rains, a woman of color from both a First Nations and Asian background whose work I have respected for a long time. In each case of working with these individuals and others during the three days of the meeting, participants were gracious and graceful with one another, receiving new persons as though the person was a family member. That sense of goodwill was a source of conversation between myself and another individual who had attended the POD conference. Many of us noted at the end of the Minnesota meeting that it had been a source of support making it somewhat easier to return to our home institutions.

Ray of Light Six: Grounded in the Research

The Saving Our Faculties Conference offered a wealth of new research on the faculty development needs of faculty of color. The plenaries and workshops introduced participants to the evidence-based situations confronting faculty of color as they seek tenure and/or retention in higher educational institutions. There was no dearth of scholarly presentations debunking the myths about why there are so few faculty of color in most higher educational institutions in the US (Davis, 1998; Smith, 1998). Those for whom research requires multivariate analysis would have had their needs met by Antonio's (1998) analysis of faculty retention factors, Turner's (1998) research on issues related to promotion and tenure of faculty of color, and Kenyon and Hune's (1998) study of factors supporting the recruitment and retention of Asian Pacific Islander faculty and students, among others. Myers' presentation, Diversity Seen from the Top and Bottom, based on national data noted that "A high minority faculty development budget is the single most important factor to increased minority hiring. Its effect is greater than the combined effects of 'excellent diversity' and increased funding for minority faculty recruitment" (1998, slide 26). As I listened to the presentations over the three days, I was reminded of a former colleague's insistence that no scientific evidence existed that diversity had any impact on learning outcomes. While the methodologies now exist to understand the nuances of classroom and institutional climates with regard to multiculturalism, the contrast between the presence of these studies at this conference and their absence at the last one was striking to me.

Allies were also found in the workshops presented during the conference. One session was hosted by faculty developers who would ordinarily have been at the POD conference. Their presentations focused on two faculty development programs in different parts of the country (one for women, one for people of color) and the politics of designing and keeping such programs open. Workshop presenters were quite candid about the obstacles they faced on their respective campuses with regards to diversity or multicultural issues: faculty, staff, and students.

Endings and Transformations

Although the majority of the conference participants were leaving the Twin Cities, we were also aware that a set of relationships had been forged that would not quickly be forgotten. We had participated in an event that could refresh and sustain rather than limit. As a final act, the participants were asked to record the moment by posing for a photograph. I have participated in taking photographs at conferences before but have only had the experience of everyone's willingness to be photographed in meetings where the participants have known and developed relationships with one another. By the end of these three days it seemed clear that relationships between participants—those of color and those from original European lineage—had been forged.

Lest the rich information presented at the conference be lost, organizers arranged to forward the conference proceedings to each participant. Now we have a set of documents that focus on the specific needs and experiences of faculty of color. The document is a useful tool for raising the unique faculty development needs of faculty of color within our home institutions.

As at the POD conference, when I left the Saving Our Faculties conference I knew transformation had taken place for many participants. At the very least, this transformation could validate our "healthy cultural paranoia" as an adaptive method given our experiences raising diversity issues on our respective campuses (whether we were or were not people of color). At the most, many of us learned what was possible for faculty development programs when issues of diversity were addressed rather than ignored.

Lessons Learned About Moving Across the Bridge

During those six days in October, I was able to move from one end of the bridge to the other. One end was exhilarating and challenging because it framed the work that had already been done on faculty development issues for faculty of color and identified the critical need for more work in the area. The other end of the bridge was also challenging as it framed the dearth of empirical evidence supporting the "no difference, no need argument."

Those of us who choose to do faculty development work addressing the needs of faculty of color will periodically find ourselves on both ends of the bridge. While some of us might attempt to strive to remain in the center, there are some lessons to be learned from those end places:

1) We can recognize reactance as an expected outcome of the introduction into our work of content about the faculty development needs of faculty of color. In this respect, backlash can have positive as well as negative effects. Our lesson as faculty development professionals is, to paraphrase Johnson Reagon (1999), that "stepping across our safety zone is necessary."

2) We must note that allies in the expected places are a source of renewal. Allies in unexpected places are a gift promoting growth within an educational institution or professional organization. External allies can support our work and, once identified, should be nurtured.

3) Methods such as intergroup dialogues, focus groups, and fishbowls are useful in airing potentially volatile subjects.

4) Faculty development professionals working on diversity issues will need to balance individual and institutional needs, experiences, and interventions for themselves and those with whom they work.

5) There is a need for faculty development work focused solely on the unique experiences of faculty and students of color.

6) Sometimes the margins are a good place to be!

Endnotes

[1]This phrase is adapted from bell hooks. (1990). Choosing the margins as a space of radical openness. In *Yearning: Race, gender, and cultural politics* (145-153). Boston, MA: South End Press.

[2]The three quotes in this section are drawn from the POD newsletter distributed to conference participants on the third morning of the conference. Names were omitted by the author.

References

Adams, M. (1992). Cultural inclusion in the American college classroom. In L. L. B. Border & N. V. N. Chism (Eds.), *Teaching for diversity* (pp. 5-17). New Directions for Teaching and Learning, No. 49. San Francisco, CA: Jossey-Bass.

Antonio, A. L. (1998, October). Faculty of color reconsidered: Retaining scholars for the future. *Proceedings of Keeping Our Faculties: Addressing the Recruitment and Retention of Faculty of Color in Higher Education.* Minneapolis, MN: Office of the Associate Vice President for Multicultural and Academic Affairs, University of Minnesota.

Bell, L. A. (1997). Theoretical foundations for social justice education. In M. Adams, L. A. Bell, & P. Griffin (Eds.), *Teaching for diversity and social justice: A sourcebook* (pp. 3-15). New York, NY: Routledge.

Bell, L. A., Washington, S., Weinstein, G., & Love, B. (1997). Knowing ourselves as instructors. In M. Adams, L. A. Bell, & P. Griffin (Eds.), *Teaching for diversity and social justice: A sourcebook* (pp. 299-310). New York, NY: Routledge.

Chan, K. S., & Hune, S. (1998, October). *Finding and keeping Asian and Pacific American faculty.* Presentation at the Saving Our Faculties Conference, Minnesota.

Comás-Díaz, L., & Greene, B. (1994). Women of color with professional status. In L. Comás-Díaz & B. Greene (Eds.), *Women of color: Integrating ethnic and gender identities in psychotherapy* (pp. 347-388). New York, NY: Guilford.

Davis, J. D. (1998, October). Retaining faculty of color: The five habits of a highly effective institution. *Proceedings of Keeping Our Faculties: Addressing the Recruitment and Retention of Faculty of Color in Higher Education.* Minneapolis, MN: Office of the Associate Vice President for Multicultural and Academic Affairs, University of Minnesota.

Figueira-McDonough, J. (1998). Toward a gender-integrated knowledge in social work. In J. Figueira-McDonough, R. E. Netting, & A. Nichols-Casebolt (Eds.), *The role of gender in practice knowledge: Claiming half the human experience* (pp. 3-40). New York, NY: Garland Publishing.

Frankenberg, R. (1993). *The social construction of whiteness: White women, race matters.* Minneapolis, MN: University of Minnesota Press.

Gutiérrez, L., & Lewis, E. (1997). Education, participation, and capacity building in community organizing with women of color. In M. Minkler (Ed.), *Community organization and community building for health* (pp. 216-229). New Brunswick, NJ: Rutgers University Press.

Gutiérrez, L., & Lewis, E. (1999). Bringing an empowerment perspective into organizational practice. In L. Gutiérrez & E. Lewis (Eds.), *Empowering women of color* (pp. 80-99). New York, NY: Columbia University Press.

hooks, b. (1993). *Sisters of the yam: Black women and self-recovery*. Boston, MA: South End Press.

hooks, b. (1994). *Teaching to transgress: Education as the practice of freedom*. New York, NY: Routledge.

Hurtado, A. (1996). *The color of privilege: Three blasphemies on race and feminism*. Ann Arbor, MI: University of Michigan Press.

Icard, L., Jones, T., & Wahab, S. (1999). Empowering lesbian and bisexual women of color: Overcoming three forms of oppression. In L. Gutiérrez & E. Lewis (Eds.), *Empowering women of color* (pp. 208-225). New York, NY: Columbia University Press.

Johnson Reagon, B. (1999, March). *Septima Clark and the sweetness of struggle*. Keynote presentation for the Center for the Education of Women, University of Michigan, Ann Arbor, MI.

Johnsrud, L. K., & Sadao, K. C. (1998). The common experience of "otherness": Ethnic and racial minority faculty. *The Review of Higher Education, 21* (4), 315-342.

Jordan, J. (1997). *Women's growth in diversity: More writings from the Stone School Center*. New York, NY: Guilford.

Kaplan, Matthew (Ed.). (1998). *To Improve the Academy, 17*.

Katz, J., & Miller, F. A. (1993). *Cultural diversity as a developmental process: The path from monocultural club to inclusive organization*. New York, NY: The Kaleel Jamison Consulting Group.

Kenyon, C., & Hune, S. (1998, October). Towards creating a successful climate for Asian Pacific American female faculty. *Proceedings of Keeping Our Faculties: Addressing the Recruitment and Retention of Faculty of Color in Higher Education*. Minneapolis, MN: Office of the Associate Vice President for Multicultural and Academic Affairs, University of Minnesota.

Lewis, E. A. (1993). Continuing the legacy: On the importance of praxis in the education of social work students and teachers. In D. Schoem, L. Frankel, X. Zúñiga, & E. Lewis (Eds.), *Multicultural teaching in the university* (pp. 26-36). New York, NY: Praeger.

Lewis, E. A. (1999). Staying on the path: Lessons about health and resistance from women of the African Diaspora in the United States. In L. Gutiérrez &

E. Lewis (Eds.), *Empowering women of color* (pp. 150-166). New York, NY: Columbia University Press.

Lubiano, W. (1996). Like being mugged by a metaphor: Multiculturalism and state narratives. In A. Gordon & C. Newfield (Eds.), *Mapping multiculturalism* (pp. 64-75). Minneapolis, MN: University of Minnesota Press.

Myers, S. L., Jr. (1998, October). Diversity seen from the top and bottom. *Proceedings of Keeping Our Faculties: Addressing the Recruitment and Retention of Faculty of Color in Higher Education.* Minneapolis, MN: Office of the Associate Vice President for Multicultural and Academic Affairs, University of Minnesota.

Patchen, M. (1999). *Diversity and unity: Relations between racial and ethnic groups.* Chicago, IL: Nelson-Hall.

Peterson-Hickey, M., & Stein, W. (1998, October). Minority faculty in academe: Documenting the unique American Indian experience. *Proceedings of Keeping Our Faculties: Addressing the Recruitment and Retention of Faculty of Color in Higher Education.* Minneapolis, MN: Office of the Associate Vice President for Multicultural and Academic Affairs, University of Minnesota.

Project on Campus Community and Diversity. (1994). *Dialogues for diversity: Community and ethnicity on campus.* Phoenix, AZ: Oryx.

Rains, F. V. (1998, October). Is the price worth the cost of survival in academic apartheid? Women faculty of color in a [white] research university. *Proceedings of Keeping Our Faculties: Addressing the Recruitment and Retention of Faculty of Color in Higher Education.* Minneapolis, MN: Office of the Associate Vice President for Multicultural and Academic Affairs, University of Minnesota.

Reed, B. G., Newman, P. A., Súarez, Z., & Lewis, E. (1997). Interpersonal practice beyond diversity and towards social justice. The importance of critical consciousness. In C. Garvin & B. Seabury (Eds.), *Social work practice* (pp. 44-77). New York, NY: Garland.

Rooney, R. (1992). *Practice strategies for work with involuntary clients.* New York, NY: Columbia University Press.

Schoem, D., Frankel, L., Zúñiga, X., & Lewis, E. (Eds.). (1993). *Multicultural teaching in the university.* New York, NY: Praeger.

Smith, D. G. (1998, October). Achieving faculty diversity: Debunking myths and other strategies. *Proceedings of Keeping Our Faculties: Addressing the Recruitment and Retention of Faculty of Color in Higher Education.* Minneapolis, MN:

Office of the Associate Vice President for Multicultural and Academic Affairs, University of Minnesota.

Statham, A., Richardson, L., & Cook, J. A. (1991). *Gender and university teaching: A negotiated difference.* Albany, NY: State University of New York Press.

Turner, C. S. V. (1998, October). Promotion and tenure for faculty of color: Promoting business as usual. *Proceedings of Keeping Our Faculties: Addressing the Recruitment and Retention of Faculty of Color in Higher Education.* Minneapolis, MN: Office of the Associate Vice President for Multicultural and Academic Affairs, University of Minnesota.

Wheatley, Margaret. (1992). *Leadership and the new science: Learning about organization from an orderly universe.* San Francisco, CA: Berrett-Koehler.

Wright, D. (1998, October). *Faculty development centers in research universities: A study of resources and programs.* Paper presented at the meeting of the Professional and Organizational Development Network in Higher Education, Snow Bird, UT.

Zúñiga, X., & Nagda, B. A. (1993). Dialogue groups: An innovative approach to multicultural learning. In D. Schoem, L. Frankel, X. Zúñiga, & E. Lewis (Eds.), *Multicultural teaching in the university* (pp. 233-248). New York, NY: Praeger.

Contact:

Edith A. Lewis
3688 Social Work
University of Michigan
1080 South University
Ann Arbor, MI 48109-1106
(734) 763-6257
(734) 936-1961 (FAX)
edithl@umich.edu

Edith A. Lewis is Associate Professor of Social Work and Women's Studies. She received her M.S.W. from the University of Minnesota (1975) and her Ph.D. in Social Welfare from the University of Wisconsin, Madison (1985). She has taught in the areas of cultural competence in interpersonal practice, family relationships, group process, behavioral theories and interventions, international social work, and community and social systems practice. Her intervention research has focused on using the strengths of populations of color to inform social work practice, policy, and research. Her publications include two co-edited books, *Empowering Practice with Women of Color* and *Multicultural Teaching in the University*, as well as numerous articles on topics that include teaching about families, community organizing with women of color, and feminist perspectives on community organizing with women of color. She is currently completing a book of case studies and exercises to be used by African and US social work students.

2

The Challenge and Test of Our Values: An Essay of Collective Experience

Kay Herr Gillespie
CKF Associates—Higher Education Development

Departing from a specific experience at the 1998 POD conference, the values of the organization—most specifically and directly the "valuing of people"—were challenged and put to the test of whether or not we genuinely and sincerely strive to actualize our values. This situation is generalizable to our daily professional and personal lives, and the essay invites readers' reflection through an examination of our values in combination with the story. The challenge continues, and the test is not finished.

This is an essay arising from experience, which is not an uncommon stimulus for what in the parlance of literature is called the *personal essay*. However, a personal essay is not what we expect to find in a professional publication such as *To Improve the Academy*.

Therefore, I invite readers to join me in stretching our understanding of the genre of "essay" and to consider these words to have arisen not just from *my* experience but also from *our* experience—that of several hundred members of The POD Network. And via this printed word, what was *my* and *our* experience also becomes the experience of *every reader*. Thus, what is offered here is no longer a personal essay; rather it is a professional and collective essay. By accident of circumstance, I happen to be the individual verbalizing these thoughts on "A Challenge and Test of Our Values," but the experience is that of each of us—whether directly or indirectly. It is a two-fold event consisting of two phases: 1) that which was actually experienced, which constitutes *the story*, and 2) that which we experience in continuing reflection.

The story began at the 1998 POD conference, where I gave an opening plenary address before the pre-conference events started. Several months before this time, I had chosen the general topic of values. My intent was to provide opportunity for participants, as well as myself, to reflect upon the values of our organization and our embodiment and living of those values. The reason I chose this particular topic was a quite personal one. I believe very strongly that it is incumbent upon us as human beings to examine our values through reflection. Values underlie our actions, and reflection allows us to assess the degree of congruence between the values we purport to espouse and our actions. To seek harmony between values and actions is to lead the examined life, which should be the hallmark of a serious professional and of a thoughtful human being.

Due to an unexpected turn of events at the 1998 POD conference, a challenge to our values was placed before us and provided us opportunity to test those values. Before we continue the story, let us consider the unexpected challenge and the test within an organizational context.

The Essence of an Organization

An organization is the creation by human beings of a collective structure—a collaborative act, a necessary response to the existence and phenomenon of society. Any organization exists because we will it to exist. It is a societal structure, which we design to serve our purposes. That means that the organization changes as we change and reflects what we are, have been, and want to become.

Keeping this foundation in mind, let's think of The POD Network in specific. It was born in the early 70s in response to a newly recognized need within the societal structure of higher education. More specifically, it was the outgrowth of the feeling of a small number of dedicated individuals who felt that we needed new ways to promote a culture of development—both for faculty and administrators as well as for institutions themselves and their internal structures—in order to respond more effectively to what higher education needed to become. One such new way was to create an association, a collective—a connected group of people working collaboratively to build a professional community with a purpose in mind. This purpose was to promote a spirit of professional development within higher education more vigorously than had existed before. The need for an organization had been recognized; it was therefore "willed" to exist by a collaborative act.

THE FOUNDATION OF THE ORGANIZATION

It is with intent that I do not use the term *mission statement* in the above heading, for regrettably it is probably true for most of us that we do not get very excited about reading a mission statement. (I don't want to lose readers in the middle of this essay!) Yet, it is also true that an effective organization must have a mission statement of some sort, even though it might be called something else, such as "goals statement" or "purpose." Such a statement of general purpose becomes the foundation of the organization; it is the stimulus of the organizational act and organizational action.

And so POD has a mission statement. Indeed, we have the long version of the mission statement and the short version, both of which have been revised over the years. The current statement was accepted in 1991, and it is here that we should find expression of our core organizational values. In reviewing the POD mission statement, three sentences stand out as most directly reflecting our values.

- The POD Network "fosters human development in higher education through faculty, instructional, and organizational development."
- "POD believes that people have value, as individuals and as members of groups."
- "Lifelong, holistic, personal, and professional learning, growth, and change for the higher education community" is central to POD's philosophy.

What values are reflected here? I asked participants in the plenary session at the conference to identify the values they found expressed in the POD mission statement, and the most frequently occurring words or phrases are listed below. They present an encapsulation of our organizational mission.

1) Lifelong, holistic human development
2) Growth
3) Valuing people
4) Positive change
5) Collaboration
6) Learning

The critical question, however, is what we do with these values, and to answer this question we must take a reflective stance.

The Reflective Stance

It is our organizational business to reflect. Readers alert to language usage will note in that sentence the absence of a preposition and an object for the preposition. I did not write "reflect upon + a noun," rather simply "to reflect." If our business is indeed faculty, instructional, and organizational development as we say it is, an inherent part of that business is reflection. Without reflection, growth and development will certainly occur, for change is a constant. However, in the absence of reflection to provide guidance, the growth and development we desire as human beings may be chaotic, accidental, unattractive, ineffective, stunted—or any other number of metaphorically appropriate adjectives that portray unguided growth. For the purpose of this *collective essay of experience* it is now time to complete the verb with its expected preposition and an object: *reflect upon* [preposition] *these values* [object of the preposition].

I think many of us probably believe that our society finds itself in a time of seeking to re-form or re-articulate values that, I hope, all would agree can be placed on the side of "that which is universally good." Such values include justice, fairness, and diversity, which includes the noble goal of valuing and respecting all persons, and we offer challenge to such values as racism and sexism. But there are among us those who lived the 60s, and I think, historically, we can point to that decade as the time within our lifetimes when we really began stirring up our values stew. Indeed, if we find what's happening around us today discomfiting, thinking about recent history might bring a bit of comfort—our dilemmas are not new ones.

As one who started professionally in the 60s, I look back upon that time as an exciting period. It forced us to begin re-examining our values, albeit often in painful, disturbing, and sometimes terribly destructive and hurtful ways. However, I think we have emerged healthier for that—whether we think of our society at large, the context of higher education, or what touches our lives personally and individually—healthier simply in that we are willing to examine and sometimes to challenge our values. We can talk about things today that only slightly over three decades ago were hardly ever expressed in public ways by our collective conscience.

The process begun in the 60s is certainly not finished. Kicking and screaming as a society, we entered an era of values foment, which is ongoing. As professionals working in faculty, instructional, and organizational development, we know and experience on a daily basis the powerful force of our individual and collective values and beliefs. We experience them as motivation of everyday actions, and to bring awareness of values to the surface, out in the open, is very healthy—in my opinion.

Other voices from our organizational past have also invited us to reflect upon our values as did, for example, Bill Bergquist, one of the "founding fathers" of POD. He presented a plenary address at the 1994 conference and commented as follows:

> I propose that when we examine organizational values . . . we are looking at "tacit knowledge." We know that these values are present and profoundly influence our life and our attitudes regarding the organization in which we work, yet these values are often not directly known to us. In other words, these values often remain "unconscious." They serve as tacitly-held templates against which we measure the "rightness" and "wrongness" of behaviors in our organization and the extent to which things have changed in our organization (Bergquist, 1994, p. 353).

Thus do we seek self-knowledge, which is seldom easy but is always imperative as we delve more deeply into that which is our humanness. The pain of this search in combination with the discovery of beauty in the searching experience itself has been exquisitely expressed by the poet Kahlil Gibran (1923/1991), who wrote as follows in *The Prophet*:

> And a man said, Speak to us of Self-Knowledge,
> And he answered, saying:
> Your hearts know in silence the secrets of the days and the nights.
> But your ears thirst for the sound of your heart's knowledge.
> You would know in words that which you have always known in thought.
> You would touch with your fingers the naked body of your dreams.
> Say not, "I have found the truth," but rather, "I have found a truth."
> Say not, "I have found the path of the soul." Say rather, "I have met the soul walking upon my path."

For the soul walks upon all paths.
The soul walks not upon a line, neither does it grow like a reed.
The soul unfolds itself, like a lotus of countless petals (pp. 54-55).

The words of the poet can comfort us and perhaps even ennoble us as we confront the glaring realities of the difficulty of assessing and re-forming our values—this is the challenge and the test.

The Challenge and the Test

In our mission statement, we officially claim that we believe all people "have value," we seek to "foster human development," and we strive to "promote change." That's what we say, but do we live by those values? That is the challenge before us, and our recent collective experience provided us with the opportunity to test ourselves. Returning to this experience through our reflection allows us to test ourselves over and over again.

At the 1998 POD conference, a publicly made remark, not by a member of POD, was understood as a denigration of a particular group of persons or, stated very directly, a racial slur. There was no immediately evident audience reaction to the comment, and it was not challenged until the conclusion of the public presentation after which there was no opportunity for public and collective discussion.

This was start of *the experience*, the start of *the story*. However, its importance goes far beyond that moment, for the substance of the particular situation is generalized every time we hear comments—or, sadly, perhaps even make such comments ourselves—that promote or reflect the stereotyping of any group of persons, thereby de-valuing them.

The first part of the two-part test question placed before us is *whether or not the silence of the immediate moment negated our purported "valuing of all persons as individuals and groups,"* and this value is absolutely foundational to all of our other statements of value as an organization and as faculty and instructional development professionals. If we do not live by that value, we are professional hypocrites.

However, I do not believe we can answer the test question of negation of our purported values with a simple "yes" or "no." All persons present were conspirators in the silence of the moment, and various perspectives emerged as we discussed the experience later. Many persons expressed their feeling of paralyzing shock and dismay. Others indicated they felt a sense of disabling shame. Some persons sitting in the back could not hear the speakers clearly and did not realize what had been said. Perhaps there were those who succumbed to the expectation we have of polite behaviors in a public setting. And we must also be fully honest and admit that, regrettably, there may indeed have been some who felt a sense of indifference. Whatever the complexity of feelings and reactions may have been, we will not be able to explain them fully despite our strong and almost overwhelming desire to do so. As we continue to keep the perspective of generalization of the situation, we must then also transfer the reflection of this complexity to other similar situations or experiences.

The second part of the test question is *whether or not we seek to affirm striving to live by our foundational values*; and this means that we must take action reflecting affirmation. In the setting of this particular experience, we did so by instituting a "difficult dialogue" as quickly as possible, whereby we came together as a community of members to discuss our feelings and reactions and concerns, taking advantage of what several called "a teachable moment." Emotions were very intense—irritation, anger, shame, confusion, hurt, pain, guilt, and also indifference. I believe the willingness, however, to engage in this difficult dialogue was indeed an affirmation of our willingness as a community to strive for living our stated values. Moreover, this process also embodied the value of fostering human development and change—critical to the POD mission and to the process of promoting faculty, instructional, and organizational development.

Our difficult dialogue yielded discussion and many written comments, some of which are very moving.[1] The following are some selected examples of comments.

- I will live forever with the profound shame that I sat in a state of paralytic shock and did nothing to challenge such a racist statement.
- Many of us are first-timers and wondered what kind of place or group this is.
- We're here out of a sense of concern and solidarity but find ourselves making many assumptions about intention and feelings on either side.
- Thanks for doing this session instead of pretending it didn't happen.
- This becomes a valuable learning lesson. For example, how do we advise faculty to handle [similar] situations in class.
- We all make mistakes, but we need to apologize and make amends.

- I am hurt! I am concerned! I am disappointed! I am ashamed to be here! But what happened today can only be a good thing for the future of POD and faculty development.

Another three of the many comments invite us to move to the important perspective of overview.

- How can we, as an organization and as individuals, create an environment that empowers us to respond to statements that hurt, shock, confuse, or befuddle us?
- We thank you for allowing us to have this difficult dialogue. All of us have been confronted with similar situations on our campuses and often respond with silence.
- Perhaps this will in-spirit us to respond in a more helpful, constructive way.

Finishing the Test

Not surprisingly, we were not done with the challenge to, and test of, our values when we completed the difficult dialogue of this experience, for the dialogue continued both formally and informally throughout the conference and even electronically afterwards on a related topic. All of these conversations were inspired by our passions in moving ways, and I hope that they continue in the minds and hearts of each conference participant and also of each reader of this "essay of collective experience."

We were not done with the test at the conclusion of the electronic dialogue, for this test will never be finished, just as a story—any and every story—is never really finished because it has unending application to who we are and how we live. That is the essence of *story* and the essence of any human experience—the particular experience reflects a general set of experiences, and the generalization includes that which had been particularized. Through the sharing of *story,* a metaphorical expression of our experiences, we allow ourselves to grow in individual and collective human richness and depth of understanding.

Conclusion

If we accept this experience as a challenge and a test and if we also believe that our response was indeed an affirmation of our organizational striving to live by our values, then I believe we have responded to a call strongly sounded by Parker Palmer, the well-known scholar of teaching, who has emerged as almost a spiritual guide for our discussions about teaching and learning. In this situation, we were indeed teaching each other and learning with each other. Palmer's comments speak powerfully to the importance of maintaining a perspective of reflection upon our values and translating that reflection into action. Valuing people means respecting them, and this is the concern he expressed. I find his words both discouraging and frightening, but they present a strong call to us for action. While his context is the university, his thoughts apply to our organization and to our individual lives as well.

> Imagine how it would transform academic life if everyone involved practiced simple respect. I don't think there are many places where people feel less respected than on university campuses. The university is a place that has learned to grant respect to only a few things: the texts, the experts, and those who win in competition. We don't grant respect to students who are stumbling and failing. We don't grant respect to tentative and heartfelt ways of being in the world, where a person can't quite think of the right word—or any word at all. We don't grant respect to silence and wonder. We don't grant it to voices outside our tight little circle, let alone to the voiceless things of the world.
>
> Why? Because academia is a culture of fear. We are afraid of hearing something that would challenge and change us. . . . we don't want to hear those voices. We carefully wall ourselves off, by means of systematic disrespect, from all those things that might challenge us, break us, open us (1998, p. B12).

I would conjecture that many of us probably agree with these statements to varying degrees of intensity. Was this what happened at the POD conference? Did we allow or suffer the promotion of the "culture of fear"? Or did we begin the difficult and ongoing process of destroying this culture?

If we accept Palmer's description, if we find within our society of higher education or our organization (or our hearts) a culture of fear, then that culture certainly negates all that higher education purports to be. It destroys the very essence of what any level of education should be about. It may be that this culture, which Palmer describes as one of *fear*, is indeed even more than that. At times it may be a culture of anger, intolerance, dishonesty with self and others, arrogance and egotism, or inappropriate and damning judgment of others who are different than we are.

Perhaps I speak strongly, but I would consider a culture with such attributes to be even worse than a *culture of fear*—if one can speak relatively in this regard. Can anything be worse than *fear*? A *culture of fear* with its tentacle-like spreading negativism—whether intentional or non-intentional—becomes a *culture of destruction of others*. I believe such a culture would be the negation of our humanness. There is a powerful line in the famous 19th-century drama *Faust* by the German author Johann Wolfgang von Goethe. This line is spoken by Mephisto, the devil figure in the drama, and he says, "Ich bin der Geist, der stets verneint," which translates as, "I am the spirit which always negates." Mephisto does not win in this drama, but the battle with the "Geist, der stets verneint" is never over.

I hope and I believe that each of the members of The POD Network in the context of daily work—with the values we espouse—will vigorously and enthusiastically seek to bring down this culture of fear or any and all aspects of a culture of negation through our work in faculty, instructional, and organizational development.

If we value others, if we cherish the concepts of human growth and development as well as the promotion of positive change, then fear and negation have no place among us or around us—as individuals or as a collective, a community of caring professionals.

Endnote

[1]A complete copy of all written comments is available from the author upon request.

References

Bergquist, W. (1994). Unconscious values within four academic cultures. *To Improve the Academy, 13*, 349-372.

Gibran, K. (1991). *The prophet* (120th printing). (Original work published 1923). New York, NY: Alfred A. Knopf.

Palmer, P. (1998, October 9). Melange. *The Chronicle of Higher Education*, p. B12.

Contact:

Kay Herr Gillespie
CKF Associates—Higher Education Development
2900 Tulane Drive
Fort Collins, CO 80525

(970) 226-3731
(970) 491-6989 (FAX)
kaygi2@aol.com

Kay Herr Gillespie is Professor Emerita at Colorado State University and holds a Ph.D. in Germanic Languages and Literatures from the University of Colorado, Boulder. Now active as an independent consultant, editor, and writer, she began working in faculty development in the early 1970s and has served as President of The POD Network. She is also heavily involved with POD publishing activities. Special interests include faculty development initiatives for new faculty, the impact of technology upon faculty life and work, and the promotion of a sense of community among faculty members.

3

On the Path: POD as a Multicultural Organization

Christine A. Stanley
The Ohio State University

Mathew L. Ouellett
University of Massachusetts, Amherst

Since 1993, the Professional and Organizational Development Network (POD) has made an increasingly stronger commitment to becoming a multicultural organization. Poised at the entrance to a new century, it seems useful to examine the current standing of this goal in the context of the overall growth and development of POD. In this article the authors take stock of the organization's history related to multiculturalism, discuss POD's current organizational strengths and challenges related to models of multicultural organizational development, and offer suggestions for further progress on the path to becoming a multicultural organization.

Introduction

Over the past decade, linkages between diversity and teaching development efforts in the field of instructional development have centered on initiatives designed to raise individual student and faculty awareness levels and on the development and dissemination of models of inclusive classroom-based teaching practices. We need look no further than past issues of *To Improve the Academy* to trace a rich and ongoing dialogue within our field on models, strategies, and resources useful in fusing the best practices in multiculturalism and teaching development. Over time, these efforts have clustered along a continuum from initiatives for encouraging individual growth (Collett & Serrano, 1992; Cooper & Chattergy, 1993; Knoedler & Shea, 1992) to those directed more broadly, such as campus-wide interdisciplinary teaching development seminars (Ouellett & Sorcinelli, 1995, 1998; Schmitz, Paul, & Greenberg, 1992).

A concurrent theme in this same body of literature is that of educational developers as organizational change facilitators (Chism, 1998; Evans & Chauvin, 1993; Patrick & Fletcher, 1998). For some time now, POD members have been sensitive to the need for increased emphasis on the "O" (organizational) in POD Network activities. In particular, there is the call for a more systemic perspective on how we, as educational developers, address diversity-related issues of individual and institutional growth and development (Border & Chism, 1992; Cook & Sorcinelli, 1999; Wunsch & Chattergy, 1991). Chism (1998) offers a model for considering our role in organizational change that eloquently reminds us of our collective talents for conceptualizing, articulating, and implementing assessment and improvement efforts and the contribution of such assistance to long-term organizational health. More recently, we have been asked to strengthen our critique of classroom diversity-related experiences of students and faculty by analyzing more directly the systemic impacts of institutional context and campus climate (Chesler, 1998; Ferren & Geller, 1993). These streams of literature point to the role that multiculturalism and diversity have played in our emerging understanding of the nature of individual and institutional change in higher education.

Based upon public and private dialogues at the most recent annual POD Network conference, we found a merging of these themes. As a result of a series of conference events, we were reminded that POD offers members a natural context within which to explore, learn, and practice new perspectives and behaviors related to the changing nature of our organization. For many, the conference propelled us both to contemplate the distance we have traveled together and to speculate on the distance to the horizon still ahead of us. We came away from this annual gathering wondering how to renew our commitment to POD as a multicultural organization and what organizational "muscles" we need to strengthen to attain our goal of POD becoming an authentically multicultural organization.

Chesler (1994) defines a multicultural organization as one that articulates "an approach to organizational change that is frankly antiracist and antisexist . . . not simply an acceptance of differences, nor a celebrative affirmation of the value of differences, but a reduction in the patterns of racial and gender oppression (racism and sexism) that predominate in most US institutions and organizations" (pp. 243-244). A multicultural organization values and *reflects* the contributions of all its members. Specifically, it constantly re-examines current organizational structures, practices, and policies and readjusts efforts constantly to better manifest a diverse and socially just organization. The process of achieving a multicultural organization is evolutionary and occurs in stages. We would like to explore, within the context of POD and our home institutions, the nature of multicultural organizational development and how our role as faculty developers is integral to organizational, institutional, and individual change. First, we will look at the organization's history with respect to these issues. Our examination will include exploring how we can advocate change, offering a model for conceptualizing a multicultural organization, and finally, inviting your call to action as we walk this path together in the future.

Taking Stock: Diversity-Related Initiatives to Date

Reflecting on our past goals for organizational growth will better prepare us to assess development as a multicultural organization, to clarify our future aspirations, and to design concrete goals and strategies for fully realizing these commitments. In support of these efforts, POD already benefits from several unique strengths. These include its history of commitment to professional and organizational development; the organizational emphasis on community, collegiality, and networking; and its leadership role in the improvement of teaching and learning in higher education.

Let's take a look at some of the initiatives and conversations that have taken place since the early years, with an eye toward how they continue to prepare us to become a multicultural organization. The POD Mission Statement, approved by the Executive Core Committee in 1991, has 16 explicitly articulated convictions relating to people and education. More specifically, related to diversity is the conviction that

> [a] self-critical stance, self-assessment, and evaluation are important as a condition for both individual and organizational effectiveness and growth. . . . POD should strive at all points to be responsive to human needs. . . . [A]s our members change and as higher education changes, so POD must change.

It is a direct result of self-assessment, critical reflection, and commitment that led POD to respond to its members' growing desire to shape a multicultural organization. Within a year of the approval of the POD Mission Statement, members helped initiate a number of specific steps to be taken by POD, including the formation of the Diversity Commission and reexamination of the goals of the organization.

The Membership Calls and the Executive Core Responds

In 1992, our annual conference was held at the Saddlebrook Resort in Tampa, Florida. At this conference 24 of our members came together to form a Diversity Interest Group. Their first action was to write a letter to the Executive Core Committee to suggest ways in which POD could encourage a more diverse membership base for the organization. At the heart of the conversations was a realization that we needed to attract a broader membership in our efforts toward becoming a more multicultural organization.

In 1993, under the presidential leadership of Don Wulff, a volunteer group began to explore organizational models for diversity. After looking at efforts within other, related higher education organizations (e.g., American Association for Higher Education), they developed and presented a proposal to the Executive Core Committee. This proposal focused on ways to make diversity a priority within POD and articulated the necessity of making diversity an explicit goal in membership outreach to underrepresented groups and institutions.

The Diversity Commission: A Focus on Recruitment

In 1994, this proposal was presented and accepted, and members who were charged with its implementation were given a budget to begin developing this work for the organization. They formed a Diversity Committee, which was later renamed the Diversity Commission. As members of the Diversity Commission, we first focused our efforts on outreach to institutions and groups that had historically been underrepresented in the organization. We began to network with Historically Black Colleges and Universities (HBCUs), Native American tribal colleges, and Hispanic-serving institutions. Between 1994 and 1998, the Commission successfully recruited 31 underrepresented institutions to our annual conference.

Between 1993 and 1997, we were aware that, although the commission was established with a recruitment goal in mind, we were increasingly consulted about other organizational efforts toward diversity, such as conference and program planning, conference site selection, publications, and the like. We welcomed these opportunities to consult across the organization. What began as a general recruitment initiative became a conceptual springboard for broader organizational assessment and changes. We know that recruitment is synergistically tied to retention. We were determined that POD not continue to recruit individuals from underrepresented groups and institutions without also paying attention to what their experiences were like once they arrived in the organization. Efforts toward valuing diversity may begin with recruitment, but not changing the nature of the organization to provide for ongoing retention of our new members is counterproductive. In fact, it sends a clear message to these members that they are invited to assimilate organizational norms and values, but not to influence or change core values and mission.

In 1995, an internship opportunity, the POD faculty/instructional development training grant program, was developed. The purpose of this program is to provide a POD member institution with funding to support an internship for a person of color who wishes to explore professional opportunities in faculty/TA instructional development. The sponsoring unit would then assist the intern in searching for a position in faculty development. To date, three campuses have received funding for this initiative: The University of Michigan's Center for Research on Learning and Teaching (CRLT), the University of Southern Colorado's Faculty Center for Professional Development, and the Center for Teaching (CFT) at the University of Massachusetts, Amherst. While admittedly supporting campus-based initiatives, this program has enabled recipients to provide education and training for faculty and TAs of color considering faculty development as a career. Grants have been used for networking activities, training in teaching consultations and assessment, and attendance at national and regional conferences.

The Diversity Commission: A Focus on Organizational Development

In 1998, another proposal was developed by the Commission and presented to the Executive Core Committee suggesting ways that the organization could work toward valuing diversity. In this proposal, current initiatives and the mission of the commission were redefined to enable more qualitative outcomes—for example, for us to become more self-reflective about how those in our organization and profession do their work. We realized that in order for us to better respond to efforts to accomplish a broader scope of involvement throughout our work and the membership, we needed to work more closely together with the Executive Core Committee, serving in both advocacy and education roles. This extended our charge to advising the Executive Core Committee on ways to increase and sustain the organization's efforts toward valuing diversity.

The Executive Core Committee: A Focus on Organizational Commitment

In the spring 1999 Executive Core Committee meeting, under the presidential leadership of Kay Herr Gillespie, leaders articulated 11 goals for the organization. These goals were then prioritized in terms of future direction. Among the important goals listed was for the organization "to enhance the centrality of diversity and multiculturalism within POD's mission." In striving to meet this goal, several objectives were shared. These included, but were not limited to, (1) conducting a multicultural values assessment of POD, (2) conducting a multicultural climate assessment of POD, (3) conducting an assessment of possible differences in perceptions between underrepresented and majority group members, and (4) increasing our sensitivity to new members of the organization so that we do not polarize ourselves into an "in-group" and an "out-group."

When one looks at the history and culture of POD since its founding in 1976, we can see regular efforts made toward valuing diversity. These efforts have been uneven, however, in terms of conference keynotes and themes; programming streams; our literature; the social, cultural, and racial identity makeup of our members; the types of institutions represented in our membership; the leadership makeup of the Core; and the level of commitment among our members. At best, our practices could be considered localized, with organizational initiatives undertaken by colleagues who not only demonstrated a strong personal commitment toward this work, but who often also were driven by compelling forces or needs at their institutions.

We remain encouraged that many of the current values, policies, and practices of POD (only some of which are described here) constitute important institutional strengths in advancing our progress toward the realization of a multicultural organization. For example, POD members value highly the spirit of collegiality and flexibility. Over and over, many first-time conference attendees remark on the generosity of POD members in sharing their ideas, programs, materials, and resources so willingly. We also have a growing historical record of formal organizational support for diversity initiatives. However, more remains to be achieved, especially at the organizational level.

Calibrating the Distance: How Do We Get from Here to There?

Attempts to understand the current context and to explore future directions for change in instructional and organizational development within POD, as well as our home institutions, might benefit from taking a multicultural organizational change perspective. As surveyed above, POD has begun to genuinely engage in creating organizational supports for diversity. We actively support outreach efforts, offer access to funds and internships, and actively nurture networks to mentor members from underrepresented institutions and racial and ethnic groups. However, the dominant values, practices, systems, politics, and guiding principles of POD continue to reflect our historically homogenous (white) character.

The theoretical perspectives and practices of multicultural organizational development provide particularly useful models and strategies as we reflect on where we are now and consider next steps as a multicultural organization. Multicultural organizational development (MCOD) offers systemic organizational change models that directly address social justice and equity issues in terms of the growth and development of organizations (Jackson & Holvino, 1988). These frameworks for addressing social justice issues in organizational development have emerged through the efforts of both practitioners and theorists since the 1970s. The work of Jackson and Holvino (1988) and field practitioners like Cross (1994) continue to directly address issues of equity and social justice in an organizational development context.

Multicultural organizational development theory enhances and extends the field of organizational development by articulating the relatedness of organizations to culture-wide change initiatives and by addressing the impact of cultural, institutional, and individual socialization (Jackson & Holvino, 1988; Katz, 1978). Like the field of organizational development before it, multicultural organizational development takes a systemic perspective and includes every aspect of an organization (mission, resources, processes, product, and people) as equally important components of growth, and it emphasizes change toward social justice.

Jackson and Hardiman (1994) have described six developmental stages through which an organization may move from a monocultural to a multicultural organization. These stages include the exclusionary organization, the "club," the compliance organization, the Affirmative Action organization, a redefining organization, and, finally, the multicultural organization (see Figure 3.1). One of the strengths of this multi-

FIGURE 3.1
Stages in the Development of a Multicultural Organization

Stage	Type	Descriptors
One	Exclusionary Organization	Mission and membership criteria openly discriminate.
Two	The Club	Mission, policies, norms, and procedures allow for a few "selected," "right" representatives.
Three	Compliance Organization	Provides some access without departing from mission, structure, culture. Maintains status quo.
Four	Affirmative Action Organization	Recruits and promotes members of social groups other than the "majority." Training provided.
Five	Redefining Organization	Actively engages in envisioning, planning, and problem-solving to find ways to ensure the full inclusion of all.
Six	Multicultural Organization	Reflects contributions of diverse cultural and social groups; acts on commitment to eradicate social oppression in all forms; all members are full participants; follows through on external social responsibilities.

From Jackson, B. & Holvino, E. (1988). Developing multicultural organizations. Creative Change: The Journal of Religion and the Applied Behavioral Sciences, 9 *(2), 14-19. Association for Creative Change.*

cultural organizational development model is that it offers multiple points of entry into systems-change and goals for a more socially just organization. For example, MCOD advocates organizational change by comprehensively addressing the organization's mission, goals, and values; structure and personnel profile; technology; management practices; and awareness and climate (Jackson & Hardiman, 1994). The model ultimately addresses the way our organization interacts with the larger societal environment in achieving our "bottom line" goals. Any one of these organizational elements provides a productive place to begin the work of transforming POD into the multicultural organization many of us envision.

In moving through different stages in the development of a multicultural organization, Jackson and Hardiman (1994) suggest a four-component process of organization-wide, long-term change strategy. These components include the creation of a multicultural change team, a support building phase, a leadership-development phase, and a self-renewing, multicultural systems-change process. We are absolutely confident that POD counts within both its general membership and the Executive Core leaders the experience, expertise, and commitment to guide our organization successfully through these endeavors.

Multicultural Internal Change Team

Dialogues currently underway within the organization provide a measure for our organization's state of readiness for further change initiatives. By better assessing how our organization currently functions, defines itself, and understands the need for change, we can develop meaningful interventions and develop practical strategies that more inclusively extend the opportunities and benefits many of us have harvested from our association with POD to others.

The Diversity Commission has played just such a powerful and important role as an internal change team. Its efforts have ranged from helping individual members increase their self-awareness to efforts to influence the organizational environment for all members. As a membership, we must realize that there may be times when we are going to feel "uncomfortable," but at the same time, we should find ways of dealing with this discomfort by having open and honest dialogues with each other. Recognizing that change is a concept integral to life and that we must continually learn in order to be effective will also help us to value the fundamental reason for becoming a multicultural learning organization.

As educational developers, we can assist our home institutions by helping groups learn of multicultural faculty development models that they can employ in creating climate change on campus. Nowhere is this call for us to be change agents advocated more strongly than by Chism (1998):

> As messengers and translators, educational developers need to be able to follow developments under discussion in the current literature and educational meetings and communicate these in a way that will be understood by their faculty and administrators, using the language that is appropriate for the context. . . . As nurturers, partners and coaches, we need to be personally centered,

> knowing our own capacity and believing in the capacity of our colleagues to recognize the need for change and be brave enough to experiment (p. 146).

Efforts of the Diversity Commission have fostered this kind of coaching for the organization's members and leadership team.

Support Building

A useful strategy for encouraging support building in an ongoing manner is to engage ourselves in a self-reflective process that continues to clarify our values and the cultural context in which these are embedded (Stanley & Ouellett, 1998). We can begin to open ourselves to change by exploring ideas, models, activities, action plans, and strategies that can be accomplished in the context of our home institutions. Some of these could involve high-risk activities such as multicultural audits, where systematic data are gathered to gain insight into an organization's life (Chesler, 1998). Equally important is to engage in candid dialogues with peers or students who have traditionally been seated on the "outside aisles" of our institutions. Lower-risk activities could involve expanding our knowledge base (Kardia, 1998) by bringing the scholarship of diversity into conversations or attending a workshop.

Leadership Development

Leadership is key to change initiatives; without it most change fails (Chaffee & Tierney, 1988; Kouzes & Posner, 1990). POD has had and will continue to have a history of strong leadership in both formal (Executive Core Committee) and informal (member-based initiatives) structures. We have had a lineage of leaders who have been instrumental in creating and responding effectively to changes within higher education in general and within POD specifically. Organizational leaders have been especially effective in creating a shared responsibility for the values and mission among the membership. Becoming a multicultural organization begins with visionary leadership for the future. We have to become more self-reflective leaders and practitioners, as we discuss successes, challenges, and intentions. It is not a static event, but rather a continuous process (Cook & Sorcinelli, 1999). It is part of being a learning community. It is part of becoming organizational change agents.

Self-Renewing Multicultural Systems-Change Process

Change is complex, nonlinear, and healthy. As we look at POD as an example, change, on one level, can be viewed in terms of increased membership, while on another, it can be seen as the way we envision our work as a national organization. At an organizational level, two modes of inquiry may be useful: One is to clarify our organizational values (what they mean to us individually and collectively), and the other is to clarify and reiterate how we express our commitment to these values (policies, procedures, resources, access). We have to continue to ask ourselves more guiding questions as we work toward this endeavor. Some might be: What do we really mean by diversity? Is it cultural diversity? Is it social diversity? Is it institutional diversity? What does the choice of conference site location or programming say to our members who are socially and culturally diverse (e.g., people of color, gays and lesbians, people with disabilities, etc.)?

As authors, our perception of POD is offered as one way to begin a discussion. A determination of POD's stage of multicultural organization development, identification of goals, and development of interventions to move us to the next stage of development require the participation of many more and diverse perspectives. What messages do we send when members of the Diversity Commission are the ones leading the charge for these issues? What are some ways that we can engage other POD committees in building diversity in their own activities? Why is it important for POD to diversify its membership to reflect faculty development efforts nationally?

In our dialogues, we cannot lose sight of the big picture. A multicultural organization allows everyone a voice to express their concerns and different perspectives about the reasons for change and the desired outcomes. Disagreement will be inevitable and should be welcomed. In developing a structure for change, leadership at all levels is important (Morey, 1997).

For example, the Professional Development Committee could develop ideas for opening the pipeline to faculty developers of color, or it could work with POD institutions who have been recipients of the diversity internship grants to involve interns in the Institute for New Faculty Developers. The Grants Committee could seek out and call for proposals that have a diversity strand. The Publications Committee could, in its guidelines, seek out and call for papers that have a focus on diversity. Similarly, the Long Range Conference and Conference Planning Committees could take into account factors that contribute to the climate of a successful conference. All committees, in their reports, budgets, and timelines for accomplishing proposed activities, could be asked to report on how goals are met with respect to valuing diversity.

A Call to Action

As we lay the foundation for becoming a multicultural organization, we can work toward self-awareness by stretching beyond our own "comfort zone" (Stanley & Ouellett, 1998) and by utilizing the experiences we share in POD to create a vital, flexible learning community. As we look toward the new century, let us not forget this goal, but rather embrace it with purpose, so that together we can build a compelling and dynamic vision for the future. As educational change agents, we can work together to develop effective communication networks and strategies in the continual search for ideas as we assess our successes and failures and decide on next steps. Jackson (1994) underscores that

> to create a vision of a multicultural system, a diversity of perspectives must be represented in a group of people who are engaged in a dialogical process such as that put forth by Paulo Freire as Praxis. . . . The people involved in this process are as important as the process itself (p. 116).

Based on our experiences and research, we would like to invite you to continue this dialogue. As we collectively shape our goal of becoming a multicultural organization, we leave you with some concrete suggestions for where to begin.

1) **Ask Questions.** We can only improve on what we have accomplished and gather information for future directions by asking questions. Talk to each other. Talk to colleagues who work at institutions that are different from your own. Talk to colleagues who are from a different social, racial, or cultural group. Articulate a vision for the future of the organization.

2) **Take More Risks.** Be an effective educational ally for change. Effective allies are supportive of, and advocates for, change. Allies have worked to develop an understanding of the personal and institutional experiences of target group members (e.g., people of color; gay, lesbian, and bisexual individuals; people with disabilities; women; etc.). Effective allies choose to align themselves publicly and privately with members of targeted groups. Often, retooled skills and reexamined perspectives are part and parcel of genuine commitment to new initiatives.

3) **Respect and Forgive.** In learning together, we will make mistakes. Hopefully, we will learn from our mistakes and our encounters and not use them as excuses for non-action. Many of us, after reflecting on our own behaviors during the last conference, have decided to be more proactive in terms of making multicultural issues more integral to programming streams and overall conference planning.

4) **Engage in Sustained Dialogue.** A vision for a multicultural organization can grow from multiple sources. We need everyone's input and perspectives if we are to make a difference.

5) **Start in Our Own Backyard.** POD offers an opportunity to practice the development of these skills and behaviors in a context that is less risky than what most of us would find at our home institutions. It provides a supportive system of collegiality and a highly expert network of professionals in a setting that values and nurtures educational development.

6) **Start Where You Are.** There are multiple points of entry into this process and we have to consider what we are ready to do publicly and what we would rather do reflectively.

Conclusion

We suggest that multicultural organizational change models, such as those by Jackson and Hardiman, can help us to acknowledge the useful contributions of current diversity initiatives in POD as well as to structure significant innovations. As we roll toward the 21st century, becoming a multicultural organization stands to benefit all of our members. The models and practices offered by multicultural organizational development theorists acknowledge an underlying commonality of forms of oppression and suggest that intervention to interrupt one manifestation (e.g., racism, sexism, anti-Semitism, ableism, or heterosexism) lays groundwork for interventions around others (Jackson & Holvino, 1988). Some POD members currently gain many advantages from the current values, beliefs, and practices of the organizational culture and, therefore, may be less motivated to act to support change. However, there are benefits for all members because participation in this process becomes an opportunity to learn and practice the skills needed in most meaningful future leadership roles both within POD and at most educational institutions.

Our experience has taught us that systemic organizational change is not without its ups and downs. To be sure, since our involvement in POD, we have seen many changes that would not have occurred without all of our efforts. As changes occur, we continue to grow and learn from the knowledge gained and the satisfaction that we have contributed to respecting and valuing human diversity. This is essential to the organizational growth and continued excellence of POD as well as to our professional and personal growth as educational developers.

Acknowledgments

The authors gratefully acknowledge the counsel and perspective of Kay Herr Gillespie, Mary Deane Sorcinelli, and Marilla Svinicki during the development of this article.

References

Border, L. L. B., & Chism, N. V. N. (1992). The future is now: A call for action and list of resources. In L. L. B. Border & N. V. N. Chism (Eds.), *Teaching for diversity* (pp. 103-115). New Directions for Teaching and Learning, No. 49. San Francisco, CA: Jossey-Bass.

Chaffee, E. E., & Tierney, W. G. (1988). *Collegiate culture and leadership strategies.* New York, NY: Macmillan.

Chesler, M. A. (1994). Organizational development is not the same as multicultural organizational development. In E. Cross, H. Katz, F. Miller, & E. Seashore (Eds.), *The promise of diversity* (pp. 240-251). Chicago, IL: Irwin Professional Publishing.

Chesler, M. A. (1998). Planning multicultural audits in higher education. *To Improve the Academy, 17,* 171-192.

Chism, N. V. N. (1998). The roles of educational developers in institutional change: From the basement office to the front office. *To Improve the Academy, 17,* 141-153.

Collett, J., & Serrano, B. (1992). Stirring it up: The inclusive classroom. In L. L. B. Border & N. V. N. Chism (Eds.), *Teaching for diversity* (pp. 35-48). New Directions for Teaching and Learning, No. 49. San Francisco, CA: Jossey-Bass.

Cook, C. E., & Sorcinelli, M. D. (1999). Building multiculturalism into teaching-development programs. *AAHE Bulletin, 51* (7), 3-6.

Cooper, J., & Chattergy, V. (1993). Developing faculty multicultural awareness: An examination of life roles and their cultural components. *To Improve the Academy, 12*, 81-95.

Cross, E. (1994). Truth-or consequences. In E. Cross, H. Katz, F. Miller, & E. Seashore (Eds.), *The promise of diversity* (pp. 32-35). Chicago, IL: Irwin Professional Publishing.

Evans, L., & Chauvin, S. (1993). Faculty developers as change facilitators: The concerns-based adoption model. *To Improve the Academy, 12*, 165-178.

Ferren, A., & Geller, W. (1993). Faculty development's role in promoting an inclusive community: Addressing sexual orientation. *To Improve the Academy, 12*, 97-108.

Jackson, B. (1994). Coming to a vision of a multicultural system. In E. Cross, H. Katz, F. Miller, & E. Seashore (Eds.), *The promise of diversity* (pp. 116-117). Chicago, IL: Irwin Professional Publishing.

Jackson, B., & Hardiman, R. (1994). Multicultural organizational development. In E. Cross, H. Katz, F. Miller, & E. Seashore (Eds.), *The promise of diversity* (pp. 231-239). Chicago, IL: Irwin Professional Publishing.

Jackson, B., & Holvino, E. (1988). Developing multicultural organizations. *Creative Change: The Journal of Religion and the Applied Behavioral Sciences, 9* (2), 14-19. Association for Creative Change.

Kardia, D. (1998). Becoming a multicultural faculty developer. *To Improve the Academy, 17*, 15-33.

Katz, J. (1978). *White awareness: Handbook of anti-racism training.* Norman, OK: University of Oklahoma Press.

Knoedler, A., & Shea, M. (1992). Conducting discussions in the diverse classroom. *To Improve the Academy, 11*, 123-135.

Kouzes, J. M., & Posner, B. Z. (1990). *The leadership challenge: How to get extraordinary things done in organizations.* San Francisco, CA: Jossey-Bass.

Morey, A. I. (1997). Organizational change and implementation strategies for multicultural infusion. In A. I. Morey & M. K. Kitano (Eds.), *Multicultural course transformation in higher education: A broader truth* (pp. 258-277). Needham Heights, MA: Allyn & Bacon.

Ouellett, M. L., & Sorcinelli, M. D. (1995). Teaching and learning in the diverse classroom: A faculty and TA partnership program. *To Improve the Academy, 14*, 205-217.

Ouellett, M. L., & Sorcinelli, M. D. (1998). TA training: Strategies for responding to diversity in the classroom. In M. Marincovich, J. Prostko, & F. Stout (Eds.), *The professional development of graduate teaching assistants* (pp. 105-120). Bolton, MA: Anker Publishing.

Patrick, S., & Fletcher, J. (1998). Faculty developers as change agents: Transforming colleges and universities into learning organizations. *To Improve the Academy, 17*, 155-169.

Schmitz, B., Paul, S., & Greenberg, J. (1992). Creating multicultural classrooms: An experience-derived faculty development program. In L. L. B. Border & N. V. N. Chism (Eds.), *Teaching for diversity* (pp. 75-87). New Directions for Teaching and Learning, No. 49. San Francisco, CA: Jossey-Bass.

Stanley, C. A., & Ouellett, M. L. (1998). Teaching for the diverse classroom. *Advocate, 1* (2), 5-8.

Wadsworth, E. (1992). Inclusive teaching: A workshop on cultural diversity. *To Improve the Academy, 11,* 233-240.

Wunsch, M., & Chattergy, V. (1991). Managing diversity through faculty development. *To Improve the Academy, 10,* 141-150.

Contacts:

Christine A. Stanley
Office of Faculty and TA Development
The Ohio State University
20 Lord Hall, 124 West 17th Avenue
Columbus, OH 43210-1316
(614) 292-3644
(614) 688-5496 (FAX)
stanley.5@osu.edu

Mathew L. Ouellett
Center for Teaching
University of Massachusetts, Amherst
301 Goodell Building, Box 33245
Amherst, MA 01003-3245
(413) 545-1225
(413) 545-3205 (FAX)
mlo@acad.umass.edu

Christine A. Stanley is Associate Director of the Office of Faculty and TA Development and a member of the Adjunct Faculty in the School of Educational Policy & Leadership at The Ohio State University. She has taught courses in College Teaching and General Biology. Her research interests include professional development in higher education, how to deliver effective consultation services to faculty and TAs, and multicultural faculty and organizational development. She is President-Elect of POD.

Mathew L. Ouellett is Associate Director of the Center for Teaching at the University of Massachusetts, Amherst. He also serves as Adjunct Professor of Social Work at Smith College, where he teaches courses on the implications of racism for clinical social work practice. His research interests include faculty development, multicultural organizational development, and equity in educational organizations. He is Vice Chair of the POD Diversity Commission.

4

The Scholarship of Teaching and Learning: A National Initiative

Barbara L. Cambridge
American Association for Higher Education

As part of the scholarship of teaching and learning, faculty members study the ways in which they teach and students learn in their disciplines, and campuses foster this scholarship at the institutional level. A national initiative called the Carnegie Academy for the Scholarship of Teaching and Learning constitutes three programs to engage and support individuals, campuses, and disciplinary associations in this form of scholarly work. This article describes the Pew Scholars Fellowship Program, the Campus Program, and the Work with Scholarly Societies and invites participation of campuses in this exciting initiative.

Dennis Jacobs has introduced cooperative learning into a large lecture course of general chemistry at the University of Notre Dame. The retention rates, test performance, and interest level of students in the cooperative learning course have exceeded those for students of similar ability enrolled in a more traditional general chemistry course on the same campus. Dennis is interested now in answers to the following questions: 1) Which features of the new course (pairing students in lecture to analyze and predict chemical behavior, small-group problem-solving activities, weekly graded homework, online quizzes, and/or increased socialization) have had the greatest impact on student learning? 2) What design elements of cooperative learning activities are most successful in stimulating meaningful discussion, promoting deeper conceptual understanding, and developing individual problem-solving skills? and 3) What is the long-term impact of such a course? Are students more successful in advanced courses if they have had a collaborative problem-solving experience in a foundational course?

Like Dennis, most faculty have questions about the impact of their pedagogical decisions on student learning in their classes. And, more and more faculty are finding answers to those questions by designing projects that build on what is known about learning and specifically about learning in their disciplines. This exciting work occurs in pockets on campuses of all kinds throughout the country. However, it often remains local, improving teaching and learning within the investigator's own classroom but not adding to the knowledge base of the discipline, partly because of beliefs about teaching that thwart its identification as scholarly work. Teaching has been regarded as private, difficult to study and critique, and less worthy than traditional research of serious regard.

Fortunately, faculty who pose, study, and begin to answer intriguing questions about their teaching can enter a newly emerging community of scholars. These scholars apply to their teaching criteria pertinent to all scholarship: clear goals, adequate preparation, appropriate methods, significant results, effective presentation, and reflective critique (Glassick, Huber, & Maeroff, 1997). They expect to go public with their findings, to receive the kind of peer review that interrogates their methods and conclusions, and to change their teaching and scholarly investigations of teaching based on that review. They also expect that their institution's reward system will acknowledge and value their scholarship of teaching and learning.

At this point, readers may be asking themselves "What planet is she writing about?" But, I did say "an emerging community of scholars." Communities must be built, and there are multiple individuals and groups committed to the building of this new community of scholars of teaching and learning. In this article I will describe one effort to enlarge this new community through support of individuals, campuses, and disciplinary associations. Dennis is a member of that effort, and you with your campus are welcome to join this growing community.

The Carnegie Academy for the Scholarship of Teaching and Learning

The Carnegie Academy for the Scholarship of Teaching and Learning (CASTL), with funding from the Pew Charitable Trusts and in collaboration with the American Association for Higher Education (AAHE), is designed to foster the practice of scholarly inquiry about teaching and learning. Its three parts attend to three ways in which faculty members enter their professional worlds: as individuals, as members of a campus faculty, and as members of disciplinary groups.

Pew Scholar Fellowship Program

The Pew Scholar Fellowship Program selects scholars from designated disciplines to pursue their work in a concentrated way through funding, opportunities for interactions with other scholars, and, most importantly, time for carrying out a scholarly project. Pew Scholars are contributing to the emergent definition of the scholarship of teaching and learning. Pat Hutchings, senior scholar at the Carnegie Foundation for the Advancement of Teaching and leader of its CASTL higher education work, suggests that the definition can begin with what the scholarship of teaching and learning is not.

1) It is not new. Faculty members have generated important work for many years upon which new scholars can build. Traditionally, however, faculty members have not become familiar with this literature, a body of work from many academic levels and many disciplines that can contribute to the foundation of new scholarly inquiry.

2) The scholarship of teaching is not for everyone for all time. Faculty members do different kinds of scholarly inquiry and pose different questions at different times in their professional lives. Some scholars will choose to focus on teaching and learning; others will not. Some will choose to do this work for all of their careers; others may move in and out of the work.

3) The scholarship of teaching and learning does not replace other kinds of scholarship. The scholarships of discovery, application, and integration join with the scholarship of teaching as one way to look at an array of scholarly possibilities.

4) Each discipline offers different ways to approach this work. For example, composition and rhetoric values narrative as a way to investigate and disseminate learning; chemistry employs a more empirical approach.

5) The scholarship of teaching and learning is not aimed exclusively at publication. Scholars of teaching and learning are exploring multiple ways of making their work public, including the Internet, faculty development activities, and public presentations.

6) The scholarship of teaching is not simply for a faculty member's own improvement. It contributes to the practice of others.

7) No one has this kind of work all figured out (Hutchings, 1999).

In fact, the work of helping to figure it out is one challenge for Pew Scholars. Ansel Adams once said that there is nothing worse than a clear image of a fuzzy concept. Knowing that a conclusive definition would be premature at this time, the Pew Scholars will over time increase knowledge about the concept of the scholarship of teaching and learning. The kinds of projects contributing to this development are as various as the scholars doing them. Here is just a glimpse of the range of work undertaken:

- Anthony Catanach, in accounting at Villanova University, is developing strategies for long-term assessment of students' use of competencies from his intermediate financial accounting course, a two-semester course considered the core of the accountancy major. He wants to determine the effects of innovative pedagogies used in his course on students' performance in subsequent classes and professional work.
- In English, Mariolina Salvatori, the University of Pittsburgh, is theorizing an approach to teaching that develops a teacher's attentiveness to her students' "moments of difficulty" for their hidden potential to produce understanding. Naming something "difficult" demonstrates a form of knowledge that is both profitable and responsible. She is studying the stumbling blocks in learning in different disciplines to understand how other disciplines confront this aspect of teaching.
- T. Mills Kelly, in history at Texas Tech University, is focusing on the ways in which student learning changes in response to the medium used to present essential source materials. Running parallel sections of the same Western Civilization course that offer materials in multimedia format or in print only, he is particularly interested in the influence of the Internet.
- Peter Alexander's "Math and Social Justice" capstone course for undergraduate mathematicians at Heritage College has the key goal of enhancing students' quantitative worldview while they work on projects that meet each student's definition of social justice and which benefit local communities.
- Stephen Chew, a psychologist at Samford University, is examining the effect of surface and structural components of examples used by teachers. Surface components, which strongly influence student understanding and ability to generalize from the example, are often given inadequate attention by teachers. Stephen aims to help faculty in multiple disciplines structure examples and problems to optimize student understanding.

- As editor of *Teaching Sociology,* Jeffrey Chin of Le Moyne College is studying the evolution of the scholarship of teaching in sociology from 1983-1998, using papers published in the journal as a database. He will compare his results with a 1983 study that extended back to 1973 to determine if progress has been made in cumulative scholarship and in a convergence of teaching-learning strategies.
- Deborah Vess, at Georgia College and State University, is examining the effects of interactive, online modules in an interdisciplinary global issues course. She is developing an assessment instrument to determine the development of students' critical abilities in the modules and interviewing students to ascertain intellectual problems faced in constructing their solutions and integrating resources. She wants to understand how students apply abstract theory to real-world situations and to document the relationship of interdisciplinary work to growth in critical abilities.

This sample of the range of projects illustrates the interesting intellectual problems that are challenging scholars in multiple fields. The Pew Scholars Fellowship Program promotes synergy among these scholars.

Campus Program

The second component of CASTL promotes a synergistic relationship among campuses. The Campus Program is designed for institutions of all types that are prepared to make a public commitment to new models of teaching as scholarly work and is implemented through AAHE. Any interested campus is encouraged to organize its efforts and then to register its process and goals so that all campuses can learn from one another.

Developing a discourse. Whenever a new community of scholars forms, the community develops language that it collectively uses to talk about what it wants to talk about. Because the term scholarship of teaching is so new, the Campus Program begins with a campus-wide focus on a draft definition of the scholarship of teaching, offered as a conversation starter. In fact, the first phase of Campus Program participation is named Campus Conversations to emphasize the need for dialogue and for developing discourse about teaching and learning. Campuses are invited to take apart and revise the draft definition so that the campus has a clearer sense of what it means by doing the scholarship of teaching and learning. The draft definition reads as follows:

> The scholarship of teaching is problem posing about an issue of teaching or learning, study of the problem through methods appropriate to the disciplinary epistemologies, application of results to practice, communication of results, self-reflection, and peer review.

Several campuses have reported their negotiated versions of a definition. These examples illustrate the thinking at three quite different campuses, two of which have generated a definition and one of which has a process in motion that suits the size and type of campus that it is.

1) *Abilene Christian University*
Following a series of departmental and college meetings and discussion on an interactive web page, Abilene Christian University decided on major changes in the definition. They feared that the language emphasized a research methodology and would exclude some practices (such as curriculum revision or teaching portfolios) that they believed are appropriately classified as scholarship of teaching. They also felt that the language of the draft definition emphasized the process more than the definition. Their definition reads:

> *The scholarship of teaching is public discourse conceptualizing teaching.*
>
> - *Public* is making our work accessible to others for critical review and use.
> - *Discourse* includes oral and written discourse in such varied contexts as curriculum committees, faculty development presentations, publications on the web, teaching portfolios, or journal articles. While both informal and formal opportunities to present findings are considered scholarship of teaching, they are weighted differently in faculty evaluations such as tenure and promotion.
> - *Conceptualizing* teaching is more than good teaching: it requires careful thought, analysis, and self-reflection about teaching.
> - *Teaching* cultivates the exchange of ideas among teachers, students, and others in and out of the classroom.

2) *Elon College*
Elon College frames a different definition:

> The scholarship of learning/teaching (a) seeks to develop new knowledge (through discovery, integration, application) in the

field of inquiry and to share what is learned widely so that insights can be built upon and oversights corrected; (b) invites collaboration throughout the process; (c) sets a direction of inquiry and commits to shared standards as to how results will be measured; (d) remains alert to the most exciting thinking in the disciplines that bear on the task; (e) invites constructive critique from the academic community (colleagues, students, and like-minded peers).

We choose to speak of the Learning-Teaching Enterprise. This shift emphasizes that what is to be examined must be a partnership of students and teachers in which both partners learn and both partners, in different ways, teach. We wanted to make learning central and also to highlight educational content in the various fields.

3) *The Ohio State University*
To root the discussion in concrete, disciplinary contexts, each member of the Executive Council of the Academy of Teaching convened a conversation in her or his own academic unit (involving similar units if desired). The proposed topic for discussion was "Learning Pitfalls in Introductory Classes." The conversations addressed such questions as: What are some common concepts that are especially confusing for students in our introductory courses? What skills are especially hard for them to master? How do we know when students are really stuck? How do we explore the nature of the problem? What do we do with the information we obtain? Are there systematic ways in which our faculty and discipline could address these issues and share our findings? Based on the answers to these questions, how do we define the scholarship of teaching for our context? Is this definition applicable to non-introductory courses as well?

A forum is now planned at which different groups will compare their results and look for commonalities across disciplines. The goal is to arrive at a university definition of the scholarship of teaching, identification of the ways in which it is supported and constrained, and a plan of action for cultivating such scholarship in the future.

Identifying conditions for doing the scholarship of teaching and learning. In the next part of Campus Conversations, campuses identify ways in which they support or inhibit the scholarship of teaching and learning. Campus groups take up such questions as, Who does the scholarship of teaching and learning on our campus? Do hiring and orienting practices locate and support faculty members committed to the scholarship of teaching? What are the most central teaching issues on our campus, and how is the campus addressing those issues? Are faculty members rewarded for doing the scholarship of teaching? How does our campus culture both discourage and affirm the scholarship of teaching and learning? What specific steps can the campus take to create conditions generative of the scholarship of teaching and learning? This environmental scan enables a campus to identify an area for study and action that will enhance its support for this kind of work.

Doing the work. Campuses that have completed their campus audit and have determined, or are deciding, on a focus for future campus-wide work are inevitably considering a range of work. Several examples signal that range.

1) *Western Washington University*

Western Washington University has drafted an action plan to profile the scholarship of teaching and learning in a way that elevates the status of teaching on its campus. With commitment from its president, who provided a summer stipend for a faculty leader to work with colleagues for planning, the campus will focus on a theme during each of three quarters of the academic year: *recognizing* the scholarship of teaching, *reflecting* on that work, and *rewarding* it. These 3-R's discussions will begin first term with main events such as a presidential luncheon for all faculty and a series of campus lectures and breakfast meetings followed by workshops.

In addition faculty members from each of the campus's 35 departments and programs are being selected to participate in a new program. They will examine the effectiveness of a case study and peer review model for developing and advancing faculty skills intended to enhance student learning in critical thinking, writing in the disciplines, symbolic reasoning, and affective development. They will try to answer the following questions: Can a faculty-based case study grounded in a peer review and self-reflective approach improve student learning in non-content domains? Will this process significantly improve instructional competence and cross-disciplinary dialogues about teaching and learning, and enhance the scholarship of teaching at WWU?

Drawing on their own teaching, faculty will generate case studies as exemplars of student learning problems and themes in non-content domain. These case studies will be used as springboards for faculty using a variety of methodologies. The campus plans to utilize electronic threaded discussions, in-classroom peer review, self-reflective writing, and the identification and development of student learning and faculty development assessment tools.

2) *Augustana College*
Augustana faculty have identified five general areas on which they would like to focus. The participating faculty (which now includes 45 of the college's 150 full-time faculty members) have affiliated themselves with one of five question groups. The five groups and some of the questions under consideration include:

- The Student. How can an instructor into tap students' internal motivation? How do various modes of learning and teaching interact with differing styles and abilities? Is students' motivation subject to change through strategies we can employ?
- The Classroom. What is the interaction between content and teaching strategy? How do gestures facilitate learning? How can teaching techniques be matched to outcomes and audience?
- The Engaging Text. What happens to students when they are assigned readings? What happens during highlighting? Is there a difference in reading comprehension from hard copy vs. screen text? Can we teach students to "talk back" to textbooks? What pre-reading approaches facilitate the reading process?
- Impact of Technology. How does technology impact learning? Do course web pages and chat groups facilitate learning? Does requiring that writing assignments be "on disk" improve the quality of writing and feedback?
- Foreign Study. How does foreign study impact students? What intellectual and social growth occurs during these experiences? What classroom experiences best facilitate learning in this context?

Resident campus experts on quantitative and qualitative research approaches have met with the participants to discuss options for structuring the inquires. Members of each group read common texts to provide a starting point for refining their research questions. By the end of summer 1999, each group will have developed a strategy for investigating a specific question.

3) *Rockhurst College*
The two central questions for Rockhurst are (1) How do we make our inquiries about teaching and learning issues public—in ways useful to

our campus colleagues and to our disciplines? and (2) Can we make this new area of scholarly discussion highly interdisciplinary to promote wider dialogue and new perspectives?

A seminar group of 15 faculty from a variety of disciplines and levels of teaching experience will follow four steps in this process. Along the way each seminar member will have access to an on-campus "consultant"—a faculty or administrative volunteer from a different discipline who has special expertise (teaching and research). These consultants will provide suggestions on resources and methods, serve as a sounding board for ideas, and occasionally join seminar discussions or make special presentations. Thus the "broadcast area" and potential impact of the seminar will be immediately increased.

The action plan for the seminar includes:

Step 1. To develop a common language, seminar members will read a core set of materials on learning theory, the scholarship of teaching and learning, college teaching, assessment, and higher education. Each seminar member will select a course they teach to serve as a practical context for exercises and discussions related to teaching as a scholarly act.

Step 2. Each seminar member will "deconstruct" the course they have selected—reexamining its component parts (objectives, assignments, assessments) in light of the readings, discussions, seminar presentations, and advice from consultants. The primary goal will be to identify discipline-based and inter-disciplinary areas of research within a course framework. Participants will present their findings to the seminar for further discussion and refinement. They will also engage in scholarly projects suggested by this process.

Step 3. Building on Step 2, the seminar will attempt to identify and answer key questions about teaching as a scholarly act, including appropriate research methods, types of evidence for such scholarship, standards and criteria for peer review, elements unique to a discipline, and interdisciplinary connections.

Step 4. Seminar members will prepare articles and presentations on the seminar experience and their course research. The workshop leader will construct a seminar workbook as a model device for subsequent faculty development activities.

Cross-Campus Communication

Occasions for sharing processes and products of campus work are part of the second phase of the Campus Program. Beginning with a colloquium prior to the 1999 AAHE National Conference on Higher Education, two-day colloquia will be held each year to enable cross-campus interaction and reports of progress both by Pew Scholars and by Campus Program participants. Meetings of campuses of similar type or working on similar issues are being held as interest and need arise.

Campuses are also supported in their work by a Web Center that offers resources, places to post drafts or finished products, sites of conversation around specific themes, and information about the work of all registered campuses and of individuals on those campuses. Faculty and staff on a Campus Program campus can sign on to make full use of all the features of the Web Center.

Work with Scholarly Societies

Faculty members often derive their primary professional identify through their discipline, a process reinforced by the current form of graduate education and by the ways in which faculty work is acclaimed. The third arena of activity in CASTL acknowledges the centrality of disciplinary and professional societies in promoting the scholarship of teaching and learning. Some associations have actively and publicly supported the work. For example, the American Sociological Association has published a book on peer review in sociology, building on work done by sociologists and others in the AAHE Peer Review project. The American Historical Association is working with Pew Scholar William Cutler from Temple University in providing examples of course portfolios on the web for response and use by other historians. The National Council of Teachers of English, the Academy of Management, and the American Chemical Society are featuring the topic of the scholarship of teaching and learning at upcoming conferences. Pew Scholar Randy Bass is leading a major project for the American Studies Association focusing on the ways in which the web opens new opportunities for both creation of, and interaction about, scholarship of teaching and learning.

These examples illustrate the ways in which scholarly societies can play a central role in fostering the scholarship of teaching and learning. At the 1999 Colloquium on Campus Conversations at AAHE, Carla Howery of the American Sociological Association challenged her colleagues who provide leadership in associations to do an association audit. In that audit associations ask themselves how they contribute not only to the professional identity but to the full range of professional work of their members, including the scholarship of teaching and learning. CASTL and AAHE have convened over 20 associations, primarily in disciplines represented in its Pew Scholar cohorts, to discuss strategies for supporting their members in this professional work and to devise their own projects for seed funding. The work of Pew Scholars like Jeff Chin and Donna Duffy offer essential information to associations about the impact of their work in this area.

What's Next?

At the 1999 Pew Scholar Institute, Peter Alexander, a mathematician from Heritage College, sparked thinking with the application of some principles of architecture to the scholarship of teaching and learning. Peter described as essential to architectural projects commodity, firmness, and delight. Commodity implies utility: The structure must serve the purposes for which it is built. Firmness includes substantiality or significance. And delight brings pleasure, joy, and satisfaction into the equation. In a later session at that same Institute, Lee Shulman picked up that language in advocating for distributed awareness, practice, and valuing of the scholarship of teaching and learning. He suggested that the standard of value for the scholarship of teaching and learning would certainly include at least utility (commodity) and delight. How will we know if this scholarship has utility and delight? Shulman answers that the work will be useful and interesting to more and more people in higher education if it is (1) generative, (2) longitudinal, and (3) collaborative.

Shulman referred to Aristotle's distinction between a face and a bag of coins. If any part of a face is removed or added to, the face changes, becoming something essentially different. If, on the other hand, a bag of coins has a few coins removed or added, the bag is recognizable as the same bag of coins. Shulman hopes that the scholarship of teaching and learning will change the face of higher education, not just alter the same old bag.

To make this change, the scholarship must first be generative, demonstrating clearly why doing the work is "worth the trouble," that is demonstrating that it is worth changing habits of mind and processes of teaching and learning that have been deeply engrained and are deeply familiar.

Second, the view of scholarship of teaching and learning must be longitudinal. Just as pool players think of the next shot as one in a strategic series, we must see individual projects as part of efforts unfolding over time. Because new questions, occasions, and circumstances will evolve, new hypotheses, projects to test those hypotheses, and ways to share conclusions will need to be developed. Along this line, Pew Scholar Randy Bass calls for a new way of viewing problems in teaching and learning as interesting and complex problems not to be solved once and for all but to be continuously explored as they emerge in different contexts (Bass, 1999).

Thirdly, the scholarship of teaching and learning is collaborative. Our rich tradition of building on research of scholars before us or beside us holds in the scholarship of teaching and learning. "It takes a village," said Shulman about the need for collaborative efforts in addressing the wonderfully complex problems that engage our intellectual and emotional abilities. This collaborative work will add to the critical mass that will serve as "an existence proof" for our colleagues who are just beginning to understand the nature of the scholarship of teaching and learning (Shulman, 1999).

In his book *The Fifth Discipline*, Peter Senge (1990) advises that transformative change can occur when genuine openness is present. He calls for "reflective openness," which "looks inward and starts with the willingness to challenge our own thinking, to recognize that any certainty we ever have is, at best, a hypothesis about the world. It involves not just examining our own ideas, but mutually examining others' thinking" (278). The efforts of the Pew Scholars Fellowship Program, the Campus Program, and the Work with Scholarly Societies all embrace the need to challenge our own deepest thinking and to do so in the company of others engaged in the same work. Teaching and learning will become central in the definition of a professor's role, the identification of a campus's function, and the heart of disciplinary associations only when we accept the challenge of exploring with commodity, firmness, and delight the complex and exciting sites of learning in higher education.

References

Bass, R. (1999). The scholarship of teaching: What's the problem? *Inventio [Online], 1* (1). Available: www.doiiit.gmu.edu/inventio/randybass.htm.

Glassick, C., Huber, M., & Maeroff, G. (1997). *Scholarship assessed: Evaluation of the Professoriate.* San Francisco, CA: Jossey-Bass.

Hutchings, P. (1999, June). *Designing the scholarship of teaching and learning.* Paper presented at the Pew Scholars Institute, Menlo Park, CA.

Senge, P. (1990). *The fifth discipline.* London, UK: Century, Business.

Shulman, L. (1999, June). *Framing questions and designing inquiry.* Paper presented at the Pew Scholars Institute, Menlo Park, CA.

Contact:

Barbara L. Cambridge
American Association for Higher Education
One Dupont Circle, Suite 360
Washington, DC 20036
(202) 293-6440 ext. 760
(202) 293-0073 (FAX)
bcambridge@aahe.org

Barbara L. Cambridge is director of Teaching Initiatives at the American Association for Higher Education. She is on leave from Indiana University Purdue University Indianapolis where she is professor of English and Associate Dean of the Faculties. At AAHE Cambridge coordinates the Campus Program, one of the three activities of the higher education program at the Carnegie Foundation for the Advancement of Teaching.

An Invitation

Videotape

A videotape titled *Fostering a Scholarship of Teaching* is now available to introduce key concepts behind the Pew Scholars Fellowship Program and the Campus Program. The video, which features, among others, Lee Shulman and selected Pew Scholars, can be used effectively to help groups of faculty understand the concept of the scholarship of teaching and learning, prompt consideration of involvement in the Campus Program, and explain CASTL to educational leaders and others interested in the quality of education.

Any campus registered for the Campus Program is welcome to a copy of the video by contacting Teresa Antonucci at American Association for Higher Education. She may be reached at tantonucci@aahe.org or (202) 293-6440.

Anyone else interested in the video may order a copy by contacting Terri Coats in the Publications Department of the Carnegie Foundation for Teaching at (650) 566-5102. The cost for the video is $9.00, including shipping with sales tax if applicable.

Booklets

Booklets about the Campus Program and about the Pew Scholars Fellowship Program are available from AAHE and from the Carnegie Foundation. Contact either site for single or multiple copies.

5

QILT: An Approach to Faculty Development and Institutional Self-Improvement

Mike Laycock
University of East London

In a climate of increasing emphasis on quality assurance and extra-institutional quality scrutiny, the author argues that faculty developers have a role in encouraging an enhancement-led culture. Faculty ownership of, and responsibility for, continuous quality improvement can help to provide an engagement with teaching and learning issues and may help to overcome resistance and mistrust. At the University of East London, UK, an enabling, whole-institutional framework called QILT (Quality Improvement in Learning and Teaching), whereby faculty create and implement funded improvement plans, has helped to generate this culture.

Introduction

The responsibility of universities for quality and standards has placed great emphasis on the monitoring and review of performance for the purposes of accountability. During 1993, the University of East London, UK, undertook a major review of its internal quality assurance procedures, particularly those associated with the academic review of courses. Two working parties were established to consider the processes of Subject Review and Teaching Review. The latter produced a policy document that radically re-defined the university's approach to quality assurance by emphasizing the importance of quality improvement rather than traditional notions of review. It was felt that quality assurance alone was of dubious value in providing a model to respond to, or to create, change and improvement.

This emphasis on quality assurance has been redressed at the University of East London (UEL) by a complementary, collective responsibility for improvement. This whole-institutional model of Quality Improvement in Learning and Teaching (QILT) was introduced in 1994/5. QILT is a process of continuous quality improvement that involves the creation of funded improvement plans by staff/student groups, the implementation of the plans, and the formative and summative evaluation of progress.

Most faculty development is about change. Continuous reflection on, and adaptation to, changing circumstances and the development of a culture of self-evaluation and self-improvement will be the hallmarks of a mature and responsible institution in its pursuit of quality improvement. However, the present arrangements for the external scrutiny of quality in higher education, it could be argued, have emphasized a static rather than transformational concept of quality. Given the range of internal and external pressures on higher education, it is likely that qualitative indicators will need to be developmental. As Yorke (1994) has succinctly put it:

> Higher education will probably need to be steered more positively towards the future than a coxless four, in which the rowers face backwards while moving forwards on the assumption that the competition lanes will not curve away from the straight (p. 7).

For some years, observers of both UK and US higher education systems have directed attention to the problems inherent in "accountability-led" regulatory frameworks for the assurance of quality. Pressures on institutions have arisen in the UK principally through government policy. At the subject level, formal accountability is exercised through a cycle of reviews of teaching quality. The Quality Assurance Agency for Higher Education (QAAHE) currently requires each subject area to undertake a self-assessment exercise every five years in the following "core areas of provision":

- Curriculum design, content, and organization
- Teaching, learning, and assessment
- Student progression and achievement
- Student support and guidance

- Learning resources
- Quality management and enhancement

At the institutional level, QAAHE undertakes a "continuation" academic quality audit. A number of UK universities are now preparing for, or have undertaken, the continuation academic quality audit under new guidelines prepared by the QAAHE. The emphasis for the audit is placed firmly on the issue of standards. There is little doubt that con-cern about standards within the regulatory framework derive from government anxiety about the movement from an elite to a mass higher education system. Unsurprisingly, some have suggested that there has been a withdrawal of trust in higher education's ability to manage that transformation without loss of standards. As Trow (1996) has described it:

> In transforming that elite system of higher education into a system of mass higher education, the British government in the past decade has gone to such lengths to deny the relevance of such claims to trust, and to subject the whole of the system and its members to what can only be seen as a mass degradation ceremony, involving the transformation of academic staff-scholars and scientists, lecturers and professors alike—into employees, mere organizational personnel (p. 318).

Similarly, Jackson (1997) has suggested that:

> The current arrangements, which emphasise public accountability through publication of results of external quality reviews, are seen by many academics to penalise openness and honesty and reward secrecy and camouflage of problems. A regulatory regime, which was focused on development, would not penalise institutions for being self-critical (p. 172).

Likewise, Trow (1996), in commenting on the accreditation process in the US, has argued that:

> To a considerable extent, external academic accountability in the US, mainly in the form of accreditation has been irrelevant to the improvement of higher education; in some cases it has acted more to shield institutions from effective monitoring of their

> own educational performance than to provide it; in still other cases it distinctly hampers the efforts of institutions to improve themselves. It encourages institutions to report their strengths rather than their weaknesses, their successes rather than their failures—and even to conceal their weaknesses and failures from view (p. 316).

It is against these increasing pressures for accountability and professional mistrust that faculty developers must try to encourage faculty development. All faculty developers recognize the complexities of their work in attempting to discharge whatever function they have set for themselves in their university. Though many different roles and approaches have been identified (in the UK see, for example, Gosling, 1996), the fundamental effort is towards encouraging faculty to reflect on, review, and implement changes to their teaching, learning, and assessment practices and approaches to curriculum development. Faculty developers also know that in some areas of their institutions they encounter resistance to their work. The Quality Improvement in Learning and Teaching (QILT) program at the University of East London has become a means of creating a culture of *engagement* with faculty development across the whole university and a vehicle for transformational change towards a "learning organization."

What Is QILT?

The QILT Program is coordinated by the university's Educational Development Services (EDS) and forms a major plank of its faculty development program. Some might argue that to try to "capture" the quality debate through faculty development is unwise. Since the university's EDS became the locus of the program, it has clearly signaled that QILT is part of the quality agenda of the university. There are, of course, risks that associating it with that agenda will prompt unfavorable reactions from faculty. But many faculty developers encounter resistance to their work, whether or not such an agenda is made explicit.

Educational Development Services has created an *enabling framework* to facilitate faculty development. Each department/subject team undertakes a regular and iterative cycle of quality improvement. The team is relatively organic and dependent on the priorities identified. It has faculty and student involvement but may also include administrative, technical, and learning support staff.

The cycle has three phases. In phase one, faculty construct an improvement plan that provides statements of areas where improvements are to be made, a timetable for achieving them, an appropriate faculty development program and, finally, identifies appropriate evaluation criteria and evidence to measure outcomes. Funding to support QILT plans is allocated by EDS from central faculty development funds. Plans are approved according to a common set of criteria that include, among others, evidence of team involvement, including students; the extent to which the proposed development lends itself to more generic applicability; and the addressing of one or more of the QAAHE core areas of provision as potential improvement areas.

Though the QILT process is the university's internal mechanism for improving quality, faculty have been guided toward the six core areas of provision. Thus, they are in a continuous and cumulative process of preparation for that exercise. Importantly, faculty are pro-actively addressing locally identified issues that can be placed in the context of the external review, rather than re-actively attempting to "defend" the subject through documentation and discussion.

Phase two represents the process of implementation and formative evaluation where the activities might include staff development workshops, the production of materials, changes in teaching methods—whatever has been identified in the plan.

Finally, in phase three, faculty evaluate whether improvements have been achieved and are effective and take action as appropriate. The outcomes of QILT improvements are then formally subjected to institutional evaluation through the annual internal departmental review.

Examples of QILT Projects

In the first year of QILT, over 50 projects were undertaken involving all departments. Some projects were vehicles for substantial change. For example, departments began to prepare distance learning materials, produce computer assisted learning (CAL) in life sciences and mathematics, improve student feedback systems (psychology), introduce student personal profiling (a joint project), implement student self-appraisal (fashion design), and improve student handbooks in the faculty of Design, Engineering, and the Built Environment (DEBE).

In the second year, faculty responded to the early experience of QILT by specifying the criteria for acceptance of QILT proposals more precisely and by reducing the number of projects to target funding more effectively. The second volume of QILT reports provides evidence of continuing innovation and development. In particular the development of Instructional Technology (IT) learning resources is well-evidenced. DEBE, for example, produced a cross-departmental IT development plan. Life sciences produced a CAL package to support a skills development module, and innovation studies evaluated particular web authoring systems for distance delivery. Other important projects include English language support in DEBE, peer-assessment of practicals in psychology, and the development of a first-year computing unit in economics.

By 1997/98, budgetary constraints had curtailed the extent to which QILT funding could be made widely available. EDS decided to focus QILT projects on identified strategic objectives, partly to ensure that developments were more aligned with recently identified institutional issues related to student progression. Although this altered the essentially voluntary nature of the early delivery of QILT, it does demonstrate the way in which the process could be used to support the delivery of aspects of a university's mission or strategic plan. The prospectus for QILT in 1997/98 identified student support and guidance and the monitoring of student progression and achievement as one priority, and the use of information technology in teaching, learning, and assessment as the second. Projects were approved to create databases for monitoring student progress in several areas of the university, to develop student profiling and self-evaluation, to establish a process for identifying students' learning needs, to create a textile design database, to further develop CAL in Life Sciences, to use IT to support lifelong learning, and to develop open learning materials. These projects, and reports on their outcomes, are published and disseminated by EDS across the university in the QILT Annual Report.

Overcoming Resistance—Ownership and Reward

That the QILT process has found little political resistance in the university is interesting. It is important to try to articulate the source of that resistance and why QILT appears to side-step it. The essential elements of ownership and reward are critical to the success of QILT.

First, the ethos through which QILT is attempting to secure change is not derived from gaining agreement at committee level about policy statements, nor by managerial dictate, nor by attempting to persuade faculty of the expertise of developers. QILT attempts to secure ownership, maximum participation, and involvement in change by the university as a collectivity. It demands an approach that relies on teamwork and consensus, which, as Taylor and Hill (1993) have suggested, is something that is problematic in higher education:

> namely, the provision of an appropriate and enriching learning experience for every student. For some establishments there may be a need to spend time reaching consensus on this point alone. This deceptively simple concept, once embraced, will effect the removal of barriers between departments, between academics and administrators arguing over points of territory or procedure and between academics entrenched in "functional foxholes" or "discipline dug-outs" (p. 24).

Whilst faculty developers ply their trade as best they can, at the institutional level wider development is often "managed" through the sector's traditional organizational structures. These structures, however, may be unsuitable for effective communication and may actually retard the process of change. Though some universities place great reliance on the democratic process enshrined in committee work or the institutional value of hierarchical management structures, the pace of change is beginning to render these organizational forms unwieldy. Both the structures, and the managerial activity emanating from them, may founder if those involved at the faculty-student interface in the institution do not have some stake in managing that change. The mistake made by the present UK administrations, and by institutions themselves, is believing that educational change can be accomplished by trying to introduce system reforms, tighter forms of planning and management, re-organization, greater accountability, and so on. All are doomed to failure if faculty do not have some stake in managing that change. It requires the empowerment of faculty to become involved in continuous improvement so that they are committed to, and own, the process of change. Of course, not all faculty will wish to take that opportunity. Many QILT projects at UEL are managed by enthusiastic faculty, whose work will nevertheless have an impact on the work of their department. Furthermore, the emphasis on a team approach means that, gradually, more reluctant faculty become involved.

Three aspects of QILT contribute to this sense of faculty ownership. First, any member of the faculty, provided a team has been identified, is entitled to submit a plan for QILT funding. The criteria for approval of plans are not based on status but simply on the efficacy (and, increasingly, the transferability) of what is proposed. Perhaps, more importantly, the process is based on trust. Funding is allocated on the basis of what is planned rather than the quality of the outcome or output, though progress is carefully monitored, and funding may be withheld if delivery is problematic.

Second, QILT re-conceptualizes traditional models of faculty development. It is not a skills-based, additive approach. Neither are faculty developers necessarily involved in giving expert advice to departments or individuals. QILT is simply a set of processes and procedures to enable faculty development to be embedded through a process of learning by doing. It demands an unconventional action-learning process. Though EDS also runs centrally organized faculty development sessions, these are beginning to emanate from concerns identified by faculty through the QILT process. Ownership of faculty development is clearly with faculty. Faculty are learners, actively engaged in constructing their own understanding of "development." The process has been described elsewhere (Ho, 1998) as "constructivism":

> Among all the complexity, the crucial idea of constructivism is that learners are actively constructing their own understanding. In the process, the learner makes reference to his/her existing knowledge and conceptions, selects information from the perceived environment according to his/her own motives and constructs new understandings in a way coherent and useful to him/her. Learning is therefore an active constructive exercise that takes place within learners. It is not a passive receiving of ready-made authoritative knowledge impacted from without (pp. 24-25).

Third, I have also argued (Laycock, 1997) that Kolb's model of the experiential learning cycle has informed the university's QILT program both as a process for faculty development/learning and as a model for the development of a learning organization. In a knowledge-based organization it is important that such a model underpins the notion of a learning organization, and here experiential learning provides the basis for continuous learning and self-renewal. Through this conceptual model, QILT is not only a process of faculty development but also one that encourages institutional change and development. As Candy (1996) has observed: "Clearly, such work carries educational developers well beyond the threshold of simply improving teaching and learning and, indeed, beyond the bounds of staff development" (p. 10).

In many ways the QILT process is also the institutional embodiment of Candy's (1996) ideas for the development of a learning organization in higher education in what he terms the CAREER model of faculty development, which comprises six key elements. Such a program is:

- **Comprehensive**. The QILT process is comprehensive and the QAAHE core areas of provision cover the majority of academic work.
- **Anticipatory**. QILT is a pro-active rather than re-active approach to quality improvement. The shift of emphasis towards an enhancement-led system provides the impetus for the university to anticipate change.
- **Research-based**. All QILT project leaders produce internal evaluative papers that are collated and disseminated by EDS annually. Some faculty have produced papers for external publication (see, for example, De Jong, 1996) or for conferences as a result of QILT projects.
- **Exemplary**. Many QILT projects, though they have been initiated in one department, have transferred to others. For example, the growth of study skills modular units in a number of departments has been a result of the transfer of developmental work from one department to another. Best practice has been modeled.
- **Embedded**. QILT is embedded in the institutional culture through the authority of the university's Quality Manual and through its reward system for staff (EDS has implemented a scheme, for example, to appoint Readers in Educational Development. Many Readers have been, or are, involved in QILT projects).
- **Reflective**. As a means of faculty development, QILT demands that faculty become critical and reflective analysts of their own practice.

QILT—Effecting Cultural Change

In providing a whole-institutional framework for change, the QILT process is also attempting to stimulate cultural change within the university towards a culture of quality that embraces self-critical reflection and the acceptance of responsibility for quality improvement. It is not a culture that, historically, has necessarily been firmly rooted in UK universities.

In summarizing the debate over the rise of the quality agenda and the historical development of universities in the UK, Barnett (1992) suggests that during the period from the Middle Ages until relatively recently, universities enjoyed privileges, rights, a social independence, and societal esteem—a period of *enchantment* when higher education was "mysterious, an activity in which only a few were engaged, but which somehow carried its own social legitimacy. Its quality was not at issue; the activity saw itself and was seen by the host society as being self-justifying" (pp. 215-216).

This self-justifying aspect of higher education culture has come under the rigorous scrutiny of the quality microscope over the last ten years to the point where:

> The host society is no longer prepared to accept that higher education is self-justifying and wishes to expose the activities of the secret garden. With greater expectations being placed on it, higher education is being obliged to examine itself or be examined by others. 'Permeability,' 'responsiveness' and 'accountability' are just some key words of the age. Against this changing mood and desire for transparency, systems of evaluation are being transported into higher education which may have a point in other spheres of modern society but which may fail to do justice to the inner activities of higher education. (p. 216)

Barnett describes this contemporary period as one of disenchantment. In part, that disenchantment is contained in faculty perceptions of the rise of managerialism (Harvey, 1995) and an attack on academic freedom or professional autonomy—an attack on the secret garden.

For the future, Barnett argues for a culture of engagement with quality:

> This is not a cosy, self-satisfied state of affairs, controlled only by the academic community through its conversations. But neither is it the imposition of inappropriate technical models and systems on a distinctive form of human activity. It is judgmental, open, binding on every participant in the academic community, critical (especially self-critical), collaborative (including the students), eclectic in its approach and willing to draw on the evidence available. However, it is driven by two principal considerations: that the central activity of higher education is that of

> educating individual students; and that it is the continuous improvement in the educational processes that lies at the centre of our concerns over quality (p. 216).

Harvey (1995) suggests that there has been renewed interest in the concept of collegialism in the UK and that it "can be characterized as having taken two paths—a conservative tendency and a radical alternative." He describes the former as "cloisterism" and the latter as the "new collegialism" (p. 2). Both have emerged as a consequence of the perceived growth in managerialism but are at opposite ends of the spectrum so far as reactions to that managerialism is concerned.

A range of concepts is used to codify the cultural and educational orientations of both. Academic cloisterism is described as "inward-looking, individualistic, self-serving and self-regulating, characterized by esoteric knowledge and opacity" (p. 35). In many respects this culture carries with it the vestiges of the self-justifying nature of the culture of the *enchantment* period.

The new collegialism, by contrast, is said to be "outward looking and responsive; emphasizes continuous improvement; professional accountability; encourages team-working; focuses on the total student experience; views students as participants in the process of learning rather than as a customer or as an end-product; and focuses on the outcomes of higher education as well as the process" (p. 35).

From Accountability to Enhancement—Seizing the Initiative

Through its particular ideological approach, QILT has attempted to encourage faculty toward a culture of self-scrutiny and self-improvement. In a sense, it has attempted to turn the accountability-led framework of the QAAHE Subject Review on its head. It has taken as a basic template for improvement the basis of the review, the six core areas of provision, and invited faculty to consider these in a process of continuous quality improvement rather than a one-off review exercise.

If the current emphasis on accountability is to be reviewed, some of the responsibility for effecting change at the national level must come from institutions themselves. As Harvey (1995) has argued:

> In a sense, this means that initiative must be grasped via the internal initiatives. This will only be feasible with an academic body

> that is prepared to adopt new-collegiate principles of responsiveness. A cloisterist approach hands the initiative to external bodies. A new collegiate approach grasps the initiative and demonstrates that accountability is achieved through a process of continuous quality improvement (p. 40).

An institutional process such as QILT could be internally audited and a cumulative product reported to external bodies in an annual quality report. The external body could arrange a periodic audit of institutional quality improvement reports in order to validate them. A similar approach could be adopted in the US where Trow (1998), for example, has also argued for a process of audit rather than accreditation:

> One answer is to urge that the regional and other accrediting bodies transform themselves or be transformed from organizations which purport to accredit the 'quality' of the institution—its teaching and learning—into bodies that have the responsibility for determining whether the institution has in place procedures and practices that enable it to learn about itself . . . What the institution would be asked to report every five or ten years is evidence (largely embodied in formal procedures) that it has developed or is developing a culture of self-scrutiny and self-improvement (p. 49).

Conclusion

I have attempted in this paper to discuss some of the more ideological purposes behind the university's QILT program rather than to evaluate its outcomes. I have argued for a more strategic, whole-institutional approach to faculty development and, thereby, the development of a culture for institutional self-improvement. QILT is a program that demands a more open, responsive, and collective approach to faculty development. In so doing it also tries to create a culture that at one and the same time urges faculty ownership, responsibility, and accountability in development, and moves toward the development of a learning organization where traditional faculty resistance is overcome.

I have further argued for a faculty development role that takes the initiative in attempting to shift prevailing accountability-led regulatory frameworks towards enhancement-led frameworks. This is not to imply that external validation of the credibility of a university's system for self-evaluation and self-improvement is not required. For systems to be publicly credible they need to be publicly recognizable. External bodies can provide that recognition. But continuous examination and assessment of the methods and procedures of quality assurance alone will not provide the impetus for change. A shift towards an enhancement-led system may provide that impetus and permit institutions to anticipate change.

References

Barnett, R. (1992). *Improving higher education: Total quality care.* Buckingham, UK: SRHE & Open University Press.

Candy, P. (1996). Promoting lifelong learning: Academic developers and the university as a learning organisation. *The International Journal for Academic Development, 1* (1), 7-18.

De Jong, W. (1996, July). *Undergraduate mathematics: Towards a new method of teaching and learning.* Paper presented at the International DERIVE and TI-92 Conference, Bonn, Germany.

Gosling, D. (1996). What do UK educational development units do? *The International Journal for Academic Development, 1* (1), 75-83.

Harvey, L. (1995). *Quality assurance systems, TQM and the new collegialism.* Birmingham, UK: Quality in Higher Education Project Report, University of Central England in Birmingham. (ERIC Document Reproduction Services No. ED 401 810.)

Ho, A. S. P. (1998). A conceptual change staff development programme: Effects as perceived by the participants. *The International Journal for Academic Development, 3* (1), 25-38.

Jackson, N. (1997). Academic regulation in UK higher education: Part II-typologies and frameworks for discourse and strategic change. *Quality Assurance in Education, 5* (3), 165-179.

Jenkins, A. (1996). Discipline-based educational development. *The International Journal for Academic Development, 1* (1), 50-62.

Laycock, M. (1997). QILT: A whole institutional approach to quality improvement in learning and teaching. In S. Armstrong, G. Thompson, & S. Brown (Eds.), *Facing up to radical changes in universities and colleges* (pp. 75-83). London, UK: Kogan Page.

Taylor, A., & Hill, F. (1993). Quality management in education. *Quality Assurance in Education, 1* (1), 21-28.

Trow, M. (1996). Trust, markets, and accountability in higher education: A comparative perspective. *Higher Education Policy, 9* (4), 309-324.

Trow, M. (1998). On the accountability of higher education in the United States. In W. G. Bowen & H. T. Shapiro (Eds.), *Universities and their leadership* (pp. 15-64). Princeton, NJ: Princeton University Press.

Yorke, M. (1994). Enhancement-led higher education. *Quality Assurance in Education, 2* (3), 6-12.

Contact:

Mike Laycock
Educational Development Services
University of East London
Longbridge Road
Dagenham
Essex RM8 2AS
UK
(0)181 849 3436
(0)181 849 3524 (FAX)
m.j.a.laycock@uel.ac.uk

Mike Laycock is a Principal Lecturer at the University of East London. In addition to coordinating the Quality Improvement in Learning and Teaching (QILT) program in Educational Development Services, he is also Director of the University's Work-based Learning Unit, which offers a cross-institutional MA/MSc/PGDip by Work-Based Learning. Former posts at the University have included Course Director of undergraduate and, then, postgraduate programs by independent study, and Director of the University's Enterprise Learning Program (funded by the DfEE). He has been a frequent presenter on higher education issues at national and international educational development conferences. He is also a member of the SEDA (Staff and Educational Development Association) Executive. Current research interests include a US/UK comparison of strategic planning in higher education institutions. He holds an MPhil from the University of East London.

The *QILT Handbook* (1995) and *QILT Improvement Plans/Reports* (1995, 1996, 1997) are available from the QILT Unit, University of East London, Longbridge Road, Dagenham, Essex RM8 2AS, United Kingdom.

6

Finding Key Faculty to Influence Change

Joan K. Middendorf
Indiana University

To succeed in getting faculty to accept new teaching approaches, academic support professionals can benefit from the literature on planned change. By understanding the different rates at which faculty accept change, we can also identify the faculty most likely to lead their colleagues to accepting new approaches. Opinion leaders can offer insight into faculty reactions to new approaches; their involvement in project planning can influence acceptance. Innovators, when selected carefully, can demonstrate and test new teaching approaches. Knowledge of when and how to involve these two kinds of faculty can reduce frustration and enhance efforts to spread new ideas about teaching and learning.

Introduction

Faculty are hired and promoted because they are committed experts in one or more specific academic disciplines. When we—as academic support professionals—work with faculty to improve their teaching, we are not asking them to give up their areas of expertise but rather to value and acquire expertise in a new area—that of teaching and learning. For faculty, this often represents a significant change. A small group of faculty seem to embrace new teaching approaches readily. Others resist new approaches and criticize their more innovative colleagues. This situation can frustrate academic support professionals, who so often work through and with faculty in making presentations, writing grants, and designing projects to enhance undergraduate education. Why are some faculty eager for change while others oppose it?

To facilitate changes regarding teaching, academic support professionals may have to expand their own expertise. They need expertise not only in such areas as instructional development, evaluation, and group process, but also in the area of planned change. Fortunately, a literature of planned change exists and can offer useful principles, as well as an increased chance of success. Havelock's (1995) work is based on diffusion research in education. Rogers' (1995) work is based on diffusion in many fields including education. Dormant's (1999) work is based primarily on corporate training and performance technology. We can apply their useful principles to a higher education setting for an increased chance of success.

This article focuses on two groups of faculty who can lend invaluable support to change efforts—the Opinion Leaders and the Acceptable Innovators. In order to better identify these key faculty, academic support professionals need to understand the overall pattern and rate of acceptance of change within a group.

Rate-of-Acceptance Categories

Not all faculty accept a change at the same rate. Some faculty are more receptive to change and accept it faster than others. Some are quite slow to accept change. Rogers (1995) notes that it is common for the rate-of-acceptance pattern to fall into a normal distribution (see Figure 6.1). Innovators accept first. Early Acceptors follow soon after. As the Majority see those who accept early, they follow along. Finally, Latecomers are extremely reticent to accept change.

By analyzing the faculty group according to rate-of-acceptance, academic support professionals can assign priorities and allocate resources most effectively. For example, if we assume that a new approach offers a good and useful change, and we introduce that change reasonably well and provide follow-up support, we can more or less count on acceptance from the first two groups—Innovators and Early Acceptors. At the other end of the curve, regardless of what we do, the Latecomers may take forever to embrace the change despite our efforts and those of our colleagues. Therefore, for different reasons—the early groups are relatively easy to influence, the last group is difficult and can consume resources without much payoff—we should probably not spend much of our limited resources on this 32% (with the exception of a few key faculty whom we will discuss below). However, by examining Innovators and Early Acceptors more carefully, we can identify the Opinion Leaders and Acceptable Innovators, two sub-groups who can influence the willing-

FIGURE 6.1
Rate-of-Acceptance Categories

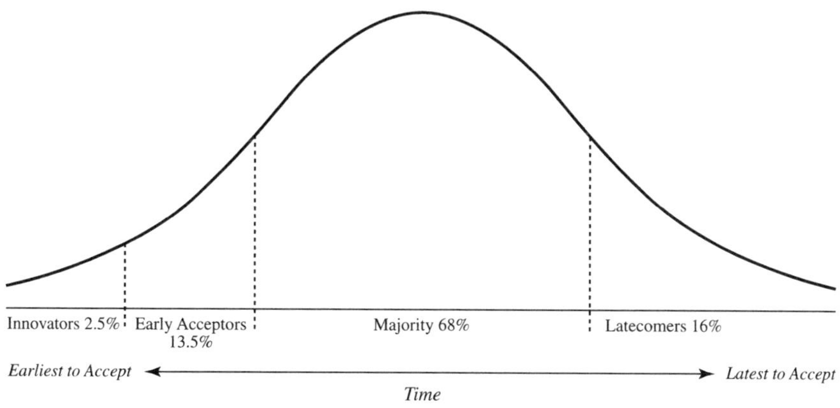

ness of the Majority to accept change. (A previous article, Middendorf, 1998, described specific steps to take for encouraging the Majority to accept a change.)

OPINION LEADERS

Opinion Leaders (Rogers, 1995) are found among the Early Acceptors. They are the most important faculty in facilitating a change regarding teaching because, even though they usually have no official position of power, they do have considerable influence over others' attitudes and behaviors. They serve as the hub of the faculty communication network. They make careful judgments and good decisions, and they decrease uncertainty because their peers trust their evaluation. For example, Professor D recently received a Fulbright Fellowship and has a good reputation for the large, introductory courses he teaches. In addition, he is described by a colleague as "a straight shooter—if he tells you something he'll do it. Also, he doesn't have hidden agendas and he's not self-aggrandizing. He doesn't speak much at faculty meetings, but when he does, he pursues his principles with persistence. Over the years he's gained our respect and we've learned to listen to him."

Faculty members who can maintain the role of Opinion Leaders

FIGURE 6.2
Rates of Acceptance and Two Key Faculty Groups

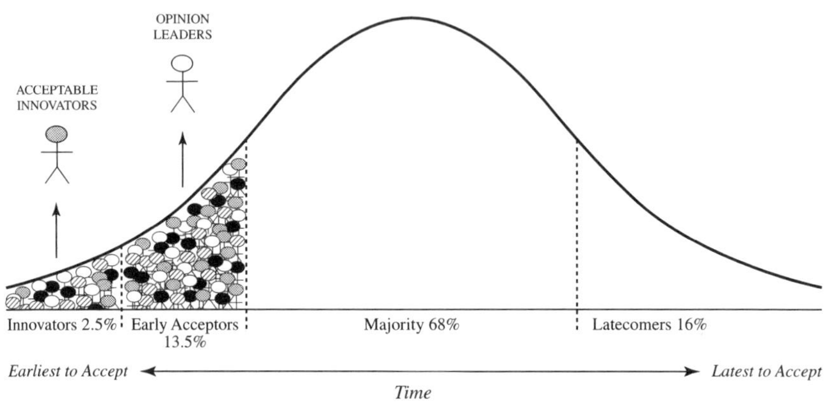

Adapted from Rogers, 1995

tend to reject an innovation that in their minds is likely to fail and to champion an innovation whose time they feel has come. When they can be brought aboard, they are natural "missionaries" for influencing others to accept new approaches to teaching.

Opinion Leaders . . .

are neither the first nor the last to make a change;
have influence within the faculty;
represent the norms of the faculty group;
are at the hub of the faculty communications network;
observe Innovators to see how an idea works or where the dangers lie;
observe Latecomers to learn about an idea's limitations;
are relied on by the group for good judgment; and
tend to be asked to serve on many committees.

They can help if you . . .

use them sparingly;
interview them to learn their attitude toward the innovation; and
involve them in planning for the implementation.

How to Identify Opinion Leaders

If you have little past experience with a faculty group, you may need to invest considerable time and effort in order to understand individuals and their relationship within the group. One way to do this is to interview members of the group. Even such simple questions as, *When you have a question about new instructional technology, whom do you consult within the department?* or, *When you have a problem grading students, to whom do you turn?* can help you identify potential leaders for your change project.

For example, in the Freshman Learning Project on the Indiana University campus, a small, interdisciplinary group of faculty were selected for a team that would examine the difficulties of teaching large, introductory classes, attempt to better understand first-year students, and implement active learning strategies to increase the quantity and quality of student thinking. Our ultimate goal was to affect not only the faculty directly involved in this project but their departmental colleagues as well. Therefore, we started with faculty who could act as Opinion Leaders within their departments. To identify likely faculty from each of eight departments, we developed a set of criteria. For our project, the potential Opinion Leader must

- Be tenured
- Teach large, introductory classes
- Be open to new ideas, though not famed for good teaching
- Be respected by colleagues (i.e., reputation as a researcher)
- Not be considered a maverick

The first three criteria are related specifically to the Freshman Learning Project. Other projects would have different criteria. The last two criteria, however, should be on the list for any change effort. When selecting faculty members to become advocates for a change, we need to be sure they already have the respect of their colleagues and are not—perhaps just because they are innovative in their teaching—considered mavericks or oddballs.

Once our criteria were clear, we asked three faculty members from each department, either in person or on the phone depending on how well-acquainted we were with them, to suggest three of their peers who met the criteria. When all three named the same person, we viewed that faculty member as an ideal Opinion Leader. In one department, when all three named different people, we went back to a very senior faculty member in the department and confidentially asked him to rank the list according to the criteria. In another department, when all the names differed, our follow-up indicated that not only was there no likely Opinion Leader, but the department was significantly lacking in cohesion. We chose not to work with that department. In this selection process we avoided getting advice from department chairs because they tend to ignore stated criteria and select faculty members for their own reasons. This method takes a great deal of initial time, but it has long-term benefits that make it worthwhile.

Once identified, how should Opinion Leaders be used?

1) Use them sparingly and efficiently. Because they tend to be sought after for all kinds of committees and projects, they may suffer from overload or overexposure.

2) Involve them as information sources. Since they represent the norms of the group, they have information about the needs of their colleagues. Interview them to find out their initial reactions to the change. If they have questions or concerns about it, we can be sure that other faculty will as well. Their reactions and responses to the change can help us identify the information we need to provide to the department and what concerns to address.

3) Involve them in planning for implementation. If they believe in the change, they can help with grant writing, planning, presentations, and discussions related to the change. Through their advocacy, we can avoid the "not-invented-here" effect (Dormant, 1999).

When Opinion Leaders Oppose Your Project

Academic support professionals face a difficult scenario when faculty who are Opinion Leaders actively oppose new teaching approaches. It can be very difficult to get faculty to change without the buy-in of the Opinion Leaders. Their open resistance can effectively block a change. To avoid this situation the academic support professional should contact the Opinion Leaders early in a project and seek their input in planning. If they demean the change, then we may need to view them as individual change projects and proceed accordingly to develop a step-by-step plan to facilitate their acceptance of the change. (See Middendorf, 1998, for a description of the stages of change and actions to take.) Granted, this entails a great deal of time and effort, but the nay-saying of those held in high regard must be defused early in order to reduce their negative impact on others. Another possibility to consider is that Opinion Leaders have a valid point, and we may have to reassess whether the innovation is worthwhile.

Acceptable Innovators

In selecting faculty for project advocacy, academic support professionals are often tempted to choose faculty who are working at the cutting edge of new technologies of teaching and learning. For example, Professor E might seem like a good candidate for an Opinion Leader. He works hard on his teaching of undergraduate political science classes, constantly revising his approach. He has instituted permanent collaborative learning groups, online quizzes, an electronic class discussion list, a web page, and group quizzes. Furthermore, he is eager to be of service to the academic support staff. Or, Professor M might be chosen. She has a national reputation for her expertise on teaching in the sciences. She travels widely, both to attend conferences on college teaching and to present workshops at other sites. She has regularly attended campus teaching workshops and has published an article about student thinking. She, too, is delighted to discuss instructional issues with academic support staff.

Professors E and M sound like ideal Opinion Leaders: They are outstanding teachers, interested in pedagogy, and accessible to academic support professionals. However, how these two relate to students or to academic support professionals is not the issue. In the role of Opinion Leaders, the issue is how they relate to their departmental colleagues. Looking further, we find that Professor E's colleagues speak derogatorily of his teaching behind his back—to each other and to administrators. ("If he knew how to teach, he wouldn't always be trying something new.") As for Professor M, her colleagues find her expertise to be off-putting and they strongly resent her. ("I've been teaching for 15 years and she had the nerve to tell me I ought to change the way I do things.") Some of the faculty who are most knowledgeable about innovations are unacceptable as models for their peers.

These two faculty members have been wrongly identified as Opinion Leaders, when they should have been identified as Innovators. While Innovators are also valuable in facilitating changes in teaching, they have different characteristics from the Opinion Leaders, and they serve a different role. Innovators are the venturesome faculty who tend to be the first to adopt new teaching approaches. They are important because they have information sources through which they learn about teaching innovations. For example, they may read journals or join email distribution lists concerned with college teaching or instructional computing. This interest leads them to frequent communication with people outside their local departments. (This outside group forms a sort of "clique" of Innovators.) Not only do Innovators learn about new teaching methods, they even try them out, which results in teaching-learning failures as well as successes.

> **Innovators. . .**
> are first to accept a change;
> are willing to take risks;
> have information sources outside their local group;
> communicate with other Innovators; and
> may be viewed as oddballs.
>
> **They can help if you . . .**
> use them for pilot testing, or
> have them demonstrate new techniques.

While faculty Innovators may bring new ideas to the group, the very things that make them innovative (e.g., information from outside their department and trying non-traditional approaches) may make them somewhat suspect to their colleagues who tend to read discipline-specific journals and develop relationships only with colleagues in their discipline. In our workshops, some participants have even called Innovators "radicals," "red-hots," or "usual suspects." Academic support professionals can help Innovators understand the negative reactions they encounter by explaining the nature of the reaction: that their advocacy for new teaching approaches may seem odd, even threatening, to their colleagues. We can encourage Innovators to show empathy for their slower-to-innovate colleagues. Innovators who are overly enthusiastic about some cutting-edge technology may sound to the faculty majority like used-car dealers and in the process turn off more people than they inspire.

However, if Innovators are carefully and appropriately involved, they can be valuable assets in a change project. How can they best be involved?

1) As demonstrators of a new technology or approach. This strategy is especially effective when faculty have asked for help. For example, if a faculty member expresses interest in collaborative learning teams,

academic support professionals can suggest that they observe an Innovator—preferably from another department or university—who has effectively designed his or her teaching around student collaboration.

2) As pilot testers. Since they are risk-takers, they are probably willing to experiment with new approaches others might hesitate to try. For example, we asked some Innovators to test several software packages for electronic class discussions. They were able to critique the software and to work out some of the problems before the program was disseminated to the rest of the faculty. Their input saved us valuable time and prevented mistakes that may have resulted in negative reactions to the software.

Return of Investment

Academic support professionals, like almost everyone else in higher education, never have all the resources that they need. How, then, can we allocate limited resources to achieve the greatest payoff? It may help to think of the situation as a two-by-two matrix—investment of resources vs. payoff (Figure 6.3).

Cell 1 represents the biggest payoff from the smallest investment. Opinion Leaders who tend to be positive toward new teaching approaches require a low investment of resources and yet result in a high payoff, since they will lead others to accept the change.

Cell 2 also represents a big payoff, but it requires a big investment. If we can work with negative Opinion Leaders and overcome their

Figure 6.3
Contingency Framework for Investment of Resources

Payoff \ Investment of Resources	Small	Big
Big	*cell 1* Positive Opinion Leaders	*cell 2* Negative Opinion Leaders
Small	*cell 3* Innovators	*cell 4* Latecomers

resistance, the payoff can be great. Moreover, they may significantly impede the process if we do not convert them. It may take a great amount of time and energy to win them over, but the payoff may be worth the investment.

Cell 3 represents a small payoff for a small investment. Innovators are quick to accept new teaching practices, but they may have limited influence on others.

Cell 4 represents a small payoff for a big investment. Latecomers can consume enormous amounts of resources with little or no results. We can't win everyone over—we can't get everyone to buy into new teaching approaches. With limited time and money, it is important to put our effort where it counts.

Conclusion

By understanding the different rates at which faculty accept change, we can also identify the faculty most likely to lead their colleagues to adopt new teaching approaches. Opinion Leaders can inform us of reactions to new approaches and concerns that need to be addressed. Their involvement in planning projects can enhance the acceptance by other faculty of new approaches. Innovators, when selected carefully, can demonstrate and test new teaching approaches. Knowledge of when and how to involve these two kinds of faculty can enhance efforts to spread new ideas about teaching, reduce frustration, and increase chances of project success.

The following questions should help academic support professionals as they begin planning change efforts.

1) What criteria should you use to select Opinion Leaders for your change project?
2) Who are potential Opinion Leaders for your group?
3) How will you gain the participation of Opinion Leaders and involve them in the project?
4) Are there Opinion Leaders who may be opposed to your project? What will you do about them?
5) Who are likely Innovators for your change project?
6) How will you involve them?

References

Dormant, D. (1999). Implementing human performance technology in organizations. In H. Stolovitch & E. Keeps (Eds.), *Handbook of human performance technology* (pp. 237-259). San Francisco, CA: Jossey-Bass.

Havelock, R. G., with Zlotolow, S. (1995). *The change agent's guide* (2nd ed.). Englewood Cliffs, NJ: Educational Technology Publications.

Middendorf, J. K. (1998). A case study in getting faculty to change. *To Improve the Academy, 17,* 203-224.

Rogers, E. M. (1995). *Diffusion of innovations* (4th ed.). New York, NY: The Free Press.

Contact:

Joan K. Middendorf
Director, Teaching Resources Center
Ballantine Hall, Room 132
Indiana University
Bloomington, IN 47405-6601
(812) 855-2635
(812) 855-6410 (FAX)
middendo@indiana.edu

Joan K. Middendorf has been the Director of the Teaching Resources Center of the College of Arts and Sciences at Indiana University for a decade. She collaborates with faculty, instructors, and administrators to diffuse pedagogical innovations. In addition, she co-directs the Freshman Learning Project. As the designer of The Change Mappings™ Workshop, she has presented on leading change at more than 20 corporations. She publishes about college teaching and change in higher education. She studies T'ai Chi for relaxation and as an exercise in learning.

Section II:

Collaboration and Partnerships

7

Student Collaboration in Faculty Development: Connecting Directly to the Learning Revolution

Milton D. Cox
Miami University

D. Lynn Sorenson
Brigham Young University

Although faculty developers have worked successfully with faculty to focus on ways to enhance learning and listen to student voices, developers have rarely formed partnerships with students. This chapter reviews established practices involving students directly in faculty development, such as student observer/consultant programs. It also describes the nature, dynamics, and outcomes of some interesting new programs involving students in teaching development activities, thereby empowering students to join developers as change agents of campus culture. Finally, this chapter raises issues for faculty developers to reflect on as they consider establishing direct connections—partnerships—with students.

Within higher education for the last 15 years or so, there has been an increasing interest in, discussion about, and movement toward a focus on student learning. Faculty developers have been attuned to this movement. For example, Cross (1987) called for individual faculty members to study student learning in their classrooms and courses, and this quickly gave rise to classroom research projects coordinated by faculty developers (Erickson & Erickson, 1988). Angelo (1989) proposed making "the 1990s the decade of faculty development for learning" (p. 37) but noted, as one obstacle, that "[m]ost faculty development programs focus primarily on teaching and secondarily on learning" (p. 43). In his article about future theories that will underlie faculty development, McKeachie (1991) states, "As I see it, the dominant theories deal with students. Our focus has shifted from instructional materials to faculty and now toward students" (p. 6).

In this decade, some have called this movement a paradigm shift from the old teaching paradigm to the new teaching paradigm (Johnson, Johnson, & Smith, 1991) or from the instruction paradigm to the learning paradigm (Barr, 1998; Barr & Tagg, 1995). In the first paradigm, knowledge is seen as transferred from faculty to students primarily through lecturing, while in the second, knowledge is jointly constructed by students and faculty through active learning. The first is teacher centered, and the second is student centered.

At the 1993 POD Conference, Zahorski exhorted:

> If students are truly at the heart of the learning process and if we really empower them—shouldn't they be actively involved in our faculty development programs? If we don't involve them, are we neglecting one of our most important resources? Indeed, do we have an ethical obligation to involve our students more actively (1993)?

As noted by Sorenson (1994), "In citing student-centered pedagogies, the empowerment of students, learning partnerships, and the student as ultimate beneficiary of faculty development, Zahorski implored faculty developers to make sure the rhetoric actually reflects the reality" (p. 97).

Usually instructional developers work directly with faculty and TAs to enable better teaching and consequently enhance student learning. Other than students' occasional memberships on advisory boards, these practices do not often involve undergraduates directly as members or consultants of the faculty development office, the teaching and learning center, or programs coordinated by these offices. Instead, developers connect with faculty, who then connect with students. Within the teaching paradigm, these practices are usually successful. For example, with respect to developer consultation with faculty about student evaluations, "the reason that student feedback plus skillful consultation often leads to instructional gains is that the consultant is able to interpret student ratings in specific behavioral terms and to recommend specific behavioral change strategies" (Seldin, 1997, p. 339). As another example, developers working with faculty also have played key roles in faculty adoption of new ways to enhance learning, such as active learning, new technology, and classroom assessment techniques (CATs) (Richlin, 1998; Steadman, 1998). To illustrate, CATs (Angelo & Cross, 1993) provide instructors with immediate student feedback on learning and, as it turns out, also enhance student learning (Cottell & Harwood, 1998; Steadman & Svinicki, 1998).

On the other hand, in the small group instructional diagnosis (SGID) process developed at the University of Washington in the 1970s (Redmond & Clark, 1982), faculty developers work *directly* with students. After consulting with the instructor to determine course objectives and concerns, the instructional consultant dialogues with students in the class—the instructor is not present—to coordinate small-group discussions and report students' responses to two questions:

1) List the major strengths in this course. (What is helping you learn in the course?) Please explain briefly or give an example for each strength.

2) List changes that could be made in the course to assist you in learning. Please explain how suggested changes could be made. (Black, 1998, p. 247).

Afterwards, the developer shares the responses with the instructor, who then discusses the results and any changes with the class in the next class meeting.

Involving students directly in faculty development usually has been overlooked as a component of faculty development practices. Wright and O'Neil (1994, 1995) surveyed key instructional developers at institutions in the US, Canada, the UK, and Australasia; respondents rated the potential of 36 practices to improve teaching at their respective institutions. Practices that involve students directly are not on this list. Other surveys (Centra, 1978; Erickson, 1986; Kurfiss & Boice, 1990; Chism & Szabó, 1996) also have not mentioned involving students (although Kurfiss and Boice did include SGID as a "practice for scrutinizing teaching"–it ranked 5/6). The omission of these practices from faculty development indicates that involving students directly in faculty development has not only been just a small component of faculty development practices—it has been virtually invisible.

Has there been a revolution this decade in faculty development practice and organization with respect to student learning and involvement?

This article reviews established practices that faculty developers are coordinating that involve students directly with the faculty development office, such as student observer/consultant programs. It also describes the nature, dynamics, and outcomes of some interesting new programs and raises issues for faculty developers to reflect on as they consider establishing direct connections—partnerships—with students in this learning revolution.

Student Observer/Consultant Programs

Just as the classroom research movement has provided college teachers with CATs for feedback on their students' perceptions and learning, student observer/consultant programs provide authentic student perspectives that connect faculty to students and enhance learning.

Serving as an introduction to formative evaluation, the student consultation model opens dialogue about teaching, learning, course design, and other important educational issues. Trained students attend class and consult with instructors. Their feedback catalyzes improvements in pedagogy, classroom climate, and course policies. As a result of participating in a student observer program, faculty may welcome observers (even peers) and become champions for "chang[ing] the status of teaching from private to community property" (Shulman, 1993, p. 6). In addition, student observer/consultant programs help connect participating faculty with important campus resources, such as media services and the center for teaching.

The following institutions have sponsored student observer/consultant programs: Carleton College; St. Olaf College; Brigham Young University; University of Chicago; DePauw University; Rutgers, The State University of New Jersey (Camden); University of Arizona; University of Illinois (Springfield); Indiana State University; Pennsylvania State University; University of Toledo; University of Georgia; and Worcester Polytechnic Institute. Some of these institutions are not currently sponsoring programs; some have provided these services for decades; and others have initiated programs only recently. The diversity of institutions sponsoring these programs ranges from private liberal arts colleges to public Research I universities. As these programs expand into an ever-increasing variety of institutions, questions regarding their viability in diverse settings (Sorenson, 1994) have been answered in the affirmative.

Despite the widespread popularity and effectiveness of these programs, an occasional skeptic will protest, "How can *they* help faculty?

They are just students!" That is exactly their strength; they *are* students. Of course they are not experts on content; that sort of formative evaluation is better left to faculty and disciplinary peers. But as students, they are experts—in their own way—about sitting in classes, doing assignments, preparing for tests, etc. For years, they have participated in dozens of classroom experiences—some of which are conducive to learning and some of which are not; that is why their voices, their views, and their perspectives are imminently valuable.

Options for Faculty: Ways to Use Student Observers/Consultants

What is it that student observers/consultants do in the classroom? The Faculty Center at Brigham Young University (BYU) sponsors a nine-year-old program, Students Consulting on Teaching (SCOT) (previously known as the Classroom Student Observer Program). Faculty select the services they want from various options. Information about the SCOT program, including the following list of ways to use SCOT (Sorenson, 1999), appears on the BYU Faculty Center web site at www.byu.edu/fc.

Recorder/observer. The student consultant records in writing what went on in the class (e.g., chronology of classroom activities, time spent in questioning, board work, small-group discussion, etc.) and gives the record to the instructor. The observer describes rather than evaluates.

Faux student. The student observer/consultant takes notes as if she or he were a student in the class and returns them to the instructor.

Videotaper. The student observer/consultant videotapes the class and gives the videotape to the instructor. The instructor may invite the SCOT to watch and discuss the videotape.

Interviewer. The instructor leaves the classroom for 15 minutes while the student consultant interviews class members about their learning in the course, as in the SGID method mentioned earlier. (This option is by far the most popular one used by instructors at BYU.)

Primed student. The student observer/consultant meets with the professor prior to class to discuss what to watch for, such as: how often certain kinds of students respond (e.g., women/men, minority/majority, traditional/non-traditional), how to involve more students in discussion, what students are doing while the instructor is manipulating a PowerPoint presentation, whether students are on task during small-group work, etc.

Student consultant. The instructor asks the student observer/consultant for evaluative feedback on classroom activities or on particular learning issues of concern. Based on this interaction, the instructor plans innovations, and the student consultant continues to provide feedback.

Other. Other methods include CATs, beta-testing of web-based course modules, etc.

These options include a wide range of activities, from simple data gathering to "continuous quality" consultation. The list of options facilitates faculty entrance to this formative evaluation process without instructors having to invent some grand project for the student observer/consultant to perform. Faculty can receive custom-fit feedback without pleading, "I need help; come advise and consult with me." As trust develops between the instructor and the student consultant, they often initiate more extensive activities (like CATs) and/or explore resources (including meeting with the campus faculty developer) to address particular issues.

Approximately 13% of BYU instructors have participated in the SCOT Program. From fall semester 1992 through fall semester 1998, nearly 300 BYU instructors used the program. About 400 classes have been observed, videotaped, interviewed, etc., affecting thousands of students. Nearly a quarter of the faculty participants are repeat users, and about half are newer faculty on their way to tenure. Both the number of participants and courses observed has increased each semester since the program began in 1990.

Managing a Student Observer/Consultant Program

To initiate and manage a SCOT program effectively, consider the following aspects:

Program coordinator. A student observer/consultant program needs one person to oversee the logistics. This might be the campus faculty developer, a professor, a graduate and/or work-study student, or a student government leader. This person (or a chair/dean/administrator) invites faculty to participate via email, flyers, or letters. From that point on, the process is both self-selecting and confidential.

Student recruitment and remuneration. In terms of recruitment, Sorenson (1999) writes that "[observers/]consultants are carefully selected students who are interested in the teaching and learning process" (p. 1). The BYU program requires student consultants to have at least a 3.0 GPA and provide two recommendations, one of which must be from a professor. (The other may be from another teacher or an employer.) At BYU, student consultants are recruited at the beginning of both fall and winter semesters.

Sources of potential SCOTs include education (and other) classes, student government and/or service organizations, faculty referrals, relatives/friends of current or past SCOTs, and articles in the student newspaper. At Carleton College the vast majority of student observers are majoring in educational studies (Morral & Tonyan, 1995). The University of Chicago program was designed to employ only MBA students.

On some campuses, student observers/consultants participate in this kind of program as a service, much as they would tutor or serve as student government committee members. Other institutions employ a service-learning model: students enroll in a credit-bearing class about teaching and learning, and their observations/consultations are part of their assignments for the class. The most common model is one in which students are paid hourly wages through student employment services or work-study programs. Nevertheless, students who participate in these programs usually value the intrinsic rewards more than the monetary ones: "Prof. XX was extremely interested in my ideas which was a valuable experience for me"; "I had a relaxed relationship with the teacher while feeling at the same time that he respected my [opinions]." Notice how validated these students feel when serving in this instructional/faculty development role.

Preparing and supporting student observers/consultants. The training of student observers/consultants can be as extensive as a semester-long course they take before or during their consultation work or as simple as a short orientation before they begin. At BYU, preparation and support consist of bi-monthly training meetings, mentoring of new consultants by "veterans," and consultation with the campus faculty developer. In addition, before a SCOT is hired, she or he must perform a prearranged "guinea pig" observation of a class and write a report, as if this were an officially assigned consultation. Copies of these reports are sent to the instructors who volunteered to be observed, but no actual follow-up meetings are held. Instead, experienced SCOTs role-play a "follow-up meeting with an instructor" for the prospective SCOTs; then each new SCOT practices a "follow-up meeting" with a veteran SCOT playing the part of an instructor. Training materials from most programs include copies of some observers' reports (without names and other identifying information) to serve as examples for novice observers.

Topics addressed in training meetings include one-on-one consultations, report writing, interview techniques, and topics from educational psychology such as Bloom's taxonomy (Harb, Hurt, Terry, & Williamson, 1995). In addition, students are provided articles/monographs such as

"Seven Principles of Undergraduate Education" (Chickering & Gamson, 1987) and other teaching/learning resources. Many times the student consultants benefit most from group discussion about issues that have arisen in their consultations. A campus faculty developer or an education or psychology professor can serve as a ready resource to the student consultants.

Those considering implementing a student observer/consultant program need not be overly concerned about providing extensive training. The fact that the students are not accomplished experts on pedagogy is not a hindrance but, in some ways, an asset to the effectiveness of their feedback.

Promoting the service to faculty. Who are the clients/participants in these programs? According to the Carleton College handbook for student observers,

> Users include faculty who are tenured and untenured, permanent and temporary. The program is used by people offering large lectures and small discussion classes, by faculty who are experimenting with something new or by faculty who simply want to ensure that their pedagogical methods are working (Morral & Tonyan, 1995).

Many faculty members participate in these programs year after year (Sorenson, 1998a).

One of the attractions of these programs is that they are "faculty driven." In other words, instructors decide whether to use a program, when and how much to use it, what options to use, and when to terminate. In addition, the data gathered is for the instructors' benefit. They decide what impact that data will make on their course design and course activities.

The promise of confidentiality is inviting to faculty who are considering participation in these programs. According to the Rutgers-Camden web site materials,

> Confidentiality is the watchword in this . . . program. . . . The results are strictly between [the instructor] and the student observer. . . . [N]o one outside [the teaching and learning center] knows that the professor is involved in the program at all (Omaha Boy, 1998, paragraph 6).

These assurances of both choice and confidentiality encourage faculty participation.

Although these observations, consultations, and reports are components of formative evaluation, some faculty members choose to display them as part of a teaching portfolio for summative evaluation. They may include student consultants' reports, the plans they developed as a result of the student consultation, and subsequent learning outcomes—but only at the faculty member's discretion and only as part of a portfolio that includes a variety of materials (e.g., student evaluations, peer reviews, syllabi, student products).

Outcomes

Student consultant programs allow faculty and student observers to experience new kinds of interactions—interactions that, among other things, value the student voice in faculty/instructional development (Sorenson, 1998b). Based on student consultants' feedback and advice, faculty often make changes. For example, instructors report modifications as simple as "speaking more loudly" or "writing more legibly on the board." Others implement more significant innovations, such as "initiating role plays" and reviewing before class "a list of things that intimidate students" in order to avoid those counterproductive behaviors. One teacher of Portuguese wrote:

> [As a result of student observations and consultations], I developed a system wherein I include student presentations along with a teaching cycle that involves a practice session after every . . . concept. [Now] the time I spend giving instruction [has] decreased to under 20 minutes, while the students' practice time [has] increased to 30+ minutes. My students [learn at] a higher mastery level. I [intend to] continue [this] in the future.

When faculty implement changes as a result of student observations/consultations, enrolled students report enhanced learning and greater teacher approachability (Sorenson, 1998a). In addition, student observers/consultants "understand more about how professors prepare, evaluate, and refine a course, [and they] gain more of a faculty perspective on how the teaching process continues throughout a course" (Morral & Tonyan, 1995). One experienced student observer stated, "I learned a lot about effective teaching and communication between a teacher and his or her students."

Through their participation in these programs, many student consultants experience personal growth: "I learned how to give *constructive* feedback"; "I'm developing person-to-person skills"; "This [experience] was valuable because it helped me learn a different, but effective style of teaching"; "I saw and learned a lot of different teaching techniques. I was able to learn how to communicate better with a professor." Consulting students feel productive when they see the positive effects of their efforts. One student reported, "I was able to see a professor [make use of] the results [of the interview]; he took notes and picked out 3-4 things to work on."

Evaluation

At the conclusion of their consultations, both SCOTs and instructors are invited to evaluate their collaboration by responding to a questionnaire in which they identify both the strengths and limitations of the program and their own interactions in the program. Nine years of evaluation data about BYU's program reveal consistently positive attitudes, interactions, and outcomes. A student observer reported, "I gained a great deal from seeing both the perspective of the teacher and the students."

Student observer/consultant programs honor both the student voice and faculty desire to enhance the learning of their own students. One elementary education professor wrote: "[SCOT helped me] improve! Great feedback and encouragement! [The student consultants] were genuine and sincerely interested in me [and my students]." A public management professor lauded the program for adding "a new dimension to the evaluation process." A music professor reported: "I have had student consultants videotape, observe, and interview students in two of my classes. I have found their assistance almost priceless in learning from my mistakes and building on my strengths as a teacher. [This program] is very conducive to improving the quality of teaching." In fact, not only do these programs improve the quality of teaching and enhance learning, they also build a campus-wide community (*including* students) that addresses important issues in teaching and learning.

Faculty Development Seminars Involving Students

In order to encourage faculty and student learning partnerships and faculty interest in student learning, developers have coordinated seminars and workshops *about* students. For example, Rallis (1994) describes a workshop in which faculty discuss their students' pet peeves about college instructors—concerns that were collected from a survey of students. One workshop outcome is that instructors develop a plan to change their teaching, for example, organizing course material in a variety of ways to honor different learning styles. However, because students do not participate in these seminars, their immediate reactions, feedback, and learning are lost. What if they *did* participate in such a seminar?

The Joint Student-Faculty Seminar on Sharing Views of Teaching and Learning

An example of a successful joint student-faculty venture coordinated by a faculty development office is the dinner seminar "Sharing Faculty and Student Views of Teaching and Learning." It has taken place for 10 years as part of Miami University's Teaching Scholars Program, a year-long faculty teaching development program for junior faculty in their second through fifth years of teaching (Cox, 1994, 1995). Each of the 11-14 junior faculty participants invites a student to attend and help prepare for the two-hour seminar. The selection of students is not limited in any way; they may be first-year through graduate, either traditional or nontraditional, from all campuses, and having various grade point averages. Most are undergraduates of traditional age and articulate—willing to speak out.

The program coordinator sends faculty participants a seminar information request form (see Appendix 1) beforehand, which asks them to list their "5 keys to successful teaching" as viewed by faculty. The students are sent a similar form asking them to list "5 keys to successful teaching" as viewed by students (the student form is the same except it is titled "Student Responses"). Each faculty member also writes two "questions to students about teaching and learning," and each student writes two "questions to faculty about teaching and learning." Both faculty and students identify a metaphor for teaching and learning.

The seminar coordinator compiles the open-ended responses, then sorts the keys by general categories and indicates the frequency of faculty and student responses in each category (see Appendix 2). (For a synthesis of 31 similar studies in which student and faculty views of effective teaching were compared, see Feldman (1988); however, only 2 of the 31 studies involved open-ended responses.) The lists of questions (see Appendix 3), keys, and metaphors are distributed to all participants before the seminar.

The seminar begins with student and faculty introductions, followed by discussion about the difference between types and frequencies of keys to successful teaching as listed by faculty and students. For example, in Appendix 2, contrast the faculty-to-student ratio of 1:2 (4 responses:8

responses) in the category of "student relations/rapport" with the ratio of 2:1 on "concrete-in-class/out-of-class activity/process." Note that in the latter category three students think teaching to a variety of learning styles is an important key, while no faculty have listed this key. Another interesting observation is the large number and variety of keys appearing on both lists. Of the 33 faculty and 31 student keys, 14 (42% and 45%, respectively) appear on both lists. These observations start a lively discussion that goes for 15 minutes or so, followed by 45 minutes of conversation alternating between student questions and faculty questions. A nice dinner (particularly to thank the students)—but a working dinner—then occurs with small-group discussion.

The usual outcome of this seminar is an increased understanding of each other's perspectives. For example, students discover how much care, interest, and fervor these faculty devote to their teaching, and they learn about other university demands on faculty time. Faculty learn about students' understanding and confusion regarding liberal education objectives, frustrations with certain teaching styles (e.g., "Why are all my instructors trying cooperative learning?"), and the variety of demands on student time.

After the seminar, each student receives a thank-you letter from the program director, and both faculty and students receive seminar evaluation forms. Out of the dozen or so seminars sponsored by the program over the year, faculty rate this seminar at or near the top when asked, "How interesting did you find this seminar?" For example, in 1996-97 this seminar received the highest rating out of all seminars (see Figure 7.1).

One factor cited for the success of the seminar is the scholarly and open climate of the proceedings. One student wrote:

> I thought the professor-student interaction was good—everyone respected everyone else's opinions—even when there were distinct disagreements. The format worked well: by having discussion first, grounds were laid for small group discussion during dinner. Overall I am happy I was able to participate in this seminar.

Another year-long Miami faculty learning community sponsored by the development office, the Senior Faculty Program for Teaching Excellence (Cox & Blaisdell, 1995), also has adopted this seminar. The procedure and format are the same. However, the types and frequencies of keys

FIGURE 7.1
Seminar Interest Ratings for Miami's Teaching Scholars Program
(0 denotes low interest, 4 denotes high interest)

Rating	Seminar Type
3.6	Sharing faculty and student views of teaching and learning
3.5	Diversity issues and opportunities in teaching and learning
3.4	Teaching goals inventory and CATs
3.4	Ethical dilemmas in teaching
3.3	Cooperative learning
3.1	Student intellectual development
2.9	All about mentors
2.9	Scholarship of teaching
2.9	Teaching projects: Selected, in-depth reports
2.7	Learning disabilities
2.7	Obtaining feedback from students
2.4	Service learning
2.0	Assessment: Meeting course and long-term learning objectives

can vary. For example, the 1998 senior faculty seminar with students revealed fewer keys appearing on both lists (29% and 33%, respectively) and different categories with unbalanced ratios (the faculty:student ratio is 1:2 in "professor knowledge/skill" and 3:1 in "abstract (less concrete) inside/outside class procedures").

Students as Chairpersons of Faculty Development Seminars

Another way to involve students in faculty development seminars is to have them chair sessions that the faculty development office or teaching center coordinates. This student involvement can assist the teaching center when several concurrent sessions occur during campus conferences or retreats. At Miami, both faculty and students have been pleased with this involvement.

A protocol for students chairing sessions has been developed over the years (see Appendix 4). The office holds a one-hour "training session" a week or so before the event. Students can receive hourly wages for their involvement in training and the seminar. Some student service organizations have their members participate as a group, with their earnings going to the organization.

This experience provides a scholarly way for faculty developers to connect directly with students. As one student reported in a reaction paper about her experiences chairing a session:

> Overall, I found the experience to be very enlightening. I was able to compare the different styles of teaching in all my classes to what [the professor] talked about. It made me grateful to know that so many teachers were actually concerned about their students.

Students as Professional Critics

The following innovative project illustrates yet another effective way to involve students in faculty development seminars. After a major science curriculum redesign at an eastern university, summer workshops were designed to prepare 25 instructors to teach new content to different students using new methods—different and new in the sense that these instructors had not experienced these situations before (Herreid & Kozak, 1995). During the first week of the program, the instructors attended seminars on student learning, such as Kolb's learning styles, and ways to use new approaches, such as case studies. During the second and third weeks, instructors developed syllabi and presentations. In the last week, the instructors delivered at least one class presentation to a group of students who had been hired to serve as critics. These 16 junior and senior undergraduates were representative of the student population (with respect to gender and ethnicity), had a wide range of grade point averages, and were majoring in 12 different disciplines in the humanities and social sciences. The students were selected from those responding to an ad in the student newspaper.

Both faculty and students were enthusiastic about the experience and recommended that it continue. Evaluations and resulting practice indicate that faculty gained a better sense of how they teach and the students of how they learn. For example, the use of small groups was carefully tried, the results analyzed, and the method adopted by many participants. Both faculty and students learned ways to communicate across very different disciplines, and they gained respect for one another.

Students as Members of Faculty Learning Communities

Learning communities provide excellent opportunities for students to learn, and learning communities of faculty are no exception. This section examines an attempt to involve students in faculty learning communities directed by faculty developers.

This is the 20th year of the Teaching Scholars Program, a learning community of junior faculty at Miami University. One of the key features of the program has been the involvement of senior faculty mentors (Cox, 1997a). Although students are members of the program's advisory committee, it was not until the 18th year of the program that the idea occurred to the director that student consultants or associates might also play an important role in actually working with junior faculty. The involvement of student consultants was also introduced in Miami's Senior Faculty Program for Teaching Excellence (now in its 8th year).

The objective of including student consultants in these two programs is to enhance the likelihood of achieving these program goals:

- Enhancing interest in teaching, teaching effectiveness, and student learning, for both faculty and students
- Advocating and developing educational and pedagogical innovation
- Interacting as an interdisciplinary community
- Discovering and incorporating ways that difference can enhance teaching and learning

Because Miami does not have a student observer/consultant program, faculty program participants select students to work with them much as the junior faculty select their senior faculty mentors (Cox, 1997a). Faculty usually invite students who have been in their past classes or are majors in their disciplines.

The program allows each faculty participant to involve his or her student consultant in joint activities similar to those described previously in the section on student observer/consultant programs. Activities can also be specific to the faculty member's participation in the Teaching Scholars or Senior Faculty Program. These joint activities include attendance at program seminars, work on the faculty participant's teaching project, and reading articles in preparation for a seminar. Members of both groups are now investigating the possibility of trying "team teaching with a student" (Gray & Hulbert, 1998).

The following guidelines about student consultants were adopted by both programs.

- Each participant selects one or two student consultants each semester. The student can be of any class standing or major. If a faculty participant selects a graduate student, then in order to ensure broad perspectives, he or she also selects an undergraduate.

- The faculty participant's role is twofold, as learner and as teacher. Faculty will learn from their students' perspectives, and students will learn about professorial life and the academy.
- Consultations between faculty participants and students is scheduled at least twice a month. Informal discussion includes, for example, classroom observations, topics raised at seminars in the program, insights about the faculty member's teaching project, responses to an article, and reactions to innovations the faculty member is considering or implementing in his or her classes.
- Faculty participants usually do not select students enrolled in their current classes. Although this could provide ongoing topics for discussion and helpful suggestions, there are ethical considerations. For example, student or faculty perspectives could be biased by the current faculty-student relationship. Students from past classes are good candidates.
- Student consultants are encouraged to participate in some of the program's seminars, such as the joint faculty-student seminar discussed earlier.
- Students are encouraged to chair sessions at the Lilly Conference on College Teaching in November and at the campus-wide Teaching Effectiveness Retreat held at Miami in February.
- Students should be rewarded/reimbursed for serving. This also helps ensure that their commitments as student consultants will last throughout the semester. Some reward/reimbursement possibilities are as follows.

Undergraduate associates. The Undergraduate Associates Program (UAP) is administered by the University Honors Program. It gives a student consultant the opportunity to work closely with his or her faculty member to explore careers in academia. The UAP is open to juniors and seniors with strong academic records. In the UAP, a student works for a semester or a year with a faculty mentor assisting with many of the tasks addressed by academics (e.g., teaching, grading, attending governance meetings, engaging in research, etc.). A student completing the UAP and submitting a final report receives the notation "Undergraduate Associate" on his or her transcript.

Independent study. Student consultants can earn an hour (or more) of independent study credit under the direction of their faculty program member.

Student wages. Faculty participants can arrange for the program to pay their students for serving as consultants. Faculty can also provide thank-you gifts (e.g., books, software) to their student consultants, purchased from program funds.

After a year and a half of piloting the use of student consultants in these two faculty learning communities, some short-term outcomes can be reported.

The senior faculty evaluations of the program report strong impact from involvement with their student consultants/associates. Each year the senior faculty participants report the relative impact of nine components of the program: release time, colleagueship and learning from the other participants, student consultants, the teaching project, retreats, national conferences, seminars, observation of others' classes, and partnership with a colleague in the program (Cox, Cottell, & Gusthart, 1998). In 1997-98, the student consultant component was rated highest in impact with an 8.3 on a rating scale of 1-10. On the comments page of the evaluation, one senior faculty participant wrote:

> This was one of the biggest surprises of last semester. My two student consultants were wonderful aides in helping me evaluate what was going right or wrong in the class. They developed a survey of the class, wrote up their own analysis, and met with me about five or six times to discuss teaching methods. I thoroughly enjoyed the group session with all the student consultants at the end of last semester. I plan to have a similar experience with two consultants (I think more would be too many) this semester.

The junior faculty, on the other hand, rated the impact of the student consultant/associate component last out of eight program components, giving it a 5.0 on the same scale as above. The junior faculty reported that their contacts with students suffered because of the following difficulties: identifying students to work with, students not following through on plans, students backing out (too busy), conflicting schedules, lack of time to meet, etc. At the midpoint of 1998-99, the evaluation results reconfirm those of 1997-98.

The impact of student consultants on junior and senior faculty differs for the following reasons. Senior faculty are experienced and familiar with campus culture, well acquainted with students in their departments, effective in motivating and rewarding student participation, and do not have the pressures of obtaining tenure. Junior faculty are at a disadvantage since there is no student observer/consultant program on campus to provide the structure for the junior faculty-student connection. Thus, the student consultant component will probably become optional for junior faculty, available for those who wish to invest the time to reap the advantages of consulting with students.

Involved Students: Potential Change Agents

Students are potential agents for change of campus culture. For example, they can help facilitate the shift from the teaching to the learning paradigm. Such a change can be a result of their faculty development activities as student consultant/observers, as professional critics, as leaders of or participants in faculty development seminars, and as members of advisory committees for faculty development programs.

Faculty developers and college teachers can go beyond just involving students in faculty development practices. When students reflect and write about their faculty development experiences, it enhances their involvement by deepening their learning and growth, and it also provides helpful feedback to developers. A reflective approach could include student reaction papers, journals, and other ways of prompting student reflection on the experience. Cox (1997b) offers this as a student portfolio option in his undergraduate mathematics courses. The following examples from these portfolios illustrate students reaching beyond their faculty development activities to affect other parts of campus.

In the excerpt below from a student reaction paper, a junior, who served as chair of a faculty development seminar, learns and then becomes an advocate for broader evaluation in his division:

> The first presentation I saw . . . was on peer evaluation of teaching. As [the presenter] began to talk about the literature on the subject, I realized how important it was. I've spent over two years participating in the governing bodies [in my division] with various faculty members, and have engaged in several conversations on the use of student evaluations. But we never once discussed the concept of being evaluated by peers. It seems that this could be an effective means of legitimizing the teaching process in the

> university. A faculty member may prove to be very knowledgeable about a given subject or topic, but his/her effectiveness as a teacher is a completely separate question.

Another student writes about her reactions as an active participant in a faculty development diversity seminar. She has grasped the complexity of adopting the learning paradigm but needs encouragement to persist in finding ways that she can support change.

> Upon looking at my newly acquired knowledge from the Diversity Seminar, I am now realizing how few of my classes incorporate inclusive teaching and learning in the curriculum. Diversity is not emphasized in the classrooms at Miami, thus the University as a whole is also having problems making the campus a diverse environment. From what I have gathered, it is necessary to start at the bottom and work your way up, so perhaps by beginning with a change in teaching styles and curriculum to add diversity, eventually it would flow to the entire campus. All of the things that would diversify the curriculum are great ideas, and from a student's view, would add new and interesting aspects to the classroom while giving new perspectives on the traditional information. Unfortunately, though, all these educationally stimulating ideas would be extremely time consuming for the individual departments, the professors, and the university as a whole to accomplish if the final goal was a complete transformation of the system.

The Oslo College Centre for Staff and Learning Development provides an excellent model for examining the issues, determining strategies, and establishing practices designed to form partnerships with students (Havnes, 1998). This is accomplished by creating contexts for educational development. Havnes examines a theoretical platform[1] for developing partnerships with students and concludes, "Changing cultures is basically what we are talking about when we discuss the opportunities of making students partners in the educational process—changing cultures among [faculty], among students, and in the relationship between [faculty] and students" (p. 9). He goes on to say that to effect this change, there will be disequilibria that threaten the existing system and challenge traditions of both teachers and students. He then asks, "Are educational developers prepared to meet this challenge?" (p. 9). Faculty developers in partnerships with students can help prepare the university community for this discussion and facilitate the shift to the learning paradigm.

Issues to Consider

The following questions will guide faculty developers considering student partnerships on their campuses:

- What goals and objectives of faculty development can students contribute toward achieving?
- How and in what ways are students qualified to serve?
- How does one initiate student involvement in faculty development programs?
- How are students identified, selected, and rewarded each year for participating in faculty development efforts?
- What are effective ways to collaborate with students in this role?
- How do faculty react to student involvement?
- How do students react to participating in faculty development?
- What ethical concerns are involved?
- How can the effectiveness of student involvement be measured?
- How can faculty developers foster connections with their student affairs divisions, and what joint efforts and objectives can be achieved?
- How can partnerships developed with students foster the transformation to the learning paradigm?

Some of these questions have been addressed in this article, but because of the diversity of campus cultures and their faculty development offices, programs, and staff, there will be a rich variety of interests, needs, strategies, and activities generated by these questions.

In the 1990s, faculty development practice has been successful in enabling faculty to focus on learning. However, "revolutionary" faculty development partnerships with students await the next decade. To transform higher education from the teaching paradigm to the learning paradigm, it is now time to examine these issues seriously and consider initiatives to form partnerships with *undergraduates.* They join together with graduate students, faculty, administrators, and developers, as learners, observers, consultants, critics, participants, advisers, associates, and leaders in educational development.

Endnotes

[1]Havnes' theoretical platform examines four approaches: the theory of levels of learning, in B. Bateson (1992), *Steps to an ecology of mind* (Canada: Ballentine Books); the zone of proximal development, in Vygotsky (1978), *Mind in society: The development of higher psychological processes* (M. Cole, V. John-Steiner, S. Scribner, & E. Souberman, Eds.; Cambridge, UK: Cambridge University Press); activity theory, in Engeström (1987), *Learning by expanding: An activity-theoretical approach to developmental research* (Helsinki: Orienta-Konsultit Oy); and the community-of-learners model, in Rogoff (1994), Developing Understanding of the Idea of Communities of Learners, *Mind, Culture, and Activity, 1* (4), 209-229.

References

Angelo, T. A. (1989). Faculty development for learning: The promise of classroom research. *To Improve the Academy, 8,* 37-60.

Angelo, T. A., & Cross, K. P. (1993). *Classroom assessment techniques: A handbook for college teachers.* (2nd ed.). San Francisco, CA: Jossey-Bass.

Barr, R. B. (1998). Obstacles to implementing the learning paradigm—What it takes to overcome them. *About Campus, 3* (4) 18-25.

Barr, R. B., & Tagg, J. (1995, November/December). From teaching to learning—A new paradigm for undergraduate education. *Change, 27* (6), 13-25.

Black, B. (1998). Using the SGID method for a variety of purposes. *To Improve the Academy, 17,* 245-262.

Centra, J. A. (1978). Types of faculty development programs. *The Journal of Higher Education, 49* (2), 150-161.

Chickering, A. W., & Gamson, Z. F. (1987). Seven principles for good practice in undergraduate education. *AAHE Bulletin, 39,* 3-7.

Chism, N. V. N., & Szabó, B. (1996). Who uses faculty development services? *To Improve the Academy, 15,* 115-128.

Cottell, P., & Harwood, E. (1998). Do classroom assessment techniques (CATs) improve student learning? In T. A. Angelo (Ed.), *Classroom assessment and research: An update on uses, approaches, and research findings* (pp. 37-46). New

Directions for Teaching and Learning, No. 75. San Francisco, CA: Jossey-Bass.

Cox, M. D. (1994). Reclaiming teaching excellence: Miami University's Teaching Scholars Program. *To Improve the Academy, 13,* 79-96.

Cox, M. D. (1995). The development of new and junior faculty. In W. A. Wright & Associates (Eds.), *Teaching improvement practices: Successful strategies for higher education* (pp. 283-310). Bolton, MA: Anker.

Cox, M. D. (1997a). Long-term patterns in a mentoring program for junior faculty: Recommendations for practice. *To Improve the Academy, 16,* 225-268.

Cox, M. D. (1997b, October). *Student learning portfolios/faculty teaching portfolios: A look at each from both sides, now.* Paper presented at the Lilly Conference on College and University Teaching, Northwest, Portland, OR.

Cox, M. D., & Blaisdell, M. (1995, October). *Teaching development for senior faculty: Searching for fresh solutions in a salty sea.* Paper presented at the Conference of the Professional and Organizational Development Network in Higher Education, North Falmouth, MA.

Cox, M. D., Cottell, P., & Gusthart, J. L. (1998, October). *Student collaboration in faculty development: Connecting directly to the learning revolution.* Paper presented at the Conference of the Professional and Organizational Development Network in Higher Education, Snowbird, UT.

Cross, K. P. (1987). The need for classroom research. *To Improve the Academy, 6,* 3-17.

Erickson, G. (1986). A survey of faculty development practices. *To Improve the Academy, 5,* 182-196.

Erickson, B. L., & Erickson, G. R. (1988). Notes on a classroom research program. *To Improve the Academy, 7,* 19-22.

Feldman, K. A. (1988). Effective college teaching from the students' and faculty's view: Matched or mismatched priorities? *Research in Higher Education, 28* (4), 291-344.

Gray, T., & Hulbert, S. (1998). Team teach with a student. *College Teaching, 46* (4), 150-153.

Harb, J. N., Hurt, P. K., Terry, R. E., & Williamson, K. J. (1995). *Teaching through the cycle.* Provo, UT: Brigham Young University Press.

Havnes, A. (1998, April). *Students as partners in educational development—Practice, policy, and theory.* Paper presented at the International Consortium for Educational Development Conference, Austin, TX.

Herreid, C. F., & Kozak, A. I. (1995). Using students as critics in faculty development. *Journal on Excellence in College Teaching, 6* (1), 17-29.

Johnson, D. W., Johnson, R. T., & Smith, K. A. (1991). *Active learning: Cooperation in the college classroom.* Edina, MN: Interaction.

Kurfiss, J., & Boice, R. (1990). Current and desired faculty development practices among POD members. *To Improve the Academy, 9,* 73-82.

McKeachie, W. J. (1991). What theories underlie the practice of faculty development? *To Improve the Academy, 10,* 3-8.

Morral, F., & Tonyan, H. (1995). *Guidelines for student observers in working with faculty.* Northfield, MN: Carleton College Learning and Teaching Center.

Omaha Boy, N. (1998). TEC: Support services. In *Rutgers: The State University of New Jersey* [Online]. Available: camden-www.rutgers.edu/Camden/TEC/Services.html

Rallis, H. (1994). Creating teaching and learning partnerships with students: Helping faculty listen to student voices. *To Improve the Academy, 13,* 255-268.

Redmond, M. V., & Clark, D. J. (1982). A practical approach to improving teaching. *AAHE Bulletin, 34* (6), 8-10.

Richlin, L. (1998). Using CATs to help new instructors develop as teachers. In T. A. Angelo (Ed.), *Classroom assessment and research: An update on uses, approaches, and research findings* (pp. 79-86). New Directions for Teaching and Learning, No. 75. San Francisco, CA: Jossey-Bass.

Seldin, P. (1997). Using student feedback to improve teaching. *To Improve the Academy, 16,* 335-346.

Shulman, L. S. (1993, November/December). Teaching as community property: Putting an end to pedagogical solitude. *Change, 25* (6), 6-7.

Sorenson, D. L. (1994). Valuing the student voice: Student observer/consultant programs. *To Improve the Academy, 13,* 97-108.

Sorenson, D. L. (1998a, April). *Student observer/consultants: Providing feedback to instructors on teaching.* Paper presented at the International Consortium for Educational Development Conference, Austin, TX.

Sorenson, D. L. (1998b, October). *Student observers/consultants as collaborators in instructional development.* Paper presented at the Conference of the Professional and Organizational Development Network in Higher Education, Snowbird, UT.

Sorenson, D. L. (1999). *Students consulting on teaching: Faculty handbook.* Provo, UT: Brigham Young University Faculty Center.

Steadman, M. (1998). Using classroom assessment to change both teaching and learning. In T. A. Angelo (Ed.), *Classroom assessment and research: An update on uses, approaches, and research findings* (pp. 23-35). New Directions for Teaching and Learning, No. 75. San Francisco, CA: Jossey-Bass.

Steadman, M., & Svinicki, M. (1998). CATs: A student's gateway to better learning. In T. A. Angelo (Ed.), *Classroom assessment and research: An update on uses, approaches, and research findings* (pp. 13-20). New Directions for Teaching and Learning, No. 75. San Francisco, CA: Jossey-Bass.

Wright, W. A., & O'Neil, M. C. (1994). Teaching improvement practices: New perspectives. *To Improve the Academy, 13,* 5-37.

Wright, W. A., & O'Neil, M. C. (1995). Teaching improvement practices: International perspectives. In W. A. Wright & Associates (Eds.), *Teaching improvement practices: Successful strategies for higher education* (pp. 1-57). Bolton, MA: Anker.

Zahorski, K. J. (1993, October). *Involving students in faculty development: A matter of value and values.* Paper presented at the Conference of the Professional and Organizational Development Network in Higher Education, Rochester, MN.

Contacts:

Milton D. Cox
106 Roudebush
Teaching Effectiveness Programs
Miami University
Oxford, OH 45056
(513) 529-6648
(513) 529-3762 (FAX)
coxmd@muohio.edu

D. Lynn Sorenson
Faculty Center
4450 ELWC
Brigham Young University
Provo, UT 84602
(801) 378-7420
(801) 378-7467 (FAX)
lynn_sorenson@byu.edu

Milton D. Cox is University Director for Teaching Effectiveness Programs at Miami University, where he founded the annual Lilly Conference on College

Teaching. He also is Editor-in-Chief of the *Journal on Excellence in College Teaching* and directs the 1994 Hesburgh Award-winning Teaching Scholars Program. He teaches mathematics and is using Gardner's multiple intelligences and student learning portfolios in his calculus and finite mathematics classes. His current research areas include faculty learning communities.

D. Lynn Sorenson is Assistant Director of the Faculty Center at Brigham Young University, where she coordinates Students Consulting on Teaching (SCOT) among other faculty and instructional development programs. She was previously with the Instructional Development Program at the University of Oklahoma. In addition, for over three decades she has held teaching positions and led teacher development programs for The Church of Jesus Christ of Latter-day Saints. A former member of POD Core, she has served as conference program chair, as conference coordinator and on numerous POD committees. Her research and publications center on new faculty careers and valuing the student voice in teaching development.

APPENDIX 7.1

TEACHING SCHOLARS PROGRAM
SEMINAR INFORMATION REQUEST

Dinner Seminar: Sharing Faculty and Student Views of Teaching and Learning
Date and Time: Monday, October 12, 7:00-9:00 p.m.
Place: Bystrom Room, Shriver Center
Please return to Milt by **October 7**

FACULTY RESPONSE

Your Name: ______________________________

My Five Keys to Successful Teaching

As Viewed by Faculty
List only **one** key per item: no run-on sentences slipping in several keys.

1.
2.
3.
4.
5.

My Two "Questions to Students about Teaching and Learning"

1.
2.

My Metaphor for Teaching

Your student's name: ______________________________
Why did you select this student?

Please return this and your student's response to Milt Cox, Office for the Advancement of Scholarship and Teaching, by **October 7.** Thank you.

APPENDIX 7.2

Miami University 1998-99 Teaching Scholars Program Seminar: Sharing Student & Faculty Views of Teaching and Learning: 10/12/98

Keys to Effective Teaching and Learning	Faculty Frequency	Student Frequency
STUDENT RELATIONS/RAPPORT		
Rapport with students: approachable, friendly, encouraging	1	1
Motivate students		1
Respect	1	1
Positive, comfortable learning environment	1	
Caring	1	2
Understanding		1
Concern		1
Encourage student input		1
Subtotals	4; 4 keys	8; 7 keys
PROFESSOR KNOWLEDGE/SKILL		
Knowledge of subject	1	1
Communication skills	2	3
Listening skill	1	
Organization/well organized	1	
Content: for career; up-to-date	2	
Competent		1
Subtotals	7; 5 keys	5; 3 keys
CONCRETE IN-CLASS/OUT-OF-CLASS ACTIVITY/PROCESS		
Get students active/interactive learning	1	2
Problem solving	1	
Experimentation	1	
Hands on approach	1	
Teach the basics		1
Available/Accessible	2	
Teach to a variety of learning styles		3
Use discussion		1
Answer questions effectively		1
Use applications of subject	3	
Use examples	2	

Keys to Effective Teaching and Learning	**Faculty Frequency**	**Student Frequency**
Cooperative/collaborative learning	1	
Use video	1	
Use case studies	1	
Subtotals	15; 11 keys	7; 4 keys
ABSTRACT (LESS CONCRETE) INSIDE/OUTSIDE CLASS PROCESS		
Relate to real world	1	
Balance		1
Model what you teach, believe	1	1
Stimulate interest	1	
Open environment in class, learning from others	1	1
Relevance, make apparent	1	
Practical: use practical activities to teach		1
Subtotals	5; 5 keys	4; 4 keys
PERSONAL QUALITIES OF FACULTY		
Humor/not so serious	1	1
Interesting person		1
Open mind		1
Flexible/Adaptable	1	2
Fair/unbiased/consistent	2	1
Enthusiasm	1	1
Supportive		1
Welcoming		1
Subtotals	5; 4 keys	9; 8 keys
COURSE/TEACHING RELATED QUALITIES OF FACULTY		
Well prepared	4	2
Clear expectations, clarity	1	
Enjoy teaching	1	1
High standards		1
Connect with one's past learning as student		1
Subtotals	6; 3 keys	5; 4 keys
OTHER		
Colleague interaction about teaching	1	
Teach small classes		1
Subtotals	1; 1 key	1; 1 key
Totals	43; 33 keys	39; 31 keys

APPENDIX 7.3

Teaching and Learning Questions Raised by Students

1. What main "drive" keeps you going each day and each year?
2. Why do you think Miami students are so grade oriented?
3. Why aren't effort and time given towards understanding a class taken into consideration (often) in grading?
4. Teaching/learning is a highly beneficial and fulfilling career. What might lead teachers to lose their desire to teach?
5. Have you ever had an extremely synergistic class, and if so, what led to this experience?
6. How often do you change or update your teaching styles?
7. Do you believe college professors should be trained in educational methods as are secondary and elementary teachers?
8. How has technology (e.g., web sites) impacted your teaching methods?
9. Why is it that at the college level all of the strategies and theories taught to education students for K-12 learning are for the most part completely disregarded?
10. Why are college professors not required to take some instruction on how to deliver instruction?
11. How can professors maintain student interest during lectures?
12. What should a teacher do when he/she is not able to answer a question?
13. What central figure is (was) key in shaping your teaching philosophy and your pedagogy?
14. What do you believe is the most important element or key to successful teaching?

Teaching and Learning Questions Raised by Faculty

1. Does reading the content for the class as listed in the syllabus help to focus your reading so you know what to read and what to scan in the reading?
2. What is the most effective method to assist you to comprehend and apply the concepts in the assigned reading?
3. What do you view as a professor's role in the learning process?
4. What are some things that might make you view a professor as a bad teacher?

5. Should a teacher structure a course in such a way that it mandates certain behaviors (e.g. regular attendance, daily preparation)?
6. Should a professor teach to the lowest level performers in a class, the highest level performers, or somewhere in between?
7. What do you expect to get from lectures?
8. How does one convince students to study systematically?
9. How do you define a good/excellent lecture that is stimulating, challenging, and informative?
10. What can a professor/instructor do to maximize retention and conversion of information/facts to knowledge?
11. How important do you think a good knowledge base is when you think about all the things which you need to be a good teacher?
12. What are the two things you value most in a professor who contributes significantly to your education?
13. What is the most effective way for you to learn theoretical/conceptual information?
14. What is the best teaching practice you've ever encountered? Why?
15. How much effort, dedication, time are you willing to commit to learning this material?
16. How do you know when you have "learned" something?
17. How important is classroom climate?
18. How much authority/flexibility do you expect?

APPENDIX 7.4

Miami University Teaching Effectiveness Programs Student Session Chair Protocol Summary

Before the Session	1. Report to registration desk 20 minutes before your session. 2. Pick up evaluation forms at desk. 3. Arrive 2 minutes before previous session ends.
Getting Ready for the Session	4-5. Help the previous session chair end the previous session & collect evaluations. 6-7. Get the room in order and check AV for your session. 8-9. Introduce yourself to your session leader and check signals. 10. Handout/place evaluation forms for your session. 11. Crowd control.
During the Session	12. Introduce the session leader(s) 1/2 minute after scheduled start. 13- Latecomers: seat and/or encourage them to move on. 14. 15. During the session: enjoy and participate.
Ending the Session	16- 3 minutes before scheduled end of session: signal the 17. presenter. 18. 1/2 minute remains: signal again, perhaps stand. 19. Time is up: lead a round of applause.
After the Session	20. Collect evaluation forms at door. 21. Thank the leader and give him or her the evaluation carbons. 22. If the next session chair fails to appear, start that session. 23. Return used and unused evaluation forms to registration table.

Thanks!

Note. The full protocol is available from one of the authors, M. Cox.

8

Transforming Introductory Psychology: Trading Ownership for Student Success

Randall E. Osborne
William F. Browne
Susan J. Shapiro
Walter F. Wagor
Indiana University East

As colleges struggle to maintain enrollments, many have shifted from a primary focus on recruitment of new students to an increased focus on retaining students once they begin attending the college or university. An examination of introductory courses on our campus, however, revealed significant differences between faculty perceptions of student skills and the actual skills students brought into the classroom. This prompted shifts in the manner in which we teach introductory psychology on our campus in order to enhance the skills necessary for success in survey courses and to provide a foundation of learning and thinking skills that would translate to other courses. These changes have resulted in enhanced consistency between sections of the course, increased cooperation between faculty teaching the course, and enhanced performance on the success measures we outlined for this project. This systematic transformation of the course and immediate and long-term outcome data are fully explored in this paper.

Introduction

College campuses are clearly concerned with retention and graduation rates for students. Although on the surface retention may appear to be a straightforward issue (either you retain students or you do not), it is not that simple. There may be an intertwining set of factors present on many campuses that could interfere with student success. Although no single factor can account for all student losses or all student successes, when variables begin confounding each other, a negative cycle can start. It is possible, for example, that (1) typical factors that inhibit student retention, (2) faculty expectations for incoming students, and (3) traditional advising of students into introductory "survey" courses during their first year may interact with each other to have a negative impact on student success. In order to illustrate how these factors can influence each other, let us quickly examine each factor and its effect on student retention and success separately.

Retention Predictors

With the major emphasis placed on assessment by accrediting agencies (e.g., North Central) over the last ten years, campuses have become more aware of factors that mediate the success of students. Along with this increase in awareness has come the realization that retention is a major concern. Traditional thoughts about retention have also begun to change (American Association of State Colleges and Universities, 1997; Hyman, 1995). As campuses build retention programs that are more active and less reactive, retention and assessment efforts can be brought together. Different types of campuses, however, may deal with different retention issues (e.g., Allen, 1993; Borden, Burton, Evenbeck, & Williams, 1997; McGivney, 1996; Pacheco, 1994; Seppanen, 1995). Residential campuses, for example, may face fewer retention concerns due to family conflicts than commuter campuses.

Commuter campuses struggle to maximize retention in the face of multiple factors that interfere with such efforts. Many of these factors were borne out on our own campus when we categorized entry data from students and made inquiries into the reasons students give for withdrawing from classes. Students cite a multitude of reasons for "dropping" or "stopping" out. These reasons include: (1) health, (2) finances, (3) changing work status, (4) childcare issues, (5) lack of preparedness, (6) lack of home support for study efforts, (7) poor time management, and (8) stress (Rickinson & Rutherford, 1995). Clearly there is only so much that can be done to aid students with some of these issues. In our experience, however, too much emphasis is placed on those things campuses cannot change and not enough emphasis is placed on developing retention efforts around those factors that can be changed.

Faculty Expectations for Students

Faculty may assume that students come to college with more skills than they do. A recent presentation at a national teaching conference (Sydow & Sandel, 1996) illustrates this very point. According to the authors, college instructors' expectations for students do not closely parallel student abilities coming into the classroom or students' expectations for what the college experience will be like.

A recent survey of faculty on our own campus confirms this misperception. Instructors teaching introductory courses (including a "first year experience" course) were asked to list the assumptions they made about students entering their classes. A majority of the faculty endorsed a consistent set of attributes or expectations for students entering the college classroom. These expectations and abilities include (1) critical thinking, (2) time management, (3) goal-setting skills, (4) the ability to apply course concepts to the "real" world, (5) active reading, (6) learning-style flexibility, and (7) intrinsic motivation to succeed. When faculty were asked to cite reasons why students do not succeed in college, the most common responses were (1) lack of effort, (2) poor time management, (3) lack of maturity, and (4) not enough time to complete all demands in their lives. Although a significant number of faculty also mentioned "underpreparedness" as a contributing factor, few offered any suggestions as to what was meant by that word.

Do entering students have the skills college faculty expect? It probably comes as no surprise that entering students are deficient in the very areas in which faculty expect them to have attained some degree of competency. All entering students on our campus must complete entry assessments, which are used to assess reading level and mathematical ability and to place students into the correct level of English composition. Herein lies the dilemma. Whereas most faculty expect students to be prepared for college-level work, 70% of our entering students place into one or more of our developmental courses. These developmental courses are considered "pre-college." This discrepancy between faculty expectations and student abilities creates the potential to exacerbate any retention problems a campus may have.

Tendency to Place Incoming Students into Survey Courses

Survey courses such as introductory psychology are often quite difficult for students. Courses that sample many topics in modest depth and then move on, as is typical in an introductory-level psychology course, are quite difficult for students with less than solid academic skills. Research also suggests that the gap between student preparedness and faculty expectations in survey courses is exacerbated in courses in which little written work is required (Boice, 1990; Rickabaugh, 1993). All of these difficulties are particularly relevant for students on our campus, many of whom are not coming directly from high school but are returning to college after an extended break in their education.

In addition to issues of academic preparation, Snowman (1996) suggests that first-year students cannot succeed without more finely developed study skills. Certainly faculty and teaching assistants can facilitate study skills development in students. But the research clearly shows that study skills are irrelevant if students do not develop metacognitive abilities (Flavell, 1979; Gardner & Boix-Mansilla, 1994). As mentioned previously, however, entrance test scores on our campus place 70% of students into one or more developmental courses (e.g., algebra, composition, reading). Given that most students need 12-15 credit hours per semester to qualify for financial aid, a typical semester for a first-semester student on our campus may include developmental math, developmental composition, college textbook reading, and a survey course like introductory psychology. As outlined already, these survey courses require many (if not all) of the skills these students do not have. At the very time they are taking the developmental courses to enhance the skills necessary to succeed in college, they are being placed in survey courses in which faculty expect those skills to already be in place.

We could be setting many students up for failure. Introductory psychology is a historically difficult course for most students. Data from our university system show most campuses report "D," "F," and withdrawal rates from introductory psychology courses as high as 45%. However, it is highly unlikely that students will stop taking introductory survey courses during their first academic year. Therefore the burden for enhancing success rates in such courses lies with the faculty teaching these courses. Seven years ago our department implemented a project to assist in the success and retention of students designated by entrance variables as "at risk." Although many of the above mentioned variables that negatively affect retention seem beyond our control, we believed there were many upon which we could have a positive impact.

Recent campus discussions with area high school counselors suggest critical thinking, a common theme in college courses, may not be emphasized in high school courses. It was our belief that focusing on and fostering entry-level students' critical thinking skills would enhance their ability to succeed in their first semester. We also thought that these increased thinking skills would translate into greater self-confidence thereby motivating retention across semesters.

The Transformation

Over the past seven years, we have made systematic revisions to our general psychology course that we believe have had a significant positive impact on student success and retention. Over the next several pages, we will outline the steps in this transformation: (1) developing a core set of learning objectives that all faculty would use when teaching the course; (2) training and employing undergraduate students as teaching assistants in the general psychology course; (3) implementing a two-credit-hour critical thinking lab that was a co-requisite with limited sections of the general psychology course; (4) deciding that all sections would be taught by three faculty, each with primary responsibility for one-third of the course material; and (5) fully integrating the course so that the three-faculty team teaches the course. This team-taught format includes team writing all assignments and exams.

Developing Departmental Objectives for Introductory Psychology

We worked as a department to develop a set of learning objectives for all students taking the introductory course. Regardless of instructor, then, the expectation was that students would learn the information listed in the objectives. We approached this task by asking ourselves, "If this is the only psychology course that a student will ever take, what do we feel this student must know about psychology?"

Given our belief that the objectives represented the most important material that students leaving the introductory psychology course should know, we decided to design and implement a departmental comprehensive final exam as well. Students in all sections of the introductory psychology course from that point on (seven years now) were given a team-written, comprehensive final exam based on those team-developed, departmental course objectives. A sample of the chapter learning objectives for this course is included in Appendix 1.

These objectives are given to all faculty who teach the course and also to students along with the syllabus for the course. Students are encouraged to use these objectives as they study for course exams and to understand what information they should be garnering from the textbook. If, for example, during the social psychology section of the course a learning objective is listed that is not discussed in class, the students are encouraged to pay particular attention to that part of the social psychology chapter and to be able to answer questions about that concept at the level at which the objective is written.

As the reader will note by reading the sample objectives listed in Appendix 1, the level of the objectives vary. If the objective states that students should be able to "apply the concepts of inhibition, excitation, and threshold to examples of neural activity," for example, then exam questions are written at this "application" level. If an objective states that students will "know the meaning of ______," then a comprehension-level question will be written based on that objective.

Each faculty member started the process of writing course learning objectives by writing objectives in his or her specialty area. These lists were then distributed to the other faculty and discussed at a departmental meeting. If other faculty had questions about the inclusion of certain objectives or the exclusion of others, the faculty member who developed the objectives for that chapter would explain his or her rationale. If there was disagreement about the inclusion of a certain objective, we attempted to reach a compromise. If such a compromise was not reached, a vote on that objective would be taken. This process continued until we had a defined set of objectives that all faculty would use.

The Use of Undergraduate Teaching Assistants

Undergraduates receive training as Teaching Assistants (TAs) by taking a course on "Psychology Applied to Teaching." This course covers basic teaching skills as well as reflective teaching, managing group work, motivating students, meeting different student needs, understanding learning styles, classroom management, developing goals and objectives, planning for attaining goals and objectives, test construction and administration, and grading student achievement.

As a final component for the course, students are required to write a reflective statement of teaching philosophy. To help students begin developing their teaching statements, we give them examples of departmental faculty members' teaching philosophies and ask them to discuss how each faculty member's approach to teaching reflects his or her philosophy. We feel that this exercise is particularly important. The course is designed to help future TAs understand the proactive nature of the educational environment. Faculty do spend a lot of time reacting to student emergencies, changing schedules, weather delays, and other unforeseen obstacles. But the majority of what occurs in the classroom needs to be developed with forethought. By having students examine others' statements and create their own, we are able to use the teaching philosophy as a basis for reflective thinking about teaching and the choices one makes about what to do or not do in the classroom.

The Critical Thinking Lab

With a newly trained cadre of TAs, we were ready to move to the next phase in the development of the general psychology course. If students were going to learn new and more effective methods for thinking, those skills would need to be practiced on a very regular basis. For this reason, we developed a two-credit-hour critical thinking lab. This lab was paired as a co-requisite with some sections of our general psychology course. Prior to the implementation of this two-credit-hour critical thinking lab, 46% of the students were receiving either "D" or "F" grades or were withdrawing prior to the end of the semester. In developing this lab, we incorporated two major themes that we felt would assist students in being more successful as learners: cognitive levels and critical thinking. Although there are many educational viewpoints on cognitive levels and many critical thinking paradigms available, we chose to adopt Benjamin Bloom's (1956) taxonomy of cognitive objectives and Randolph Smith's (1995) seven characteristics of a critical thinker.

We adopted Bloom's (1956) cognitive levels to assist students in reflecting on their own thinking. Bloom suggests that many students are unpracticed in going beyond the knowledge level of information. This matched our own thinking about the challenges faced by students in many survey courses. If those courses simply ask students to recall facts, most students can do so competently. If, however, such courses expect students to apply those facts and use them in novel ways, most students will be unprepared to do so. We also felt, however, that such skills can be taught. The two-hour lab course provides us with the appropriate environment for teaching such skills and allows students to practice them multiple times and in multiple ways.

For example, we expect students to go beyond mere memorization or recitation of facts and expect them to assess their comprehension and analyze interconnections among ideas. An important aspect of the analysis process is the ability to break information down into subparts and retain and utilize only those subparts that are meaningful. Any extraneous information should be discarded. Teaching students how to break information down into meaningful units aids them in assessing what information is most important to retain and what can be discarded or, at least, ignored.

Our desire to emphasize student's thinking skills led us to search for a useful definition of critical thinking. For our approach to critical thinking, we adapted Smith's (1995) definition of the seven characteristics of a critical thinker. According to Smith, critical thinkers (1) are flexible—they can tolerate ambiguity and uncertainty, (2) identify inherent biases and assumptions in their thinking, (3) maintain an air of skepticism and ask, "What am I being asked to believe?", (4) are able to separate opinions from facts, (5) do not oversimplify or, in our opinion, make things overly complicated, (6) use logical processes to make inferences and connections, and (7) examine all available evidence before drawing conclusions. We felt that, regardless of degree program, student success would be enhanced if they could develop these seven characteristics.

It is important for the reader to note that we do not believe critical thinking can be taught as "content." Instead, it is taught as a process. It is a goal that is approached with systematic and continuous practice. We felt it was important to put critical thinking within a context. For this reason, we paired the critical thinking lab with the introductory psychology course. This pairing allowed us the additional benefit of being able to explore the degree to which fostering such abilities might impact success in our introductory course.

We developed critical thinking assignment sheets and group activities that encouraged students to expand their thinking in relation to content issues from the introductory psychology course. These assignments encouraged students to think in non-traditional ways. Group work was the primary mode of instruction, with faculty and teaching assistants "working" the room to encourage debate and keep the groups on task. Many of the activities were taken directly from Smith's book. One such activity, for example, asks students to imagine that they are on Clinton's re-election team. Their task is to devise a survey that would yield results favorable to Clinton's re-election. After completing this part of the assignment, the same groups are required to develop a survey that would lead to results unfavorable to Clinton's re-election. Such an assignment reinforces many of the concepts covered in the research methods section of the introductory course but places that information within the context of critical thinking.

To help make this formalized method of thinking more automatic, we decided to engage students in frequent and systematic analyses of their own thinking and designed a scoring rubric that reflected the comprehensive thinking we were striving to model. During one class period, for example, students watch a television news magazine show and are asked to use Smith's characteristics of critical thinking to analyze the program. Did the presenter, for example, analyze the information and discard meaningless information? Once students use the scoring rubric to analyze the program, they are put into groups to discuss their analysis. We use this scoring rubric as the primary method of evaluation to encourage students to reflect continuously on their thinking and the thinking of others. Whenever students turn in an assignment, we use this rubric and return the completed form with the student work. A copy of this rubric is included in Appendix 2.

We also encourage self-reflection by requiring students to turn in a daily "exit card" at the end of the class period. On these cards, we ask students to describe which critical thinking characteristic the activities from the lab reinforced, what cognitive level we had attained that day, and a rationale for their answers. In addition, any assessment comments are welcomed from students. The course faculty member and the TAs read these cards and then write personal responses on each, returning the cards the next class period.

A Sample In-Class Activity

One particular activity was listed by 88% of the students as the most influential in illustrating how challenging critical thinking can be. Four cards were placed on a sheet of paper and then copied onto an overhead transparency. The cards (from left to right) were (1) the king of hearts, (2) the three of clubs, (3) the jack of hearts, and (4) the five of clubs. Students were placed into groups and asked to look over the sequence of cards and to generate a hypothesis that would predict what the next several cards would be. Once students decided on what they believed the sequence to be, they were instructed to test the hypothesis by telling either the instructor or one of the teaching assistants what they believed the next card would be. In return, they would receive a "yes" or "no" response. A "yes" response, of course, would simply indicate that the card they chose fit the sequence.

On the surface this may seem easy, but it proved extraordinarily difficult for students. Most groups immediately predicted that the fifth card would be the nine of hearts (based on the hypothesis that the sequence was descending and skipping heart cards). Shocked expressions greeted the faculty member and TAs when they told students that this answer was incorrect.

This process continued for over 20 minutes and groups were gently nudged and prodded to try different hypothesis testing approaches. The activity clearly illustrated for students that they needed to be more flexible in their thinking. When students were told that a good scientist would approach this task by trying to pick cards that might prove her hypothesis wrong rather than trying to prove herself right, performance started to improve.

The typical approach of believing that it was the suit of the card that mattered could result in many "false positive" responses. Students might believe they had accurately determined part of the sequence because they had guessed the fifth, sixth, and seventh cards only to be told "no" when they guessed the eighth card. By trying to prove themselves right, or changing too many variables at once (like changing from a face card to a numbered card as well as changing the suit in the same guess) students had to start over when they received a "no" response.

Once students tried to prove themselves wrong by inserting other suits, they made quick progress. Ultimately, all groups completed the task having discovered the hypothesis statement that the instructor and teaching assistants had decided upon prior to the activity. The sequence that would always receive "yes" responses was "a face card followed by a numbered club."

The themes of challenging what is known, exploring one's hypotheses, and trying to prove oneself wrong are carried throughout all activities in the course. Students are taught to "invest" in their critical thinking and to understand how to reap the benefits of making that investment. Critical thinking requires more time and effort and may force one to reveal biases and assumptions inherent in one's thinking. But, in return for such an investment, students learn they gain more pure knowledge and can be more certain of what they know and why they know it. These skills, we believe, aid students as they take other courses within their degree programs.

Results of the First Transformation of the Course

A recent analysis of our data supports our notion that emulating Smith's seven characteristics of critical thinking enhances student success. Students completing the critical thinking course along with the general psychology course outperformed the matched sample on all variables regardless of academic major.

Ninety-two students completed the critical thinking lab with a paired general psychology course across those five semesters. In order to assess the impact of the critical thinking lab we created a matched sample cohort. The matched sample, drawn from regular sections of the general psychology course during the same semesters, was created based on entering scores on the campus entry assessments, high school rank, gender, ethnicity, declared major (if applicable), and semester in college.

Recall that prior to this project the average "D," "F," and withdrawal rate in our introductory course was 46%. The average "D," "F," and withdrawal percentage across the five semesters in which the critical thinking lab was attached to the introductory course was 24%.

In addition, the graduation rate of students who completed this version of the introductory psychology course (recall that these students were also designated by the university as the most "at risk" for academic failure) was 14% higher than for the matched cohort of students who took the traditional introductory course during the same semesters. Lastly, upon graduation, students who had completed the combined introductory psychology/critical thinking course had an overall GPA that was over one letter grade higher than the matched cohort sample.

The Second Transformation of the Course

Once we realized that the critical thinking laboratory could have such a powerful impact on student success and retention across semesters, we felt obliged to implement changes that would bring those advantages to all students who enrolled in the introductory course. To accomplish this, we knew we had to develop a method for ensuring consistency of coverage and expectations across the sections of the introductory course. Since we had recently developed an entire set of learning objectives for this course, a set that all faculty teaching the course would be held accountable to, it seemed the right time to expand the critical thinking experiences into all sections of introductory psychology.

At this point, the need for our own professional development as teachers became quite obvious and relevant to us. Many faculty felt they should have full control of the classroom and the content. Academic freedom was mentioned many times when faculty felt they were being "told" what to do or not do in the classroom. But we had data in hand suggesting very strongly that changes we had made on an experimental basis in some sections of our introductory psychology course were having profound positive effects on students. We could not ignore the obligation that came with such a discovery.

With the newest phase in the transformation of the course, the faculty moved to larger sections (up to 90 students when the previous enrollment cap had been placed at 50) with the continued aid of our undergraduate teaching assistants. These larger groups of students, however, were also required to enroll in a one-hour, content-based activity lab. Our campus policy requires 2½ hours of contact per week for a three credit hour course. We reduced our "lecture" class time to two hours and converted the additional half hour of lecture time into one hour of "lab time." The faculty designed "content" laboratories that supported course content covered during the preceding week.

In addition three faculty now team-teach the course, with each faculty member taking primary responsibility for teaching one-third of the course and designing the lab activities that support her/his content weeks. We offer two sections of the course each semester. One section meets twice a week for one hour each day. The second section is a night section that meets once each week for two hours. During each section of the course, the faculty persons not having primary teaching responsibility alternate attending the day and the night sections. The undergraduate teaching assistants also attend one of the course sections in addition to conducting at least one of the weekly activity labs.

We begin the lab sessions with sessions on study skills and critical thinking. Beginning in the third week, labs involve hands-on experience with course material covered the previous week. The week following the presentation of social psychology, for example, students are taught how to recognize persuasion cues and analyze television commercials. The week following the presentation on memory, interactive activities on memory (such as demonstrating primacy and recency effects) are presented. In addition, we now teach all sections of the introductory psychology course in our full-technology classrooms. All class sessions and presentations fully incorporate our available technology, and all lectures are now presented via PowerPoint. We are beginning to incorporate QuickTime video presentations and additional graphics within the PowerPoint presentations as well.

The Results from the Latest Transformation

We have implemented this team-taught procedure for two semesters and are now ready to report on the preliminary results. During the fourth week of classes we are required to send "early warning" reports to students who are in danger of performing poorly in the course due to poor attendance, poor exam grades, incomplete work, etc. During the early warning this past semester (the second semester of the "team taught lab activity" project), the average attendance percentage in the introductory course was up by 22%. In addition, the average withdrawal rate was down by 19%. Three semesters ago (prior to implementing the new, revamped introductory course with undergraduate teaching assistants leading lab sessions) the average grade of students in the introductory psychology course was 71%. After implementation of the required lab and the new team-taught format, the average course grade for the day sections (with a majority of "traditional" aged students) was 78%, and the average course grade for the night section (with more "non-traditional" aged students) was 80%. During the second semester, the average day section mid-term grade was 83%, and the average mid-term grade for the night section was 82%.

Conclusion

By placing our own control over content aside and working as a team, we have developed an approach to teaching the introductory psychology course that appears to be having positive short-term (higher course grades, better attendance, fewer "D," "F," and withdrawal grades) and long-term (overall higher GPA upon graduation, increased graduation rate) effects on students. Student course performance is an entire letter grade higher even though we are utilizing the same battery of test questions, the same departmental final exam, and the same categories of assignments we have used in previous years. By engaging in research on the impact of the critical thinking lab course and the team-taught version of the general psychology course, we have discovered information that has caused us to reexamine how our introductory courses are taught.

We feel that we have also gained better insight into the teaching/learning process. Students comment about enjoying the variety of lecture and activities. The faculty work closely to write exams, to solve problems, make decisions about student emergencies, and continuously monitor the process. Although it is difficult to "give up" some of our favorite things to teach in the class, we feel obligated to do so to the extent that such material is not a part of the agreed-upon objectives.

As we continue to move forward with our assessment model, we intend to find newer and ever more creative ways to enhance our own professional development as educators by trading ownership for student success. Much of our "affective" data comes from the students themselves. Students complete written work during every class period and are asked to complete assessment instruments many times throughout the semester as well. Overall, the response to the new format is quite positive. Eighty-seven percent (N=104) of students rate themselves as "agreeing" or "strongly agreeing" with the statement, "The activities helped me with the content, and I can use what I have learned." In addition 88% "agree" or "strongly agree" with the statement, "The teaching methods used helped me gain important information and understanding of the unit topic."

In addition to enhancing students' feelings about the general psychology course, anecdotal feedback from students and the teaching assistants about the team-taught approach is quite positive. Other faculty in other disciplines are asking us about the new format, and some have mentioned that students enrolled in the course have responded favorably to them about the approach. Teaching assistants state that numerous students have talked about the excitement and collegiality in the department.

We include brief written reflection in every class period and end each unit of material by asking students to share the strengths and areas in need of improvement from that unit. These end-of-unit assessment cards have provided a wealth of information for our continual improvement of the course and our team-teaching approach. Under strengths some representative comments include:

- "I like having three instructors teaching—it keeps things interesting."
- "Each instructor is different, but it is obvious each of you knows your stuff."
- "I like the use of in-class activities and many, many examples."
- "I can see how this information is going to help me as a future nurse."
- "I didn't realize psychology included so much. This really opened my eyes."

Comments about areas in need of improvement have been very helpful as we attempt to fully integrate the team-taught format. During the first semester of team-teaching, we utilized a form of "tag-team-teaching." Each of us was responsible for one-third of the material and we organized that material into units. During "our" unit, each of us took primary responsibility for teaching the material, scoring assignments, and writing the exam.

Multiple student comments identified a particular exam by using the instructor's name such as, "the question about Social Comparison on Osborne's exam. . ." This kind of comment suggested to us that students did not truly perceive our course as a team effort. We now attend all class sessions together, use scoring rubrics for all assignments, divide up the grading, and write the exams collaboratively. Student assessment comments suggest this collaborative approach embodies the type of team work we want students to recognize.

- "I really like having three instructors to teach me. I can ask any one of you for help."
- "Three teachers for the price of one—what a deal!"
- "It is very informative when the three of you teach together."
- "It is interesting how your perspectives differ yet it helps me learn."

As we peruse assessment comments, several themes emerge. The most important for us centers on students' positive reactions to the benefit of having three teachers. As we discuss course concepts, all three faculty will offer suggestions, ways to approach the concept, and advice for how best to learn the nuances of each concept. This is reflected in student comments such as, "When the three of you describe something there is bound to be one description that really works well for me."

A second theme centers on excitement. We want the students to be excited about the discipline and we wish to model that excitement. General psychology courses are recruiting grounds for new majors. If we can share some of our excitement with students, not only will they learn the course material better, they may be motivated to apply that material beyond this one, simple course and may sample additional coursework. Comments such as, "It is pretty obvious that the three of you are excited about what you do," provide evidence to us that students are, indeed, perceiving this excitement.

By developing ourselves professionally and trading traditional academic "ownership" for a more consistent and well-designed set of courses, we are ensuring more success for the students who take our courses. In addition, we are mentoring and role-modeling for the next generation of professionals who will teach in our discipline by taking our undergraduate TAs to teaching and research conferences and helping them as they present their ideas for professional critique.

We are now turning our attention to our lifespan development course. This is another multiple section course. We have already developed a set of departmental themes for the course and are considering a team-taught, integrated approach to teaching it as well. We have developed a cadre of assignments that appear to better meet the needs of our students. Although psychologists write the textbooks for such a course, and the course is taught by those of us in the psychology department, the majority of students who take the course are education, nursing, and social work majors. The assignments we have designed allow students to apply course concepts to solving problems they might encounter in their chosen profession. Student evaluations of these assignments are quite positive and advisors from the aforementioned disciplines have commented favorably on the preparedness of students completing the lifespan development course.

FINAL THOUGHTS

Transforming a course from multiple sections with no explicit consistency to one that is team-taught is difficult at best. Faculty perceptions of "owning" the classroom come into direct conflict with the desire to ensure consistency between sections of the introductory course. As we have experienced this transformation over the past seven years, we have identified several issues that could either interfere with such efforts or enhance the potential for success of these efforts. We leave you with these things we have learned.

- Make a careful decision about what method to use for developing the list of course learning objectives. We began by letting faculty develop learning objectives for those sections of the course about which they cared the most. Only after allowing faculty to defend their choices did we make attempts at compromise. Looking back, this may have resulted in unnecessarily long lists of objectives that we trim annually. Another tactic might be to have faculty develop the learning objective lists for chapters that are outside their areas of expertise. Thus, if someone else wants a certain concept to be included, he or she would have to argue convincingly for its inclusion.
- Such efforts need to be rewarded. Reference to these efforts should be made in annual service reports, and recognition of the difficulty of team-teaching such sections should be made when calculating faculty teaching loads.
- Continuous assessment is absolutely essential with constant vigilance over what the desired outcomes might be. If student learning is the desired outcome, then constant assessment data should be gathered and analyzed to determine if student learning is increasing.
- If the department is large, only those interested in the introductory course should be required to be a part of the process. As long as departmental faculty are willing to have the proposed product brought forward for a vote upon completion, the primary work is best handled by those most concerned with the introductory course.

- Efforts must be taken to allow faculty to utilize their preferred methods for achieving course goals. Lectures need not be used, for example, if the faculty member is more comfortable with first exposure methods (e.g., reading the chapter before it is discussed, completing a chapter quiz, and then discussing it during class).
- The focus must be kept on the outcome goals and not the process each faculty member uses to move students toward those outcomes.
- A firm commitment must be made by a departmental dean or chair to invest in the transition. In other words, the risk involved must be formally recognized and a commitment must be made to see the course through several transformations before decisions are made about the success of the new method. Such change will not bring about desired outcomes overnight. The department must invest in a long-term process of change.
- The faculty working to revise the course cannot work in isolation. By knowing what the other faculty will teach, they can design a more integrated course. Having faculty attend all sections of the course and holding weekly meetings can significantly increase the cohesiveness of the course.
- If a "team-taught" persona is desirable, it is best not to have a single faculty member teach large portions of the course. It is better to have faculty rotate weekly to reinforce for the students that the effort is an integrated one.
- It is imperative for faculty to prepare for the impact team-taught sections will have. We have gone from maximum enrollments of 50 per section (when taught individually) to sections of 90. Although this may seem minimal given that three faculty team-teach the course, it makes learning students' names much more difficult and also limits the amount of interactive work that can be done during the regular class sessions (as opposed to the activity labs).

References

Allen, B. A. (1993). The student in higher education: Nontraditional student retention. *Community Services Catalyst, 23,* 19-22.

American Association of State Colleges and Universities. (1997). *Policies and practice: A focus on higher education retention.* Washington, DC.

Bloom, B. S., Englehart, M. B., Furst, E. J., Hill, W. H., & Kratwohl, O. R. (1956). *Taxonomy of educational objectives: The classification of educational goals. Handbook 1: The cognitive domain*. New York, NY: Longman.

Boice, R. (1990). Faculty resistance to writing-intensive courses. *Teaching of Psychology, 17,* 13-17.

Borden, V. M. H., Burton, K. L., Evenbeck, S. E., & Williams, G. A. (1997). The impact of academic support programs on student performance and persistence. *Research Brief, 4,* 1-16.

Flavell, J. H. (1979). Metacognition and cognitive monitoring: A new area of cognitive developmental inquiry. *American Psychologist, 34* (10), 906-911.

Gardner, H., & Boix-Mansilla, Z. (1994). Teaching for understanding—within and across disciplines. *Educational Leadership, 51* (5), 14-18.

Hyman, R. E. (1995). Creating campus partnerships for student success. *College and University, 7,* 2-8.

McGivney, V. (1996). Staying or leaving the course: Non-completion and retention. *Adults Learning, 7,* 133-135.

Pacheco, A. (1994). Bridging the gap in retention. *Metropolitan Universities: An International Forum, 5,* 54-60.

Rickabaugh, C. A. (1993). The psychology portfolio: Promoting writing and critical thinking about psychology, *Teaching of Psychology, 20,* 170-172.

Rickinson, B., & Rutherford, D. (1995). Increasing undergraduate student retention rates. *British Journal of Guidance and Counseling, 23,* 161-172.

Seppanen, L. (1995). *Implications for retention strategies of differential student progress rates and the literature on student retent*ion. (Research Report No. 95-4). Olympia, WA: Washington State Board for Community and Technical Colleges, Education Division.

Smith, R. A. (1995). *Challenging your preconceptions: Thinking critically about psychology*. Pacific Grove, CA: Brooks/Cole Publishing.

Snowman, J. (1996). Research in action: Becoming a better teacher. *Midwestern Educational Researcher, 9* (2), 28-31.

Sydow, D. L., & Sandel, R. H. (1996, May). *Making student retention an institutional priority*. Paper presented at the National Institute for Staff and Organizational Development Conference on Teaching and Leadership Excellence. Austin, TX.

Contact:

Randall E. Osborne
Indiana University East
Middlefork Hall #352
2325 Chester Boulevard
Richmond, IN 47374
(765) 973-8445
(765) 973-8508 (FAX)
reosborn@Indiana.edu

Randall E. Osborne is Associate Professor of Psychology at Indiana University East. His teaching interests include Social and Abnormal Psychology and specialty courses on self-concept and self-esteem development and Psychology in the Courtroom. Dr. Osborne's research interests focus on self-concept, self-esteem, and factors that influence student success such as the relationship between pedagogy and student learning.

William F. Browne is Professor of Psychology at Indiana University East and Chair of the Behavioral and Social Science Division. His primary teaching focus is on training future college teachers, specifically undergraduate teaching assistants. Dr. Browne's research interests center on child and adolescent development and a cross-cultural analysis of adolescent self-concept and attitudes toward life.

Susan J. Shapiro is Associate Professor of Psychology at Indiana University East. Her primary teaching responsibilities include sensation and perception, behavioral neuroscience, and an online general psychology course. Dr. Shapiro's scholarly interests include applying the discipline of psychology to improve classroom interactions, student learning, and interactions with technology.

Walter F. Wagor is Associate Professor of Psychology at Indiana University East and currently serves as Assistant Vice Chancellor for Assessment. In addition to General Psychology, he regularly teaches Life Span Development, Learning, and Cognitive Psychology. Dr. Wagor's scholarly interests include student learning, assessment, teaching improvement, and youth violence.

APPENDIX 8.1

SAMPLE OF DEPARTMENTAL OBJECTIVES FOR INTRODUCTORY PSYCHOLOGY

I. Introduction

A. Definition and History

Formulate an accurate definition of the science of psychology.

1. Identify its goals.
2. Outline and discuss the development of Psychology as a science.

B. Contemporary Perspectives

1. Compare and contrast the major assumptions and methods of the five contemporary perspectives: psychoanalytic, behavioral, humanistic, biological, and cognitive.
2. Recall or recognize important names associated with the various perspectives.

C. Research Methods

1. Classify variables in examples as independent and dependent.
2. Differentiate between experimental and control variables.
3. Justify the use of random subject assignment.
4. Compare and contrast experimental and non-experimental research techniques.
5. Describe and explain bias and placebo effects in psychological research.
6. Classify research as ethical or unethical in accordance with the principles of the American Psychological Association.

D. Statistics

1. Identify and define mean, median, and mode.
2. Define variability and explain how the Standard Deviation and Range are used to measure it.
3. Describe the normal curve and discuss its use in psychology.
4. Explain the concept of statistical significance as it is used in evaluating research hypotheses.
5. Interpret correlation coefficients.

E. Interpret information when presented in tables, diagrams, and graphs.

II. Biological

A. Describe the neuron

1. Describe the basic structure of the neuron and the relationship of this structure to its function
2. Comprehend the process of neural communication and demonstrate this by being able to:

a. Describe the structure and function of the synapse.
b. Describe the function of neurotransmitters and give an example.
c. Apply the concepts of inhibition, excitation, and threshold to examples of neural activity.

B. Peripheral nervous system

1. Discriminate between the structures and functions of the sympathetic and parasympathetic nervous systems.
2. Define homeostasis and give examples of mechanisms which promote it.

C. Central Nervous System

1. Name and locate the basic structures in the central nervous system on a diagram or model.
2. Describe the function of named structures.
3. Apply knowledge of function in the central nervous system to understanding the effects of brain injury by describing the effects of injury to a particular structure in the brain.
4. Structures to be identified and described include:
   a. Corpus callosum
   b. Localization of function
   c. Somatosensory
   d. Motor cortex
   e. Primary Visual
   f. Primary Auditory
   g. Thalamus
   h. Hypothalamus
   i. Limbic System

D. Endocrine

1. Name the structures which make up the endocrine system.
2. Describe the function of the structures which make up the endocrine system.

E. Genetics

1. Discuss the interaction between Nature and Nurture.

APPENDIX 8.2

Project/Assignment/Activity Grading Sheet for B252—Critical Thinking

Content = ________
(Average Scale Point Circled Equals Points Earned)
Scale Used:

1--------------2--------------3--------------4--------------5--------------6--------------7

Major Problems in Most Areas	Major Problems in Many Areas	Major Problems in Some Areas	Minor Problems in Most Areas	Minor Problems in Some Areas	Few Problems	Little or No Problems

1.) The material presented was understandable.

1--------------2--------------3--------------4--------------5--------------6--------------7

2.) The content covered was covered accurately.

1--------------2--------------3--------------4--------------5--------------6--------------7

3.) The assignment was well organized.

1--------------2--------------3--------------4--------------5--------------6--------------7

4.) Student work met defined criteria.

1--------------2--------------3--------------4--------------5--------------6--------------7

5.) The material being presented was understandable.

1--------------2--------------3--------------4--------------5--------------6--------------7

Critical Thinking Characteristics = ______
(Average Scale Point Circled Equals Points Earned)

1--------------2--------------3--------------4--------------5--------------6--------------7

Major Problems in Most Areas	Major Problems in Many Areas	Major Problems in Some Areas	Minor Problems in Most Areas	Minor Problems in Some Areas	Few Problems	Little or No Problems

1.) Project showed flexible thinking.

1--------------2--------------3--------------4--------------5--------------6--------------7

2.) Project identified inherent biases and assumptions.

1--------------2--------------3--------------4--------------5--------------6--------------7

1--------------2--------------3--------------4--------------5--------------6--------------7

Major Problems in Most Areas	Major Problems in Many Areas	Major Problems in Some Areas	Minor Problems in Most Areas	Minor Problems in Some Areas	Few Problems	Little or No Problems

3.) Project maintained skepticism with accepting statements from others.

1---------------2---------------3---------------4---------------5---------------6---------------7

4.) Project separated opinion from fact.

1---------------2---------------3---------------4---------------5---------------6---------------7

5.) Project did not oversimplify.

1---------------2---------------3---------------4---------------5---------------6---------------7

6.) Project utilized logical inferences.

1---------------2---------------3---------------4---------------5---------------6---------------7

7.) Project examined available evidence before drawing conclusions.

1---------------2---------------3---------------4---------------5---------------6---------------7

Bloom's Cognitive Objectives = _______
(1 point for each "yes" checked)

1.) Appropriate mount of knowledge demonstrated. ___ yes ___ no
2.) Knowledge was correctly used to demonstrate comprehension. ___ yes ___ no
3.) Information was applied to real world problems. ___ yes ___ no
4.) Information was analyzed into meaningful units. ___ yes ___ no
5.) Information synthesized into new knowledge. ___ yes ___ no
6.) Student evaluated learning to test for accuracy. ___ yes ___ no

Total Grade = Content + Critical Thinking + Bloom

9

TEACHnology: Linking Teaching and Technology in Faculty Development

Mei-Yau Shih
Mary Deane Sorcinelli
University of Massachusetts, Amherst

As a coordinator of teaching technologies and director of a center for teaching in a large research university, we have worked collaboratively over the last year to achieve a common goal: to implement and refine several faculty development initiatives that create linkages among the domains of teaching, learning, and technology. In this case study, we will describe the kinds of programs we've developed and summarize lessons we've learned. We hope that faculty developers on other campuses who are grappling with how to define their mission related to technology and how to work with faculty to integrate teaching and technology can adapt some of what has worked well for us.

The use of instructional media in the classroom has long been identified as a "fourth revolution" in education (Ashby, 1967). It has the potential to reshape the role of the instructor from a knowledge conveyer to a guide and coach, while students take a more active role in the learning process. No longer are the textbook and instructor the sources of all knowledge; instead, the faculty member becomes the director of the knowledge-access process (Heinich, Molenda, Russell, & Smaldino, 1996). In this way, instructional technology refers not so much to the actual use of technological tools as much as it does to the process of developing overall goals and strategies for enhancing teaching and learning that incorporate these tools. At its best, technology-based learning can help teachers support a wider range of learning styles, facilitate active learning in the classroom, use faculty time and expertise more effectively, and familiarize students with technology that will be vital for their futures in the world of work.

In our experience, faculty are both greatly excited and daunted by the promise and power of teaching technologies. Our students have grown up in a "high technology" environment and are well adept at the use of TV, videotape, computers, and the Internet as information exchange tools. Many faculty, on the other hand, struggle to learn new technologies and to see how they might be useful to them as teachers. At the same time, administrators, eager to better use limited resources, are ramping up resources for technology and urging that faculty get on board. This combination of faculty members' intrinsic interest in learning something new, fear of falling behind in understanding of instructional technology, and awareness of institutional pressures to use technological innovations has presented faculty developers with a variety of instructional challenges. How can we best work together with faculty to explore methods for integrating teaching and technology in ways that create a better learning environment for students?

As a coordinator of teaching technologies and director of a center for teaching in a large research university, we have worked collaboratively over the last year to achieve a common goal: to implement and refine several faculty development initiatives that create linkages among the domains of teaching, learning, and technology. In this case study, we will describe the kinds of programs we've developed and summarize lessons we've learned.

Needs Assessment

The Center for Teaching's (CFT) efforts began in 1995-96 with a needs assessment of faculty chosen because of their visibility as "early innovators" who had already attempted to use technology in their teaching. A total of 20 interviews were conducted with faculty representing nearly all of our nine schools and colleges. Our discussions focused on how faculty were using teaching technologies, what was going well, and what wasn't working so well (see Appendix 1).

In summary, the needs assessment suggested the following. In order to implement teaching technologies, individual faculty need time, resources (equipment, support services, appropriate classroom space), and a higher degree of communication and coordination with other users. On an institutional level, the university needs to work toward reframing its reward structure to recognize efforts to use technology. There also should be a broad discussion of the value and implications of technology for our mission of teaching and learning.

Setting out a Mission

In response to the assessment, the CFT expanded its mission to address issues of instructional technology and its implications for teaching and learning. Clearly, the Center had neither the resources nor desire to become technology providers on campus. Instead, we defined our mission as follows:

- To support individual faculty efforts in their use of instructional technology by consulting on issues of good practice and clarity of teaching and learning goals, and to direct faculty to other relevant campus resources.
- To increase communication among users of technology in hopes of improving the human infrastructure related to this rapidly changing field.
- To coordinate efforts with other units on campus that provide technical expertise and support for instructional technology.
- To advocate for institutional support of individual efforts to create and implement instructional technology.
- To recognize and reward excellence in the use of instructional technology (Butcher, 1997).

Early TEACHnology Initiatives

We decided that our long-range plans should include several tiers of activities that would provide multiple points of entry into the use of teaching technologies. We sketched out ideas on a continuum—from "lower risk" activities (e.g., a written and web-based guide to resources, teaching and learning roundtables) to a program that asked faculty to engage in more intensive training (e.g., a year-long faculty fellowship).

During the 1995-96 academic year we began by offering a Teaching Well with Technology campus-wide workshop series that included topics such as The Active Voice: Classroom Learning and Student Involvement, The Paperless Class: Teaching and Research Via the World Wide Web, and Engaging Students as Active Learners: Using Technology to Promote Learning in the Classroom. During the 1996-97 academic year we published and distributed a print and web-based resource, *TEACHnology: A Guide to Teaching Technology Resources*, and followed up with a series of Teaching-and-Learning-with-Technology roundtables. Each roundtable explored one of the key teaching technologies featured in the guide—presentation tools, computer-based instruction, classroom communication systems, and distance teaching and learning tools. We used faculty, listed as "peer innovators" in the guide, to facilitate the discussions. These three initiatives all offered accessible, low-risk ways for faculty to gain awareness of the wide variety of teaching technology resources available to them as teachers. We were now ready to launch the cornerstone of our teaching technologies initiative, an intensive, year-long TEACHnology Senior Faculty Fellowship. The following section describes the development of this key program. We believe it is unique in the field in terms of goals, design, format, and outcomes.

TEACHnology: A Senior Faculty Fellowship Program

For over a decade, the Center for Teaching and the Provost's Office at the University of Massachusetts, Amherst have sponsored a Lilly Teaching Fellows Program, a highly successful faculty development program for promising junior faculty members. After initial funding of a three-year grant from the Lilly Endowment, the university committed the necessary resources to continue the program over the past decade. Former teaching fellows report a number of benefits derived from a year in the program and in their ensuing academic careers—new teaching skills and attitudes, collegial contacts, greater understanding of institutional expectations, and professional confidence (List, 1997).

From its inception, the Teaching Fellows Program was limited to pre-tenure faculty. Over the years, however, there have been many tenured faculty who felt that they, too, could gain from a similar experience. As noted earlier, teaching in the 1990s has presented unique challenges that were not present in the past. We felt that senior faculty would benefit from a forum in which they could share information, discuss classroom experiences, and learn from each other.

Beyond the teaching technology activities occurring in our Center, several campus initiatives allowed us to move our vision of a senior faculty fellowship closer to reality. Our chancellor's multi-year strategic planning process included, from the start, a significant information technology initiative. This initiative spearheaded the development and renovation of facilities; the installation of state-of-the-art equipment in lecture halls, classrooms, and computer labs; and a modest laptop computer loan program. The next step seemed to be to increase the human infrastructure of resources on campus. The university had focused on hardware and software; it was time to focus on "peopleware."

In 1997-98, we proposed and started our TEACHnology Senior Fellowship Program, building upon the goals and framework of the Lilly Teaching Fellows Program. Why focus on providing senior faculty with increased opportunities and support for integrating teaching technologies? Based on our earlier needs assessment, we found lots of evidence that it was our tenured faculty who were particularly interested in developing new computer-based paradigms for teaching and learning. In fact, nearly all of our faculty who were identified as "early adapters" were tenured. Rogers (1995) offers an explanation of faculty adoption of new technologies. He proposes that "innovators" and "early adapters" constitute 15 percent; traditional faculty—"the majority or mainstream"–constitute 70 percent; and "nonadopters" form the last 15 percent of the total faculty. Rogers emphasizes that the majority of faculty need assistance in "crossing the chasm" from the mainstream to the adapters. We found that tenured faculty at UMass included both a small group of "early adapters" and an enormous group of "mainstream" faculty seeking assistance in "crossing the chasm" (Sorcinelli, in press).

Goals of the Program

The major goals of the TEACHnology fellowship are to help senior faculty apply the capacities of technology to teaching and learning, particularly at the undergraduate level; to foster teaching innovations through technology; to increase communication and collaboration among users of technology; and to provide a special opportunity for renewal to senior faculty.

Selection of Fellows

The TEACHnology fellowship includes ten tenured fellows who are selected from across the nine schools and colleges on campus. The award is competitive; nominations are made by department chairs and reviewed by a selection committee. The program seeks tenured faculty who are teaching undergraduates, have a plan for integrating teaching technologies into a course, and are interested in disseminating what they have learned throughout their home departments and colleges. During the first two years, the program has attracted senior faculty who are both outstanding teachers and scholars. Fellows are awarded a state-of-the-art laptop computer with instructional software, funded by the deans of their schools and colleges.

Program Elements

The structure of the TEACHnology fellowship is a simple one. Each fellow chooses one course to work on and the goal is to integrate relevant teaching technologies and other teaching innovations into the course. Regular interaction among the fellows is a key ingredient. We open the fellowship year at a one-day retreat in the fall where fellows meet each other, learn about the project's goals and activities, and identify personal plans. Throughout the year, they participate in a seminar that meets every other week. Here fellows are introduced to instructional concepts that broaden their perspectives both as teachers and users of technology. They also share experiences, work on projects and examples, and practice implementation of course materials. Topics for such sessions include enhancing traditional teaching through technology (e.g., presentation tools such as PowerPoint); changing pedagogy with technology (e.g., collaborative learning, computer-assisted instruction); accommodating individual differences with technology; and connecting in- and out-of-class learning with technology (e.g., email, World Wide Web). Outside of sessions, fellows consult individually or in small groups with our Center's coordinator of teaching technologies and other campus service providers. At the end of the academic year, the fellows have an integrated course designed, developed, tested, and evaluated. They also offer demonstrations of instructional materials to other colleagues through a department, college, or campus-wide forum.

Program Outcomes

Over the past two years, 20 faculty members have participated in the TEACHnology program. They report a number of benefits in terms of professional development. First, they indicate that they are much more informed as to what technologies are available to them and which service providers can best help them when they require assistance. The TEACHnology program also provides a supportive community in which the fellows interact with other fellows both during and beyond their year in the program. In addition, the program encourages senior faculty to form a cadre or network of "peer innovators" who can share expertise with colleagues. Most importantly, the program promotes renewal and vitality in teaching by offering an opportunity for senior faculty to become learners again, rethinking their instructional objectives and their approaches to teaching, trying out new technologies, and integrating these ideas into their classes.

Eight Lessons Learned

We continue to work at figuring out the best options for promoting teaching development through teaching technologies. We have gleaned a few ideas about what it takes to make a program like this really work in terms of supporting faculty, especially in their role as teachers in the information age.

1) Provide Incentives for Development

Our senior fellows reported that one key attraction to the TEACHnology fellowship was that the grant required a simple application and provided a concrete award: a high-performance laptop computer, either a Power Mac or Pentium PC. Each laptop was loaded with software such as Claris Home Page, Publisher, and MS Office for their project development. We also built training in the use of each application into the program.

2) Keep the Emphasis on Pedagogy vs. Hardware and Software

Although our Center provides various mini, hands-on training sessions to faculty as they develop their projects, the program continually focuses faculty attention on the pedagogical implications of using technology. At the bi-weekly seminar, concrete examples about ways in which technologies can benefit, or detract from, teaching and student learning are freely shared among the fellows.

3) Offer a Range of Individual Support Services

We soon recognized that the all-group seminars needed to be supplemented with individual support services. These support services included ongoing, one-on-one consultation with a trained teaching technology consultant in the Center, special access to other services providers on campus who could offer specific training (e.g., web design and multimedia projects), and access to a network of peers from the previous year's program. This structured yet flexible design was successful because faculty wanted to share ideas and also wanted training targeted directly to their individual needs. (They clearly indicated that they would not engage in activities that wasted time or were unrelated to their instructional situation.)

4) Create Collegial Structure That Facilitates Dialogue

Many faculty members experience a sense of isolation and express a desire for more collegiality, particularly in their roles as teachers. Our fellows also noted that they typically have few opportunities to interact with faculty members outside of their department or school/college. Fellows reported that the TEACHnology fellowship encouraged them to connect with, and help, each other by providing opportunities for peer learning during the bi-weekly seminars and by creating "networks" across the disciplines for research and teaching.

5) Focus on Acquiring New Skills

The TEACHnology fellowship is an ideal avenue for faculty development because it focuses on an area in which many faculty are novices (sometimes knowing less than their students) and are challenged as learners. At the same time, many faculty are eager and intrinsically motivated to learn technology applications necessary for their teaching and scholarship. They especially appreciate learning skills that take them to a new level (e.g., creating an instructional web site to support a large class, using presentation technology to engage students in the classroom, or forming email discussion groups for their classes). Like most adult learners, our senior fellows also responded best to learning through lots of "hands-on" practice rather than listening to presentations.

6) Pay Attention to Non-Technological Teaching and Learning

Technology is merely a tool to enhance learning; technology alone will not solve instructional problems. Instructional issues such as learner characteristics, learning outcomes, physical setting, and teaching style are at least as important as knowledge and skills in using technology. Dialogues among participating faculty across disciplines facilitated a better understanding of these non-technological issues; at the same time, our Center offered individual consultation to faculty to respond to specific instructional needs that extended beyond the use of technology.

7) Seek Ways to Assess Teaching Technologies

Our Center provides each fellow with opportunities for mid-term classroom assessment during the fellowship year. TEACHnology fellows each choose one course in which to get student and/or consultant feedback on their incorporation of teaching technologies. These sources of feedback (e.g., student focus groups or surveys, classroom observations) allow them to identify what is going well and what might merit attention. For example, when one fellow asked students what would make a PowerPoint presentation a better learning experience, some students suggested that the faculty member needed to slow down the pace while presenting the slides, and others suggested that the instructor engage in more interactive discussions associated with the presented information. When another faculty member used the PRS (an interactive Personal Response System) to promote active learning in class, most students responded positively in terms of the collaborative practices facilitated by the PRS. At the same time, some students perceived such interactive exercises as distracting. Such feedback opens up useful dialogues that go beyond the technology to instructional issues such as teaching goals, pacing, student learning differences, and peer and collaborative learning strategies.

8) Create Ample Measures of Recognition and Reward

Beyond modest financial support, our faculty expressed a need for something often vaguely described as respect or recognition. Senior faculty who have been "good citizens" and have put considerable time into developing as teachers and researchers, often remark that they receive little acknowledgment for such efforts. Beyond resources provided through the program, fellows are recognized in campus publications, awarded plaques, and acknowledged at our annual Celebration of Teaching Dinner, which draws several hundred students, staff, faculty, and administrators. This spring semester, a campus-wide teaching technology roundtable was hosted by the fellows from the first two years. They presented the range of teaching ideas and strategies that they have gathered from integrating technologies in their classrooms.

Final Thoughts

We learned a lot during the first two years of the TEACHnology Fellows Program, from development to implementation, from teaching to learning. At an individual level, participating faculty have learned to use computers and other instructional media to make their teaching more effective. They have become aware that the integration of technology involves more than physical setup and technical support; it requires some curricular modifications and instructional strategy shifts. Also, our tenured faculty fellows report positive effect in terms of an improved sense of collegiality, community, and morale. At the departmental level, the TEACHnology fellows have begun to emerge as exemplars who are eager to take risks and become mentors to colleagues who express interest in instructional technologies. Finally, the program has gained administrative support, particularly at the department, college, and provost levels and has raised awareness of the need for more faculty development opportunities that create linkages among teaching, learning, and technology.

Acknowledgments

The authors would like to acknowledge former CFT Coordinators for Teaching Technologies, Amy Butcher and Lisa Isleb, who provided early leadership for this program.

References

Ashby, E. (1967). Machines, understanding, and learning: Reflections on technology in education. *The Graduate Journal, 7,* 359-373.

Heinich, R., Molenda, M., Russell, J., & Smaldino, S. (1996). *Instructional media and technologies for learning* (5th ed.). Englewood Cliffs, NJ: Prentice-Hall.

Butcher, A. (1997). *TEACHnology: A guide to teaching technology resources at the University of Massachusetts, Amherst.* Center for Teaching: University of Massachusetts, Amherst.

List, K. (1997). A continuing conversation on teaching: An evaluation of a decade-long Lilly Teaching Fellows Program 1986-1996. *To Improve the Academy, 16,* 201-224.

Rogers, E. M. (1995). *Diffusion of innovation.* (4th ed.). New York: NY Free Press.

Sorcinelli, M. D. (Fall, 1999). Post-tenure review through post-tenure development: What linking senior faculty and technology taught us. *Innovative higher education.*

Contacts:

Mei-Yau Shih
Center for Teaching
301 Goodell Building
University of Massachusetts Amherst
Amherst, MA 01003
(413) 545-1225
(413) 545-3829 (FAX)
mshih@acad.umass.edu

Mary Deane Sorcinelli
Center For Teaching
301 Goodell Building
University of Massachusetts Amherst
Amherst, MA 01003
(413) 545-1225
(413) 545-3829 (FAX)
msorcinelli@acad.umass.edu

Mei-Yau Shih is Coordinator of Teaching Technologies at the Center for Teaching, University of Massachusetts, Amherst. She works with faculty on integrating technologies for teaching and learning in the classroom. She is currently coordinating the TEACHnology Fellows Program at the UMass Amherst campus. She joined the CFT in August 1998; before that, she was employed at Westmar University in LeMars, Iowa, as Associate Academic Dean, Associate Professor, and Director of the Telecommunications Programs. She has developed and taught various instructional technology and telecommunications courses in the past seven years; some of her classes were offered over the interactive (fiber optics) network and the Internet.

Mary Deane Sorcinelli is Associate Provost, Director of the Center for Teaching, and Associate Professor, adjunct in the Department of Educational Policy and Research Administration, University of Massachusetts, Amherst. She also serves as visiting scholar to the American Association of Higher Education (AAHE) in Washington. She has consulted with hundreds of individual faculty members on teaching and has worked at departmental, school, campus-wide, and national levels to encourage support and recognition for good teaching. She publishes widely in the areas of academic career development and teaching improvement and evaluation. She also directs a number of external teaching development grants and teaches at the graduate level.

APPENDIX 9.1

A total of 20 half-hour interviews were conducted with faculty from nine different colleges and schools of Natural Sciences and Mathematics, Humanities and Fine Arts, Engineering, Education, Food and Natural Resources, Nursing, Social and Behavioral Sciences, Public Health and Health Sciences, and Management. Our assessment focused on the following questions:

What went well?

- Reaching more students, connecting in surprising ways through technology, and seeing the students actively engaged in learning.
- Access to appropriate technology resources and ability to collaborate across units.
- Using technology to increase dynamic and cooperative teaching and learning.
- Increased productivity for both students and faculty.

What did not go well?

- Using/implementing technology makes incredible demands on faculty time.
- Logistics of accessing/using/moving equipment was daunting.
- Impersonal nature of technology (lack of face-to-face contact) and lack of student access to necessary resources (e.g., CD-ROM drives in public labs) inhibits the creation of excellent teaching and learning environments.

What resources could you not find?

- Almost all expressed frustration about access to resources.
- Support services were often inadequate even though they may have tried hard and meant well.
- Classroom space was inadequate to implement instructional technology.
- Lack of coordination and communication across campus about instructional technology. Who is doing what?

- Lack of institutional support both in terms of incentives and rewards and in terms of physical resources.

What made it possible for you to start using instructional technology?

- When asked what allowed them to implement instructional technology, the most frequent response was "tenure." They felt that the effort required such a commitment of time and energy that it would never have been possible until they had that freedom.
- Others attributed their start to serendipitous early encounters with technology.

What are the special pedagogical challenges?

- Evaluation of instructional technology projects, especially distance education.
- Incredible time demands of creating and implementing instructional technology.
- Positive and negative impacts on students learning. Technology can create dynamic demonstrations and opportunities for a wider variety of learning styles, but it can also deprive students of personal contact and support. How does one balance the conflicting experiences?

What topics of instructional technology would you like to discuss with other faculty?

- Why are we trying to use technology? Is it worth it? What is the administration's real goal? How does it fit our mission?
- How do we find access to necessary resources? How are funds allocated?
- Does it really improve teaching?
- What is the new role of faculty when using instructional technology (sage on the stage vs. guide on the side)?
- How do we build communication/community on campus around technology?

(Butcher, 1997)

10

From Transparency toward Expertise: Writing-Across-the-Curriculum as a Site for New Collaborations in Organizational, Faculty, and Instructional Development

Philip G. Cottell, Jr.
Serena Hansen
Kate Ronald
Miami University

This paper will inform readers about a comprehensive approach to collaborative efforts between faculty developers, discipline specific faculty, and writing specialists. Miami University's Richard T. Farmer School of Business Administration has begun to support a team of writing specialists, led by a faculty developer. This team has worked with business faculty to build a model of collaboration for using Writing-Across-the-Curriculum that addresses some of the shortcomings of earlier models. This paper recounts the successful use of this new model in one accounting class.

Writing-Across-the-Curriculum (WAC) celebrated its 25th anniversary in 1996, according to Barbara Walvoord (1996), one of its most prominent advocates and leaders. This celebration marks only the latest incarnation of attempts to re-integrate and recuperate what was once at the heart of almost all academic curricula. More interesting, perhaps, than any anniversary the "modern" WAC movement might mark is the question of how writing got out of the curriculum in the first place.

David Russell (1991) ascribes writing's absence from academic disciplines to increasing specialization at the end of the 19th century, the "ideal of research" that came to dominate higher education, and to what Russell calls the "transparency" of rhetoric within individual disciplines.

Russell carefully documents the reasons why "disciplines never acquired a conscious knowledge of the rhetorical conventions they used daily and expected their students to use; hence, the discursive strategies in any given discipline remain 'transparent,' so bound up with the activity of the discipline and acquired so subtly in the learning of the discipline that they are rarely thought of as writing instruction" (p. 17). Because apprentices learn written conventions gradually and as a part of their socialization into a disciplinary community, the process of learning to write these conventions seems invisible, common-sensical, or "transparent." When students struggle with these conventions, faculty have tended to view their struggle as lack of writing ability, which may be attributable to sheer ignorance on the part of the students or to a failure of writing specialists to do their jobs properly. Moreover, Russell blames the absence of writing from the curriculum (beyond first-year composition courses) on the isolation of faculty from one another in the modern university: "The isolation [of new academic specializations] required that people continually talk past each other, failing to listen to what others were really saying. . . . [The modern university] required barriers to frank communication which are stylized into courtesy. . . . [We are] tacitly obeying the need to fail to communicate" (p. 23).

This collaborative essay tells a story about making that rhetoric less transparent and more explicit for students in an introductory accounting class during the 1996-1997 academic year. But it also tells a story about how collaboration across disciplines helps faculty as well as students understand how learning and language are inextricably connected. We offer our experience as collaborators from different disciplines in the context of current debates about the place of writing instruction in college curricula, about disciplinary integrity, and about the possibility of interdisciplinary cooperation. Finally, this essay suggests that an integration of faculty, instructional, and organizational development offers the best chance for lasting change in writing-across-the-curriculum.

WAC's Collaborative and Developmental Models

WAC has always relied on collaborative, interdisciplinary efforts among faculty, and its 25 year history reveals the tensions that accompany any effort at cooperation across academic departments. In chronicling WAC's recent history, researchers identify three main "stages" through which it has passed. Most of these histories focus on how definitions of effective writing have changed over the years; in summarizing this history here, we want to highlight two aspects of WAC: (1) the models for interdisciplinary collaboration that underlie changes in cross-disciplinary writing instruction and (2) the ways that each model seeks to make transparent rhetoric more visible for students and disciplinary faculty.

WAC began as a response to a perceived problem—that students were not writing well enough, or often enough, beyond the first-year required composition course. The earliest efforts to remedy this problem (the "First Stage" 1970-1980) relied on the use of informal "writing-to-learn." Writing specialists from English departments typically invited faculty from other disciplines to workshops designed to showcase how writing, mostly informal writing, could help students learn course material necessary to accomplish disciplinary course goals. Class journals, personal response papers, and attention to processes of writing (drafts of papers, revision strategies) mark this version of the WAC movement. Such workshops were usually "successful" in helping faculty outside of English see how writing could help students learn. However, without changes in institutional structures and rewards, faculty often had difficulty sustaining the kinds of changes suggested, since these early methods were *not* connected to disciplinary content or goals. Moreover, this first-stage model cast the English professor in the role of missionary: WAC consultants described themselves as "strangers in strange lands" (McCarthy, 1987) sent to distant, exotic, and dangerous shores to convert the natives without engaging in collaborative inquiry with disciplinary professors. These initial efforts did little to combat what Russell (1991) describes as the tendency of academics to see writing as a single, elementary skill, a "transparent recording of speech or thought or physical reality, rather than a complex rhetorical activity, embedded in the differentiated practices of academic discourse communities" (p. 9).

In the "Second Stage" of WAC (1980-1990) attention shifted back toward the disciplines and possible ways of making writing a permanent part of all departments. Called "writing-in-the-disciplines," rather than writing-to-learn, in this stage of WAC, writing specialists recruited disciplinary faculty and together they began to investigate, for example, what writing "well" in economics might mean, apart from writing-to-learn the material being taught in economics. In this model, writing specialists learned from disciplinary faculty how writing worked in particular disciplines and from there devised ways to introduce students to those conventions. This later stage in WAC moved a bit closer to helping both writing specialists and disciplinary faculty together look more closely at how writing shapes disciplinary knowledge. But, as Russell (1991) explains, faculty tend to speak different languages, both with each other and with the students:

> The transparency of rhetoric in the disciplines makes it much more difficult for faculty to see and intervene in the students' socialization into the discipline. . . . [The] instructor has been so gradually and thoroughly socialized into the symbolic universe of the discipline that he often cannot see or understand why others, who are writing about the same "content," do not "make sense." Though the students may understand the "facts," they may not understand the essential rhetorical structures: specialized lines of argument, vocabulary, organizational conventions, tacit understanding of what must be stated and what assumed—in short, the culture of the discipline that gives meaning to the facts (p. 18).

Although writing-in-the-disciplines helped disciplinary professors begin to pay attention to the rhetorical structures of their disciplines, many remained unconvinced that the investment of time and energy in teaching those structures resulted in increased student learning of the material. Writing specialists, too, became frustrated by this model's limited attention to form and stylistic structures too often separated from a study of the disciplinary culture.

The chroniclers of WAC's history have either told the story of these stages in evolutionary terms, with writing-in-the-disciplines replacing writing-to-learn, or they have described these movements as oppositional theories that cannot usefully co-exist. As Flynn, Remlinger, and Biulleit (1997) describe it,

> Writing to learn is often seen as hopelessly romantic and individualistic in its conception of the writer as an isolated individual who must be released from the fetters of institutional constraints. Writing in the disciplines is often seen as hopelessly conservative in its conception of learning as a matter of internalizing the relatively stable conventions of a relatively stable discourse community (p. 360).

These authors posit a new model of "interactionalism," and the term echoes the latest research in WAC, suggesting that these two approaches need not be in conflict. Kirscht, Levine, and Reiff (1994) posit a new model of WAC that not only helps students learn a discipline but also demands that they study the epistemological and rhetorical conventions and foundations of the field. This "Third Stage" suggests that a "rhetoric of inquiry" approaches the disciplines as "centers of inquiry" (p. 374). Instead of seeing the teaching of the memo or lab report, for example, as a static, fixed form, this new view would use the study of the form—both writing it and writing about it—as a way both to learn the disciplinary content and to place it within disciplinary and professional contexts. In other words, such a "rhetoric of inquiry" makes discourse conventions less transparent, more visible:

> If conventions are seen as rhetorical, as the ways that questions are asked and answers sought in a given field, writing becomes a way not only to interact with declarative knowledge, but also to develop procedural knowledge concerning that field—to learn how knowledge has been constructed as well as what knowledge is. WAC thus becomes a way into the inquiry practices of the field (Kirsch, Levine, & Reiff, 1994, p. 374).

In other words, helping students integrate their learning into the rhetorical structures of the discipline collapses the false distinction between learning-to-write and writing-to-learn a particular body of knowledge.

These debates about the methods and purposes of WAC and the possibility of maintaining disciplinary goals while collaborating across disciplines play out in real contexts, in actual classrooms, and among real-live colleagues (Walvoord, 1997). WAC is always, first, a collaborative enterprise. The next section of this essay describes how three people collaborated to design, teach, and understand how one particular writing assignment might accomplish these interactive goals: learning accounting, learning how accountants communicate in actual business contexts, and understanding how the rhetoric of that communication contributes to the knowledge being learned. To accomplish these goals, we relied on individual, departmental, and institutional structures of development. At each level, we worked to make our individual, disciplinary assumptions less transparent and more accessible to each other and to the students whom we were trying to teach.

Local Context

The collaboration we document here was part of the Howe Writing Initiative, a collaborative project among faculty, graduate, and undergraduate students in the department of English and School of Business Administration. Its goal is to enhance the quality of student writing and the teaching of writing in the School of Business. Institutionally, this effort is supported by the Howe Professorate in Written Communication, an interdisciplinary tenured position endowed by generous alumni. Organizationally, this professorship means long-term commitment to writing resources, including support for graduate assistants who work within the framework of the Howe Initiative. Instructionally, this initiative provides in-house writing consultation to all business faculty, year in and year out, meaning that faculty development relies not on one-time workshops or teaching experiments, but on continual conversation, observation, and collaboration. Yet the Howe Writing Initiative is not a top-down mandate; faculty support for this initiative has been shown through its adoption as a school-wide plan for integrating writing across the School of Business Curriculum. As the Howe Professor, a faculty member in a particular discipline, and a graduate assistant writing specialist, we offer the following as an example of that integration in one particular course during one particular semester.

Collaborating on Writing and Accounting

In response to calls for educational reform in the discipline, the department of accountancy began a lengthy process of curriculum reform. Among the changes incorporated into the new curriculum was the call for writing in many of the revised courses in order to fulfill recommendations for writing across the curriculum. These recommendations were part of the curricular changes that led to the Howe Writing Initiative.

Principles of Accounting, a required introductory course for all School of Business students, was one of the courses in which writing was mandated. The Accounting professor assigned to this course had used some informal writing assignments in the past as part of various cooperative learning structures. However, he soon realized that the WAC mandate seemed to oblige a more formal project. In the past, the professor had found the traditional term paper to be mostly a waste of student time and an anathema in terms of grading requirements. He thus sought a fresh approach. In the midst of this planning, the Howe Professor learned of the assignment and assigned one of the Howe writing specialists to assist with its planning and implementation.

The Principles of Accounting class consists primarily of sophomore college students. For the most part, these students have never before been exposed to any concepts of accounting or finance. Most come to the course completely naive as to the purposes or processes of business organizations. Therefore, a writing assignment that encourages students to engage in the vocabulary and rhetoric of accounting, the language of business, can enhance their understanding of the discipline.

Accounting has, indeed, been described as the language of business. As such it seeks to view events that occur in the business community and translate these events into financial information useful to readers. Therefore, the Principles of Accounting course should educate business students about the language of the business community in much the same way that a student who wishes to travel in a foreign land would be educated about that country's language. The better one understands the language of any community, the better that person can understand the community culture. In the business community this understanding can define the line between success and failure. The question, therefore, is how a writing assignment can enhance student understanding of accounting, the language of business.

The accounting professor and the Howe writing specialist came to realize that the assignment would have greater value if the "transparency" problem raised by Russell (1991) could be overcome. One obvious avenue for making the transparency of writing in accountancy more overt for students lay in exploiting the fact that the course focuses upon teaching financial accounting from the perspective of the user, as opposed to the preparer, of financial statements. Obviously students needed to learn how to analyze financial statements. A person entering the business community must have the ability to read and interpret financial information by using the tools of financial analysis. Yet the actual use of these tools remains for most students an abstract exercise. No matter how much the professor insists that students think like a user, the impact of financial analysis typically remains transparent and tacit for most students (and professors) since students usually write simply to demonstrate to their teachers that they have mastered the necessary tools and information. One way to teach students the impact of financial analysis was to make the user less transparent and more overt.

The professor and the writing specialist decided to have the students write the assignment in groups in which they would role-play financial advisors writing to clients. For the first paper the client was a bank considering loan applications from two customers in the same industry. The second paper dealt with a client considering an investment in stock. This time students would compare two companies in different industries. The financial statements the students analyzed were real-world ones from companies chosen by the accounting professor. The professor and the writing specialist agreed that for the writing assignment to be effective, the students should write two papers. In this way they could improve the second paper based on the feedback they received on the first one.

These two types of audiences have differing needs from the accounting point of view. Investors in debt securities are more concerned with risk relative to return. Investors in equity securities focus their attention on growth. If the assignment were successful in motivating student learning as they wrote, they would begin to discern the rhetoric of the accounting discipline. Successful papers would intelligently discuss risk, return, and growth as well as how these concepts could impact future cash flow. These concepts, perhaps transparent to students before they wrestled with the writing assignment, would begin to come into focus.

One indication of student knowledge of a subject can be measured by ability to communicate concepts to someone outside the discipline. The assignment for the second paper stressed that the required memorandum was to be written to a client who was not an accountant. The purpose here was to restrict student use of "buzz words" that could mask lack of conceptual understanding.

The Role of the Howe Writing Specialist

Early in the process the Howe writing specialist began to learn about the accounting professor's course, goals, attitudes, and assumptions about writing. She consulted with him about the nature and role of the two papers assigned within the larger context of his course. She also began to serve as a resource to the professor as he assigned, discussed, and evaluated the assignments. Thus the accounting professor could draw upon the writing specialist's experience assigning, conferencing about, and evaluating student writing to help this assignment be a positive learning experience for both professor and students.

The writing specialist began by studying the syllabus, textbooks, and policies of the course. She also evaluated the initial assignment proposed by the accounting professor. She drew on her own experience composing writing assignments and reading the resulting papers to make some predictions about the likely success of the assignment. She initially felt that the assignment was very well written. It defined a specific audience and explained what both the writer's and reader's purposes would be. It listed the elements the memo would need to include in order to accomplish the task and set forth the criteria by which the teacher would evaluate the writing. However, experience had taught the writing specialist that a productive learning experience isn't ensured by a well-written assignment. The context in which the assignment is given—the other kinds of work the students are used to doing in the course, the professor's attitudes (often those she is unaware of communicating) toward the subject matter, and significantly, the disparity between the culture of school writing and disciplinary discourse enter to produce various and often unsatisfactory interpretations of even the best assignment.

The Discourse of the Discipline

Because the writing specialist had little prior knowledge about accounting, she observed classes to get a better understanding of the classroom dynamics, what kinds of discussions went on, etc. She learned several things about the discourse of accounting. She discovered that numbers (just like any evidence) mean different things to different people, depending on their particular theories and agendas. For example, leverage, a measure of risk in a company's capital structure, can be a positive for an investor seeking growth but a red flag indicator for a creditor. On one occasion the writing specialist expressed to the accounting professor that ratios were not numbers but relationships, an aspect of accounting rhetoric that had previously been transparent to him.

The familiarity of the writing specialist with the nature of disciplinary discourse allowed her to understand some of the expectations of the professor. He wanted to know that the students could perform the correct calculations, correct definitions, etc. But a test can find this out. Why writing? Writing requires that the students use the calculations together to evaluate a particular situation, assigning significance and interpreting the values as good or bad as they applied to the particular scenario, then use these numbers and the explanation of their significance to fashion an argument supporting their recommendation.

On the other hand, her experience with students led her to predict the kinds of written responses they might make to these instructions. Given that this was an accounting course and given students' experience with "fact or number" courses, including the experience of being tested on their mastery of facts and ability to perform isolated calculations through exams, she reasoned that the students would first interpret the purpose of the assignment to fall in line with the purpose of all the other work in the class—to demonstrate knowledge/mastery. In order to accomplish this task they would react to the written assignment as a checklist, probably writing an isolated paragraph about each ratio or in answer to each question, and having done that, state the "answer" (their recommendation), assuming that the magical numbers and ratios of accounting that they had listed above provided adequate support and explanation. They would probably not see that much of the work the assignment asked them to do was to verbally interpret the ratios' significance in a larger context and to a particular audience.

As the writing specialist and the accounting professor collaborated together for this project, the awareness of the professor about the importance of discourse was heightened. The professor began to understand several aspects of writing more fully. First, the notion of an audience was consistently raised. He saw that the writing assignments should not just test students' ability to comprehend accounting, but that these contextual assignments also challenged students to tailor their knowledge to particular purposes and particular audiences. The accounting professor realized that students learned more when their instruction included discussions of the rhetoric of the discipline. In other words, the disciplinary professor began to move away from traditional methods of incorporating writing into a content course, where, as Russell (1991) says, "the transparency of writing masks that the rules of the game, are, in many ways, rhetorical; written discourse plays an important (at some points, crucial) role in professional advancement" (p. 18).

The accounting professor began to grasp the concept of transparency. At first transparency appeared positive to him, that is, synonymous with clarity. But through dialog with the writing specialist, he began to understand that in writing, transparency could mean that students were using words without really understanding their meaning. Thus they were missing the key point from the accounting perspective, to understand the language of business. As the professor and the writing specialist worked together to craft the assignment, they attempted to ensure that students would "see" the language they were using.

In order to operate on more than just assumption, the accounting professor asked his students to write down the questions they had about the assignment. He then collected these answers and gave them to the writing specialist. Although the assignment had been very specific about format requirements, the majority of the questions revealed that the students were having a hard time imagining what writing in accounting should look like. The things they thought they would be "graded on" were surface characteristics. They did not have a picture of themselves as making an argument.

The writing specialist visited the class and walked the students through her reading of the assignment. She expressed to them that it was okay not to know immediately how to write the assignment but that a consideration of their purpose and their audiences' needs could answer most of their questions, including format and surface features. She explained how to make educated guesses about audience needs and appropriate format choices.

Second-Stage Collaboration

After the students had written and handed in the papers, the collaboration between the accounting professor and the writing specialist moved onto another plane. The writing specialist and the accounting professor decided to read the same set of papers separately and to rank them in order of strongest to weakest. They compared their impressions and were able to use examples from the students' writing to enhance their discussion. While they did not always esteem the same things, they mostly agreed on the ranges, and through their discussion each educated the other about what they valued as very different readers.

As they worked together, the writing specialist was able to clarify to the accounting professor what it was that he liked or disliked in the papers. In other words, the accounting professor began to discern the lens through which he viewed the writing. They worked together to develop descriptions of the characteristics of papers in the middle and lower range as well as the upper range papers (Appendix 1). Through this collaborative effort, the accounting professor began to recognize the rhetoric of his discipline in a very different and more precise way. The writing specialist helped the accounting professor transfer his ideas about the papers to the students through concise comments that listed a few positive aspects of the papers along with recommendations for improvements.

Perhaps the most important outcome of this collaboration was that the accounting professor felt much more capable of evaluating his students' writing, as he saw that his own knowledge of disciplinary discourse could guide his judgment of the effectiveness of the papers for intended audiences. While the writing specialist could not have served as a competent grader for the assignment, she could help the accounting professor describe features of the paper. She was also able to suggest some of the conflicts or gaps that students were not able to resolve because of their limited experience using the language of business. Through increased understanding of the rhetoric of accounting, students gained an appreciation that even within the framework of a class in which there seemed to be straightforward and definite answers, much depended on the surrounding context.

Success of the Project

The collaboration we've described participates in all levels of professional development. Of course the accounting professor engaged in "faculty development" when he began to work with the writing specialist and as he began to see how teaching the rhetoric of accounting could help his students learn its methods and concepts; however, the writing specialist was also challenged and "developed" as she learned how accountants communicate and worked to help make the rhetoric of accounting less transparent for both teacher and students. And this project also is part of a larger instructional development project; currently, every section of introductory accounting assigns these two memos to students. Moreover, the collaborative work surrounding this writing assignment now serves as a model for other departments, which, as part of the Howe Writing Initiative, are developing new writing assignments for their courses. This collaboration between individuals, then, was also supported by, and in turn influences, the School of Business Administration's commitment to leading the next stage of Writing-Across-the-Curriculum. Russell (1991) says that "unless spurred by external pressures, disciplines have not found it necessary to examine, much less improve, the way students are initiated into their respective symbolic universes. Given the lack of incentives in specialized structures of reward, writing instruction in the disciplines has tended to remain an informal and largely unconscious dimension of disciplinary teaching, a transparent part of business as usual" (p. 18). Our collaborative project succeeded in large part because the institutional context mandated a change from business as usual and provided individual support and organizational structures that helped formalize the work of making the tacit and transparent assumptions about writing more visible and useful for everyone, including the students.

The students learned that writing enhanced their learning of accounting, but they also learned that accounting is more than numbers, that accounting knowledge must be used rhetorically. When asked in a follow-up study to this project about their reactions to these writing assignments, students responded with sophisticated reflections on the connection between rhetorical and disciplinary knowledge. For example, 35 out of 42 students surveyed named introductory accounting as the course with the "most helpful writing assignment this semester." They explained why:

> The group project in accounting tied writing—professional business writing—to what we learned in class.
>
> I liked the ARP projects. They made the concepts and terms easier to understand because they were used with real companies. Also, to be able to write the paper well, you had to fully understand the concepts.
>
> The ARP projects were most helpful because they encouraged us to truly understand the information we were learning and apply it to real world situations.
>
> The ARP reports allowed me to do some common business writing and professionally relate my knowledge to real audiences. This class emphasized writing techniques more than any other I've had in Business.

The writing specialist also interviewed students to get a fuller picture of what they had learned from these assignments. Excerpts from these conversations show even more clearly how students had been able to see and use the transparent connection between writing and knowledge:

> Writing seemed unusual in accounting but it really helped me learn. This was a very long report, so it got you really practicing a lot of writing and thinking like an accountant. I think that was very helpful—it made you convert from a different type of thing to this thing. It was looking at a table of numbers and then trying to convert that into words. I think it was a pretty unusual thing, but it really helped overall.
>
> Another thing I just remembered that was important was that each report we had to do was from a different perspective, not just writing from the student's perspective.

> There was a lot besides the writing that went into these reports. I think that since you are writing these memos to potential investors, it's kind of like you're writing them for yourself because you don't know much about it and you're trying to explain it to someone else. When you had to prioritize and figure out what you need in those three pages and what was important, that also aided in learning accounting because you're like "Well, what is really important to this reader?" and that's what I want in these three pages.

Considering the needs of particular readers is a clear indication that students are learning to make the transparent more overt, learning to think like experts.

Reflections on Collaborations: Becoming Experts

A rhetoric of inquiry is aimed at making what's tacit, assumed, and transparent about disciplinary discourse more visible—both for students who must learn it, and for teachers who often don't know how to teach it. Academic writing has too often been confined only to school exercises, such as essay exam answers or research reports. In these exercises, the teacher serves as the sole audience for student writing, and the demonstration of knowledge, not communication, as the sole purpose for writing. Traditionally, writing is modeled in academic settings as the container or package for the content or knowledge that students acquire in their courses: writing occurs after thinking; information is put into writing according to prescribed formulas and rules learned through imitation. Our experience suggests another model for academic writing: immersion in contexts that require real communication.

Geisler (1994) suggests that this kind of situated knowledge distinguishes an expert from a novice. Geisler defines an "expert," first, as someone who is able to abstract from what she calls "domain content representation" and is also able to "adapt abstractions to case specific data." These two abilities—abstraction and application—lead to *expertise*, but there is another, connecting factor that Geisler insists is an essential part of expertise—rhetorical awareness.

In other words, it's not enough to know your subject or to be able to relate abstractions to specific cases; you must also know how, when, where, to whom, and why to communicate that knowledge. Geisler's study shows that most students develop "domain content" expertise—the ability to work with more and more abstract representations of the "problem space" of disciplines and to apply these abstractions to particular data or cases—during their undergraduate years. But they are not yet experts, because during this time the "rhetorical problem space remains basically naive" and "knowledge still has no rhetorical dimension" (p. 87). For example, a student may comprehend the concept of financial leverage but be unable to use that concept effectively to convince a client about the risk of investing in a highly leveraged firm.

Geisler blames academics' tendency to present (and to view) texts (and textbooks) as "autonomous," or transparent, existing without context, silent containers of information with no agenda of their own. Students tend to view their professors, their lectures, and their classes in much the same way: as transparent sources of knowledge. However, usually somewhere after undergraduate school—either on the job or in graduate studies—students begin to see these kinds of texts and sources differently, as documents in context, with authors who have agendas, claims that can be argued and refuted, and styles that tell much about hierarchical relationships. This awareness, finally, that people write "not simply to say things, but to do things: to persuade, to argue, to excuse" (Geisler, p. 87), blends with disciplinary knowledge and leads to expertise. It is not enough, then, to learn the concepts and tools of a discipline *(knowing that)*. One must be able to use and apply and communicate that knowledge in particular *(knowing how, why, when, and for whom)*. That's what we think our work together has helped us to do—transform our separate, transparent knowledge into collective, overt expertise that is useful for us, our students, and, we hope, other faculty who not only want to help students write more effectively but to learn how writing and disciplinary knowledge are intimately and usefully connected.

The larger lesson for faculty developers in general is to mobilize collaborations between skill-based experts and disciplinary faculty across their respective fields. Faculty developers must maintain an awareness of tacit transparent assumptions embedded in disciplinary knowledge. Creating and supporting initiatives such as the one we have described enable faculty, their colleagues, and their students to move from transparency to expertise.

References

Flynn, E., Remlinger, K., & Biulleit, W. (1997). Interaction across the curriculum. *Journal of Advanced Composition, 17* (3), 343-361.

Geisler, C. (1994). *Academic literacy and the nature of expertise: Reading, writing, and knowing in academic philosophy*. Hillsdale, NJ: Lawrence Erlbaum.

Kirscht, J., Levine R., & Reiff, J. (1994). Evolving paradigms: WAC and the rhetoric of inquiry. *College Composition and Communication, 45* (3), 369-380.

McCarthy, L. (1987). A stranger in strange lands: A college student writes across the curriculum. *Research in the Teaching of English, 21*, 233-265.

Russell, D. (1991). *Writing in the academic disciplines, 1870-1990: A curricular history*. Carbondale, IL: Southern Illinois University Press.

Walvoord, B. (1996). The future of writing across the curriculum. *College English, 58* (1), 58-79.

Walvoord, B. (1997). *In the long run: A study of faculty in three writing-across-the-curriculum programs.* Urbana, IL: National Council of Teachers of English.

Contact:

Philip G. Cottell, Jr.
Department of Accountancy
Miami University
Oxford, OH 45056
(513) 529-6214
(513) 529-4740 (FAX)
cottelpg@muohio.edu

Philip G. Cottell, Jr. is Professor of Accountancy at Miami University. He has served as coordinator of Miami University's Senior Faculty/Program for Teaching Excellence. This fall he will be leading a new learning community centered on cooperative learning. He and Barbara Millis are co-authors of *Cooperative Learning for Higher Education Faculty* (ORYX Press).

Serena Hansen graduated from Miami University with a Ph.D. in English in May 1999.

Kate Ronald is the Roger and Joyce L. Howe Professor of English at Miami University. She teaches graduate and undergraduate courses in composition and rhetoric. She works with faculty in the Richard T. Farmer School of Business to improve the teaching of writing.

APPENDIX 10.1

Grading Criteria

- *Demonstrate awareness of audience.*
  The best papers specify an audience with specific investing goals and requirements.
- *Demonstrate clear understanding of purpose.*
  The best papers provide meaningful context for conclusions based upon financial analysis.
- *Organize with audience and purpose clearly in mind.*
  The best papers prioritize information important to the reader through headings, subheadings, and appendices.
- *Write in a concise, clear business language.*
  The best papers use active voice, strong verbs, and easily readable prose.
- *Prepare final copy in professional form and style.*
  The best papers demonstrate careful proofreading and attention to conventional business formats.

11

Faculty Teaching Partners and Associates: Engaging Faculty as Leaders in Instructional Development

Myra S. Wilhite
Joyce Povlacs Lunde
Gail F. Latta
University of Nebraska, Lincoln

Special interest discussion groups provide opportunities for faculty to address specific instructional issues in a variety of areas including technology, distance learning, general teaching topics, pre-tenure issues, honors teaching, and the like. In 1995, to leverage the Teaching and Learning Center's resources, outstanding classroom teachers were invited to provide leadership for discussion groups by serving as Partners or Associates. This chapter describes how an inexpensive faculty discussion-group leadership program maximizes a teaching improvement center's resources, makes innovative teaching visible, and provides peer models for other faculty while helping promote an overall institutional culture that actively supports teaching excellence.

Individualized instructional consulting is a major tool of teaching improvement centers, as numerous handbooks and resources for practitioners demonstrate (e.g., Lewis & Povlacs, 1988; Wadsworth, 1988; Brinko & Menges, 1997). Its effectiveness has been demonstrated by empirical studies (Cohen, 1980; Menges & Brinko, 1986). However, as most faculty developers know, one-to-one individualized consultation is labor-intensive, especially if it moves through the four phases of initial contact, conference, information collection, and information review and planning (Brinko, 1997). In the face of budget constraints, re-allocations, demands for assessment, post-tenure review, and the like, faculty developers in teaching improvement centers must look for ways to expand the impact of their work, without resorting to superficial solutions.

The purpose of this paper is to describe how an inexpensive faculty discussion-group leadership program leverages a teaching improvement center's resources, makes innovative teaching visible, and provides peer models to other faculty while helping promote an overall institutional culture that actively supports teaching excellence.

Faculty as Leaders in Instructional Improvement

TLC Partners

Over the years the Teaching and Learning Center at the University of Nebraska, Lincoln has asked selected faculty, such as recipients of distinguished teaching awards or former clients with special expertise, to lead workshops. However, when we wanted to offer more faculty an expanded leadership role (e.g., panelists, discussion group leaders, etc.), we had trouble identifying capable and willing faculty. We tried publishing a general call for volunteers in our newsletter and in a special mailing, but the response was discouraging. When we reflected on our inability to attract faculty, we were struck by Boice's words: "When senior faculty are asked why they have not participated in faculty development programs, their answer is nearly uniform: it is because, in their view, no one has asked them in a meaningful way" (Boice, 1992, p. 314). In an effort to find "a more meaningful way" to encourage more faculty to take a leadership role in our programs, we established the TLC Teaching Partner program.

We launched the Partner program in 1995 by sending a flyer to all faculty saluting those who had recently contributed to TLC programming and providing an opportunity for faculty to sign up to become a Teaching Partner. Potential partners were asked to share their teaching expertise, experiences, and insights in our discussion groups and conversation series by serving as panelists or facilitators/presenters. Faculty were asked to indicate topics of interest. The response was very encouraging. Faculty who had never before participated in TLC events (as leaders or participants) volunteered to take a leadership role in instructional development activities. Faculty seemed to appreciate the special recognition of "partnering" with the university's faculty development center and eagerly identified a special interest or particular area of expertise to share with colleagues. In the three years prior to the initiation of the Partner/Associate program, 75 faculty served in leadership roles. By 1997, more than 40 faculty representing 34 academic units were participating *each semester.*

TLC Associates

We developed the TLC Associates Program as another means of recruiting faculty to take a leadership role in instructional improvement. These leadership roles usually require special expertise and a more extensive time commitment than partners. In recent years, as campus and faculty needs have changed (e.g., instructional technology, distance education, the Comprehensive Education Program) and Center staff has remained constant, alternatives to in-house expertise were needed to best support faculty in these new areas. The TLC Associates Program was launched in 1994 when, with little additional funding available, we created the position of TLC Associate for Instructional Technology. Center staff lacked experience and expertise in instructional technology. To provide faculty development opportunities in that area, we went outside the Center, naming a faculty member from the teachers college to lead the faculty development effort. With the approval of his college dean and funding from the office of academic affairs, the new TLC Associate took a leadership role in facilitating workshops and discussion groups and in providing individual consulting in instructional technology. Because the TLC Associate was successful in meeting the needs of faculty, we extended his appointment a second year. Since that time, five other faculty members have been invited to serve as Associates: two for the Distance Education Learning Group, one as leader of Let's Talk Teaching (a discussion group for general teaching issues), one for the Comprehensive Education Program (a university-wide general education program), and one replacing the first Associate for Instructional Technology. Most Associates plan and facilitate a monthly discussion group. They may contribute an occasional newsletter article, conduct faculty surveys, form and moderate email special interest groups, collaborate with TLC faculty on workshops and grants, or provide individual consultation in their area of interest.

To prepare faculty for their leadership role, Center instructional consultants establish a close working relationship with Partners and Associates from the planning phase through evaluation and follow up. TLC consultants meet each faculty leader to discuss interests and expertise, explore effective format, and determine schedules. Consultants attend each session and provide follow-up on request. Center staff handle publicity, room reservations, registration, duplicate handouts, and evaluation forms. Leaders receive an evaluation summary of each discussion group session to facilitate ongoing planning. With the help of faculty Partners and Associates, the number of discussion-groups sessions increased from 10 in 1992-93 to more than 80 in 1997-98.

Special Interest Discussion Groups

As indicated, Partners and Associates become leaders in special-interest discussion groups. These discussion groups are scheduled to meet over a semester or an academic year. They are organized around specific topics providing faculty an opportunity to become familiar with the literature and to explore instructional issues and strategies around that specific topic. This sustained interaction among colleagues often fosters a sense of community, a collegial environment of exploration, and a safe place for examining one's current teaching practices and exploring alternatives (Jarvis, 1991; Boice, 1992). As a result, special-interest discussion groups can be particularly helpful to faculty who wish to make substantive changes in their teaching.

Because teaching tends to be an isolated activity (Green, 1990), an important benefit of group activities sponsored by a teaching improvement center lies in bringing together faculty from different disciplines and of different ages and ranks. Discovering common interests in a discussion-group setting helps reduce a sense of professional isolation that some faculty members may feel. "It is helpful to know that other faculty members struggle with the same issues and have different insights based on their experiences" (Green, 1990, p. 58), or, as Jarvis puts it, "Professors enjoy the chance to escape their professional boxes and to discuss larger issues" (Jarvis, 1991, p. 61).

Since discussion groups often transcend disciplines in their membership and offer a collegial environment for exploring and improving practice, developing and supporting special-interest discussion groups is a worthy faculty development program objective. They are cost effective, time efficient, and can extend the opportunities a small staff can provide. Discussion groups introduce faculty to theories of effective teaching, model good teaching techniques and strategies, keep teaching at the forefront of academic work, and help promote a culture that actively supports teaching excellence.

Between 1992 and 1997, the Center sponsored the seven discussion groups listed in Figure 11.1. Seventy-eight sessions were offered (Wright, Banset, Bellows, & Wilhite, 1997). Figure 11.1 also summarizes information about the purpose of the groups, participation, and the number of discussion-group sessions held. Beginning in 1995, faculty Partners or Associates provided leadership for the groups.

The Century Teaching Club, for teachers of large classes, was one of our first and most popular discussion groups. Dormant for several years in the late 1980s, the group was reestablished in 1992 as more faculty were assigned larger enrollment classes. The group remained active through 1995, when some members began participating in First Tuesday, a technology discussion group. In response to faculty requests, the Center once again organized the group in 1997 under the leadership of a teaching Partner. Historically, members of the Century Teaching Club

FIGURE 11.1
Special Interest Groups and Faculty Partners/Associates

Group Name	**Purpose/ Audience**	**Partner/ Associate Involvement**	**# of Mtgs. Annually**	**Avg. # Participating**
Century Teaching Club	for teachers of large classes	facilitator	6	10
Conversation Series for Pre-Tenure Faculty	personal, professional, and instructional development	panelists	4-6	13
First Tuesday	technology-novice	facilitator	5-6	37
Technology Group	technology-advanced/ technical	organizer/ presenter	9	15
Distance Education	for faculty teaching on TV or online	facilitators	4-6	20
Let's Talk Teaching	teaching and learning issues	facilitators	3-5	21
Teaching Matters	teaching topics for TAs	panelists	2-4	15

have been actively involved in projects that extend beyond monthly meetings: providing opportunities for peer classroom visits for faculty new to large-class teaching, conducting a large lecture hall survey to determine faculty perceptions about physical facilities, sponsoring workshops, and publishing an occasional newsletter. In 1994-95, members of the Club also provided leadership in exploring the use of multimedia in the large class and beyond.

The Conversation Series for Pre-Tenure Faculty (1992-95) provided collegial support for new faculty members: the opportunity to meet with colleagues not only to explore instructional issues, but to examine professional and personal development concerns, especially balance between tasks. Faculty served primarily as panelists at the monthly sessions. New faculty spent time networking over breakfast before exploring personal and professional issues. Participants explored such topics as Balancing Career and Personal Life; Balancing Teaching, Research, and Service; Tips on Testing and Grading; Promoting Discussion in the Classroom; Documenting Effective Teaching for Promotion and Tenure; Classroom Rapport; and Assertiveness: How to Take Charge in a Nice Way. The group met four to six times during the academic year.

The Pre-Tenure Conversation Series was discontinued in 1995 as other issues emerged on campus. To better meet the needs of the general faculty population, the organizer of the Conversation Series initiated two new discussion groups: First Tuesday (technology-related issues) and Let's Talk Teaching (general teaching issues). In addition, the instructional consultant for TAs developed Teaching Matters, a teaching strategies discussion group originally intended for TAs but soon opened to all faculty. The needs of the pre-tenure group were effectively met by these new discussion groups, and during the next two years, TAs and pre-tenure faculty explored general classroom teaching concerns in the Teaching Matters discussion group (e.g., Organizing and Guiding Group Work; The Teaching Portfolio; Encouraging and Evaluating Student Writing; Classroom Assessment Techniques).

Technology topics accounted for 33 of 78 discussion group sessions between 1992 and 1997. Technology topics seem to draw the largest number of participants, probably because such topics are of current interest to faculty and offer personal as well as professional value. This growing interest among faculty led to the formation in 1995 of First Tuesday, a discussion group focusing on general technology issues in teaching. In addition to First Tuesday, faculty could explore technology issues by participating in the Technology Group. The Technology Group attracted mostly "early adopters" and, unlike First Tuesday, focused primarily on the technical aspects of using technology in the classroom. This group was led by the TLC Associate for Instructional Technology, a professor in the teachers college who has been a campus leader in the area of multimedia for classroom use since 1990 and was instrumental in establishing the UNL Teaching, Learning, and Technology Roundtable.

In 1996, a discussion group for Distance Learning faculty was organized on the basis of a needs assessment and interest survey, as well as on the advice of the Distance Learning Advisory Group. In spring 1997, as interest in the UNL Honors Program grew, the TLC formed a new discussion group to provide faculty a forum for exploring issues related to teaching honors students.

Recognition

It is important to support and recognize the work of discussion group leaders who are the pacesetters for excellence across our campus. Partners and Associates are recognized each year in *Teaching at UNL*, the Teaching and Learning Center newsletter. Associates' responsibilities usually require special expertise and a more extensive commitment of time than Partners. Associates are given $1,000 for professional development in acknowledgment of their contributions. Being recruited and participating in these leadership roles give faculty the sense that they are valued by their colleagues and the institution.

Evaluations of Partners/Associates Programs

In 1997, we gave our discussion group Partners and Associates the opportunity to provide feedback on the impact their leadership role has had on their own teaching and learning by completing a brief questionnaire (see Appendix 1). In a separate survey, discussion group *participants* evaluated session effectiveness and identified future topics of interest. All participants who responded to the survey agreed that sessions were well organized, relevant to their professional needs, and gave them new ideas and applications for teaching. Participants also reported increased student involvement in their classes.

Impact on Teaching and Learning

Although the intrinsic rewards of contributing to the development of colleagues might be reason enough to participate in a leadership role,

Partners and Associates agreed that their participation as leaders also had a positive impact on their own teaching and learning. When asked to indicate ways in which their leadership role affected their teaching, Partners and Associates reported affirmation of their own efforts, increased self-confidence, increased reflection on teaching, and use of new teaching methods. When asked in what ways they had noticed the effects of these changes beyond their own observations, respondents most often indicated positive comments from faculty and awards and recognition.

As faculty members have become more effective teachers, they have welcomed the opportunity to become partners in instructional development activities and to learn from the expertise and experience of their colleagues, as well as Center and external "experts." One Partner noted: "I've not participated as a leader for recognition, but for my own learning and sense of keeping up with new points of view to see if they agree with my own. Interactions with members of the audience nearly always are profitable." Another faculty leader reflects the sentiments of most: "My participation as a TLC Partner has increased my contacts with others across campus who share interest and expertise in improving the quality of teaching and learning at UNL. . . . Every year there are things from the Teaching and Learning Center that help me. Presenting is something I do as a payback."

A corollary benefit of faculty leadership is the fact that those who lead sessions tend to draw participants from their own departments—often faculty who ordinarily would not attend our activities but come to support or hear their colleagues. One leader noted, "My participation in the Partners/Associates program has heightened awareness of others in my department and college of the importance of innovation in teaching and learning. This is significant!"

Benefits

Although it takes a considerable amount of TLC staff support and flexibility to coordinate the Partners and Associates program, the overall benefits to faculty across campus, as well as to the leaders, far outweigh the effort required. Originally conceived as a means of extending the ability of Center staff to meet the needs of faculty, the Partners and Associates program has provided additional benefits for Partners, Associates, participants, and the Teaching and Learning Center. The program provides select faculty the opportunity to play a leadership role in instructional development activities, share innovative approaches to teaching, and receive feedback from peers in a non-evaluative setting. It is an effective and efficient way for faculty leaders to network with faculty from across campus and collaborate with, and learn from, TLC staff. The program heightens faculty awareness of, and support for, TLC's activities and mission and creates a cadre of faculty who may be tapped to support other TLC functions. In addition, participation results in recognition by colleagues and administrators for service to the academic community, often stimulates faculty development activities within the Associate's own department or college, and provides funding for professional development.

Barriers

Partners and Associates said time was the most difficult obstacle to overcome. Home departments are not likely to provide release time for this activity. Thus, balancing participation in the program with daily demands of teaching, research, and service is problematic. Other potential roadblocks include scheduling, session format, and location.

We have found that a particular day each month works well to keep the date in the minds of faculty. However, a fixed time prevents some faculty from participating because of scheduling conflicts. Although sessions are typically kept short (60-90 minutes) to enable more faculty to work these meetings into their schedules, such time constraints prevent adequate coverage of some topics. For example, this format is not conducive to skills acquisition, only the demonstration and discussion of some possibilities. In addition, there is rarely enough time for Partners or Associates to provide systematic follow up. However, TLC addresses this concern by offering more in-depth activities as follow up to discussion groups as requested.

Technology-based presentations also create unique problems and issues. Media-equipped classrooms are in high demand throughout the day. Because of the limited number of such classrooms, it is always a challenge to find sites that can support these technology-based presentations at a convenient time for faculty.

Conclusion

Based on our experience at the University of Nebraska, Lincoln, a program that links special issues and priorities across campus with faculty in the role of Associates and Partners can achieve significant outcomes. Individual consultation for teaching improvement is important in helping faculty diagnose and improve teaching while a class is in progress; however, it is a time-consuming process that requires considerable skills (Brinko & Menges, 1997). Although they may not be formally trained in instructional consulting, Teaching Partners and Teaching Associates have their own expertise to offer in targeted areas such as curriculum, technology, or assessment. Faculty Partners and Associates can extend the impact of individual consulting by offering specialized instructional improvement and development services to targeted groups. In following up with individual clients, Teaching Associates can take some of the burden of individual consulting off the shoulders of faculty developers, especially in the area of technology. At the same time, the teaching improvement center offers the service and organizes the development activities. Such a program is cost-efficient and effective, helps the institution achieve goals and priorities in curriculum and instruction, provides professional development opportunities for individual faculty members, breaks down isolation of faculty across disciplines, and improves teaching and learning on a class-by-class basis across the campus.

References

Boice, R. (1992). *The new faculty member.* San Francisco, CA: Jossey-Bass.

Brinko, K. T. (1997). The interactions of teaching improvement. In K. Brinko & R. Menges (Eds.), *Practically speaking: A sourcebook for instructional consultants in higher education* (pp. 3-8). Stillwater, OK: New Forums Press.

Brinko, K. T., & Menges, R. J. (Eds.). (1997). *Practically speaking: A sourcebook for instructional consultants in higher education.* Stillwater, OK: New Forums Press.

Cohen, P. A. (1980). Effective use of student-rating feedback for improving college instruction: A meta-analysis of findings. *Research in Higher Education, 13* (4), 321-341.

Green, M. F. (1990). Why good teaching needs active leadership. In P. Seldin & Associates (Eds.), *How administrators can improve teaching: Moving from talk to action in higher education* (pp. 45-62). San Francisco, CA: Jossey-Bass.

Jarvis, D. K. (1991). *Junior faculty development.* New York, NY: Modern Language Association of America.

Lewis, K. G., & Povlacs, J. T. (1988). *Face to face: A sourcebook of individual consul-*

tation techniques for faculty/instructional developers. Stillwater, OK: New Forums Press.

Lunde, J., & Wilhite, M. (1996). Innovative teaching and teaching improvement. *To Improve the Academy, 15,* 155-167.

Menges, R. J., & Brinko, K. T. (1986, April). *Effective use of student evaluation feedback: A meta-analysis of higher education research.* Paper presented at the meeting of the America Educational Research Association, San Francisco, CA. (ED 270 408).

Wadsworth, E. C. (Ed.). (1988). *A handbook for new practitioners.* Stillwater, OK: Professional & Organizational Development Network in Higher Education, New Forums Press.

Wilhite, M., Latta, G., & Lewis, D. (1998, May). *A faculty discussion group leadership program: Promoting teaching excellence in a climate of financial austerity.* Paper presented at the Faculty College, Mahoney State Park, NE.

Wright, D., Banset, E., Bellows, L., & Wilhite, M. (1997). *Self-study report of the Teaching and Learning Center prepared for program review.* Lincoln, NE: University of Nebraska-Lincoln, Teaching and Learning Center.

Young, R. E., & Eble, K. E. (1988). *College teaching and learning: Preparing for new commitments.* New Directions for Teaching and Learning, No. 33. San Francisco, CA: Jossey-Bass.

Contact:

Myra S. Wilhite
Department of Agricultural Leadership, Education, and Communication
300 Agricultural Hall
University of Nebraska, Lincoln
Lincoln, NE 68583-0709
(402) 472-5991
(402) 472-5863 (FAX)
mwilhite@unl.edu

Myra S. Wilhite is an Associate Professor in the Department of Agricultural Leadership, Education, and Communication at the University of Nebraska, Lincoln. She previously served as instructional consultant with the Teaching and Learning Center where she introduced the Partners and Associates program.

Joyce Povlacs Lunde is a Professor Emerita, Department of Agricultural Leadership, Education, and Communication at the University of Nebraska, Lincoln.

She formerly served as an Educational Development Specialist in the Office of Professional and Organizational Development at UNL.

Gail F. Latta is a Professor in the University Libraries, Teaching and Learning Center Associate for Instructional Technology and Chair of UNL's Teaching, Learning, and Technology Roundtable.

APPENDIX 11.1

STAFF AND PROGRAM EVALUATION TEACHING AND LEARNING CENTER

[December, 1997]

Our essential business involves meeting UNL's instructional development needs. You have contributed to this effort by participating in a leadership role in one of our fall semester activities. (List of TLC activities attached.)

Please take a moment to reflect on this experience and provide feedback in two areas:

- Evaluate the TLC staff with whom you interacted in preparation for your leadership role.
- Assess the impact your participation had on your own teaching and learning.

Describe your role: (Check all that apply.)

____ Facilitator
____ Panel Participant
____ Presenter
____ Table Host
____ TLC Associate

Part I: Staff Effectiveness

Indicate your response by using the following scale: SA=Strongly Agree; A=Agree; N=Neither Agree nor Disagree; D=Disagree; SD=Strongly Disagree; NA=Not Applicable.

TLC staff I worked with:

____ 1. were well organized.
____ 2. were competent and helpful.
____ 3. communicated clear expectations to guide my preparation/participation in the TLC event.
____ 4. were flexible and open to suggestions.

Part II: Impact on Teaching and Learning

1. How much has your participation in a leadership role affected your teaching?

☐ Very Much
☐ Somewhat
☐ Not Very Much
☐ Not At All
☐ Not Applicable

2. In what way(s)? [Mark all that apply]

- ☐ Increased self-confidence
- ☐ Use of new teaching methods
- ☐ Affirmation of my own efforts
- ☐ Change in course content
- ☐ Change in assignments or exams
- ☐ Improved teaching methods
- ☐ Better understand learning
- ☐ Increased reflection on teaching
- ☐ Change in course structure
- ☐ Other: __________

3. Besides your own observations, how have you noticed the effects of these changes?

- ☐ Improved student performance
- ☐ Improved student ratings
- ☐ Awards and recognition
- ☐ Increased student involvement
- ☐ Positive comments from faculty
- ☐ Other: __________

4. Based on your experience, would you encourage colleagues to take a leadership role in TLC activities?

- ☐ Yes
- ☐ No

5. To what degree do you believe your participation in these activities is valued by your department?

- ☐ Highly valued
- ☐ Moderately valued
- ☐ Minimally valued
- ☐ Negatively valued

Comments:

Thank you!

12

Creating a Culture of Formative Assessment: The Teaching Excellence and Assessment Partnership Project

Roseanna G. Ross
Anthony Schwaller
Jenine Helmin
St. Cloud State University

In a year-long, grant-supported collaborative effort, St. Cloud State University's Assessment Office and Faculty Center for Teaching Excellence created a Classroom Assessment Techniques (CATs) faculty development project. This project was targeted at departments across campus at St. Cloud State University, with the intent of creating a university climate of formative assessment while improving teaching and learning. This article describes the purposes, stages of implementation, and results of the project as measured by a pre-test and post-test survey. The pre- and post-test surveys indicate that the project was highly effective in impacting the use of CATs among participants and their departmental colleagues.

Introduction

The Partnership

St. Cloud State University has both a Faculty Center for Teaching Excellence and an Assessment Office. Although these two offices were established to operate independently, it was recognized that projects dealing with both improvements of teaching and learning as well as assessment in the classroom of student learning offer rich opportunities for collaboration. This project was an initial effort at collaboration between the two offices. The Teaching Excellence and Assessment Partnership Project entitled "Enhancing Student Learning Through Formative Assessment" was designed to assist faculty in developing and integrating strategies for obtaining useful feedback about student learning and teaching effectiveness. This project was intended to enhance classroom learning through formative assessment using Classroom Assessment Techniques, also called CATs. CATs are designed to involve and empower both teachers and students to improve the quality of learning in the classroom. In addition, CATs can become part of a classroom research plan for faculty.

The purpose of the Faculty Center for Teaching Excellence is to promote useful conversations about good teaching by providing resources and strategies to support, strengthen, and recognize excellent and innovative teaching for active learning. The mission of the Assessment Office is to encourage and facilitate assessment practices on campus within all programs and departments. The directors of both the Faculty Center for Teaching Excellence and the Assessment Office felt that a project dealing with formative assessment might, in fact, help to meet various goals and objectives in both offices. Thus, the two offices worked together to secure a grant and develop this formative assessment project to improve teaching and learning.

Statement of the Problem

The Assessment Office recognized that there was not a campus culture of assessment at SCSU—faculty seemed wary of the word "assessment" itself and were only aware of the summative nature of assessment. The Assessment Office felt that there was a need for further education about the many forms, styles, and types of assessment. The Assessment Office also identified a lack of support within departments for faculty to take the initiative in assessment efforts within their own classrooms.

In addition to these stated problems, the Faculty Center for Teaching Excellence wanted the faculty to see more clearly the connection between formative assessment and the potential for enhanced teaching and student learning in the classroom. This partnership project provided a strategy for meeting goals and objectives for both offices.

Definition of Terms

To help the reader understand the meaning and value of this project, several terms need to be defined. These terms include the definitions of formative assessment, classroom assessment techniques, and classroom research, which are drawn from the work of Angelo and Cross (1993) and Cross and Steadman (1996).

- **Formative Assessment.** Unlike summative approaches to assessment, which are intended to provide evidence for evaluating or grading students at the end of a learning experience, formative assessment in the classroom involves students and teachers in the continuous monitoring of students' learning throughout the term.

- **Classroom Assessment Techniques (CATs).** CATs are a formative assessment tool intended to be learner-centered, teacher-directed, and context specific. CATs are simple, yet systematic classroom teaching strategies that provide faculty with feedback about their effectiveness as teachers and give the teacher a measure of the students' progress as learners (Angelo & Cross, 1993). Faculty can then use this information to redirect their teaching strategies to help students make their learning more efficient and more effective. CATs can be considered an assessment technique as well as a teaching strategy.

- **Classroom Research.** Classroom research refers to a teacher's conscious planning, gathering, analysis, and evaluation of feedback from students for the purpose of appraising the effectiveness of some part of any course being taught by a faculty member. Classroom research is, more often than not, qualitative rather than quantitative. Classroom research is formative rather than summative, learner-centered rather than teacher-centered, and beneficial to the students who give feedback as well as to the teacher who asks for it. Classroom research should be thought of as an ongoing process rather than just a single event (Cross & Steadman, 1996).

Design of the Project

Goals of the Project

The goals of this collaborative project are directly related to the mission and goals of both the Faculty Center for Teaching Excellence and the Assessment Office as well as to the problems that have been identified by these two offices in the "Statement of the Problem." These goals include:

1) To promote formative assessment for enhanced classroom teaching and learning.

2) To teach university faculty about CATs.

3) To create a culture of formative assessment on campus.

Objectives of the Project

From the development of the stated goals, the authors developed specific objectives that were used to guide the design, implementation, and assessment of the project. Objectives of the project included:

1) To secure involvement of a large number of departments from a variety of colleges. Each department would then identify departmental representatives to participate in the project (the grant limited participation to 15 departments).

2) To perform a pre-project, "profile" survey of participating departments.

3) To teach CATs and formative assessment techniques to representatives of those selected departments.

4) To support the participants' use of CATs within their respective classrooms throughout the year.

5) To encourage the participants to share insights from the project with colleagues in their departments.

6) To analyze the impact of CATs training and application on participants and their departments.

Description of the Project

Based upon these goals and objectives, the project was organized around ten stages of development and implementation.

Stage one: Introduction, promotion, and design of project. To market and publicize the project across the university campus, we developed a brochure (which announced the project and introduced the concept of formative assessment and CATs) and disseminated it to all faculty within the university. In addition, the directors of the project met with each of the college deans and chairpersons to define and explain the purposes of the project. The goal of the Faculty Center for Teaching Excellence and the Assessment Office was to secure participation and faculty representation from at least 15 departments. At the same time, the authors recognized that campus-wide distribution of the brochure was an initial step in educating the campus community on formative assessment. During this initial stage, two Minnesota consultants, recommended by Thomas Angelo as experts on CATs, were engaged to help with the project. These two consultants were asked to help design the formative assessment profile survey (which was to be used as a pre- and post-test), to present a university-wide address on assessment, and to facilitate two workshops for the project participants—a workshop at the beginning of the project and a follow-up workshop half-way through the project.

Stage two: Participant application and selection. After the project was adequately advertised, application forms were sent to approximately 700 faculty and 70 departments or programs (see Appendix 1 for letter to departments). The application form was designed to encourage at least three members from any one particular academic department or program to become involved in this project. Within the application form, the applicants were also asked to describe how they proposed to disseminate information learned within the project to the remaining members of their department. We made the dissemination plan a major requirement of the project in order to encourage those participating in the project to begin discussions and communications with other faculty members within their department about formative assessment and CATs. Such discussions were imperative to expanding the reach of the program and to creating a departmental support system for future use of CATs. It should be noted that each faculty member who was selected for the project was provided with an honorarium within the grant of $250. As it turned out, 44 faculty members were part of the project, and 13 departments or programs were represented. Of the 44 faculty members, eight decided to be involved as individuals not necessarily associated with a department.

Stage three: Participant and department profile survey (as pre-test). Once the faculty and departments were selected, faculty from all selected departments or programs (or individual faculty members) were asked to complete a formative assessment profile survey (see Appendix 2). The survey was designed to identify the attitudes of participating faculty concerning classroom assessment and research as part of their teaching practice. This survey was given both before the project began (to establish a base-line) and again after the project was completed (for comparison purposes). This survey was designed by the two outside consultants and contained questions about faculty members' familiarity with formative assessment, attitudes about assessment, and use of activities to enhance formative assessment in the classroom. A 1-to-5 Likert scale was used to help identify these attitudes. In addition, various demographic data were collected to help in classifying faculty respondents.

Stage four: University-wide address on classroom research. In February of the project year, the two consultants were invited to address the university faculty on the project and specific concepts dealing with assessment. Their presentation, "Enriching Your Teaching: Classroom Research through Classroom Assessment," was interactive and focused on avenues for involvement in classroom research and assessment. The purpose of the presentation was to kick off the project and to help educate faculty campus-wide on classroom research and assessment. Although this was an open address, participating faculty selected for the project were required to attend as part of their training in the project.

Stage five: Initial training of participants. Immediately following the university-wide address, the 44 individuals selected for the project met with the two consultants to learn more about the value and purposes of formative classroom assessment and the use of CATs. This four-hour, interactive workshop was designed to show faculty how Classroom Assessment Techniques can be used to improve the teaching and learning environment. During this time, faculty identified specific CATs that could be used in their courses over the next three months.

Stage six: Implementation of CATs. For approximately three months after the initial university-wide address and the workshop with the consultants, faculty selected for the project began the process of implementing CATs within their classrooms. It was during this time that faculty actually experienced the value of CATs and formative assessment. A brown-bag lunch was held for any participant wanting additional support during this time. Each participant received a copy of *Classroom Assessment Techniques: A Handbook for College Teachers* (Angelo & Cross, 1993). The 13 participating departments also received a copy of *Classroom Research: Implementing the Scholarship of Teaching* (Cross & Steadman, 1996). Occasional communications were sent from the Center to encourage continued participation.

Stage seven: Continued training of participants. In April, the project participants met again in a four-hour, follow-up session to work with the two consultants and to share their successes and failures with CATs and formative assessment. This time was also used to correct any misconceptions about CATs and formative assessment. It was anticipated that based upon this follow-up session the faculty in the project could continue improving their use of CATs in their classrooms.

Stage eight: Dissemination in departments. Near the end of the spring term, project participants disseminated the information learned from the project to other faculty members within their departments and/or programs. The method used for dissemination was originally described in their application form and was one criterion in the selection process for participation in the project. These dissemination methods included presentations at faculty meetings, writing and circulating reports or specific classroom applications, use of email interaction with colleagues, and writing newsletter articles.

Stage nine: Participant and department profile survey (as post-test). After completing all departmental dissemination efforts, project participants, as well as the members of their departments, were given the formative assessment profile survey as a post-test. The data from the pre- and post-test surveys would later be used to help assess the impact of this particular project.

Stage ten: Reporting of classroom implementation and continued support. Finally, each participating member of the project submitted either a one-page report to the Faculty Center for Teaching Excellence on the implementation of CATs in the classroom or wrote an article for publication in the Minnesota State Colleges and Universities Center for Teaching and Learning publication entitled *Open to Change.*

To extend the impact of the project beyond the first year, in the subsequent year participating faculty presented information about their use of CATs in Center-sponsored campus forums. Center representatives and participants have also shared the project at state and national conferences. Participant reports on the use of CATs are available to faculty as a resource through the Center and will soon be published on the Center's web page (http://www.stcloudstate.edu/~teaching/index.html).

Design of the Study Using Survey Data

The pre- and post-test survey on the knowledge of, attitudes toward, and behavior in using CATs and formative assessment was ideal for comparing several groups of faculty involved with the project. Mean and t-Test analyses were conducted on the survey data. The mean is the average and the t-Test is the comparison of means (the greater the difference between the means, the greater the difference between the groups). The significance was measured at the .05 and .01 levels.

In this project, two groups were tested in various comparisons to each other. The first group, called "participants," were those departmental representatives and individual faculty specifically selected for the project. These participants attended the two workshops on CATs and formative assessment and implemented this knowledge in a specific course(s). The second group, called "colleagues," were those additional faculty within the 13 selected departments. The "colleagues" were not directly involved in the project but may have attended the university-wide address and/or may have been involved in departmental/program dissemination efforts. Four tests were designed to compare the attitude of these two groups toward CATs and formative assessment.

- ***Test 1*** is a comparison of all respondents, including the "participants" and the departmental "colleagues," simply comparing the pre-test survey results to the post-test survey results of all faculty involved in any way with the project.
- ***Test 2*** is a comparison of only the "participants," or those directly involved with the project, by comparing their pre-test survey results to their post-test survey results.
- ***Test 3*** is a comparison of only those "colleagues," or those departmental faculty not directly involved with the project, comparing their pre-test survey results to their post-test survey results.
- ***Test 4*** is a comparison of the "participants" to the "colleagues," examining whether there was a significant difference in change of attitude and behavior between the two groups.

Results of the Project

Participant Numbers

Based upon the participant numbers, the project advertising was a success. At the beginning of the project, during the university-wide address, a total of 67 university faculty attended the presentation (this included participating department representatives and their departmental colleagues). A total of 44 faculty participated in the project training and CATs implementation in courses. Of this number, 36 faculty "participants" were identified as departmental representatives, representing 13 departments. (The remaining eight faculty participants—from eight different disciplines—requested to be involved as individuals since their departments chose not to participate. Because funds were available, and their participation fit the overarching goals of the project, it was decided to support their participation and request dissemination in professional arenas other than their departments.)

Survey Results

The pre- and post-test surveys indicated that the 44 participants' knowledge, attitudes, and behaviors around CATs had been positively impacted at significant levels of .01 and/or .05. The surveys also indicated that this project had a slight impact on colleagues' attitudes toward CATs. The questions showing significant change in knowledge, attitude, or behavior for each of the groups are described below (see Appendix 3 for the table reporting the probabilities for all four tests).

Test 1: A comparison of all respondents' (participants and colleagues) pre- and post-test survey responses. A comparison of the mean scores on the pre- and post-test surveys shows that these faculty reported an increase in the following activities at the conclusion of the CATs project:

- Attend more presentations and read books on assessment (survey question 5)
- Believe in more ongoing assessment (survey question 14)
- Structure time within the class for written feedback (survey question 16)
- Analyze and discuss written feedback with students (survey question 17)

Test 2: A comparison of the participants' pre- and post-test survey responses. A comparison of the mean scores on the pre- and post-test surveys shows that these faculty reported an increase in the following activities at the conclusion of the CATs project:

- Attend more presentations and read books on assessment (survey question 5)
- Believe more information is needed than just at end of term (survey question 14)
- Have discussions with students about assignment effectiveness (survey question 15)
- Structure time within the class for written feedback (survey question 16)
- Analyze and discuss written feedback with students (survey question 17)
- Have discussed written feedback from classes with colleagues (survey question 18)

Test 3: A comparison of the colleagues' pre- and post-test survey responses. A comparison of the mean scores on the pre- and post-test surveys shows that these faculty reported an increase in the following activities at the conclusion of the CATs project:

- Analyze and discuss written feedback with students (survey question 17)

Test 4: A comparison of participants' responses with colleagues' responses. A comparison of participant and colleague mean scores on the pre- and post-test surveys shows that participants, in comparison to colleagues, reported a significantly greater increase in the following activities:

- Attend presentations and read books on assessment (survey question 5)
- Believe in ongoing assessment (survey question 6)
- Believe in making the effort to gather data (survey question 7)
- Believe information is needed more than just at end of the term (survey question 8)
- Seek written feedback other than at end of the term (survey question 9)
- Believe feedback should be sought frequently (survey question 10)
- Are comfortable taking time for discussions about class effectiveness (survey question 11)
- Are willing to change course in response to feedback (survey question 12)
- Seek written feedback other than end of term (survey question 14)
- Analyze and discuss written feedback with students (question 17)

Participant Comments While Using CATs

During the second workshop in April, participants were asked to comment on their experience with their use of CATs in the classroom up to that point. The following statements represent a summary of many of project participants' responses:

- CATs act as a classroom activator, leading to positive and broad interaction among students and faculty.

- CATs help to change student and teacher expectations, to determine where students are, and to adjust accordingly.
- CATs help to increase student ownership of their learning, taking more responsibility for their learning.
- CATs help to develop an unexpected depth of understanding and creativity in the teaching/learning process.
- CATs help to show how perceptions differ between students and faculty.

Conclusions

After reviewing the results and observing the implementation and completion of the project, the project directors feel confident in making several concluding statements. First, it appears that the project helped to bring the concept of classroom assessment to the forefront within the university setting. With the major promotional campaign, it was inevitable that faculty, campus-wide, would be more aware of formative assessment in general and Classroom Assessment Techniques in particular. The project was also instrumental in facilitating faculty conversations about assessment, thanks in large part to the participation of departmental colleagues during dissemination efforts. As reported in the surveys, faculty participation in the project directly enhanced instruction in the classroom. Finally, the project functioned to bring the Faculty Center for Teaching Excellence and the Assessment Office together in a collaborative effort, which, in turn, helped faculty to see assessment as less intimidating while impacting the teaching and learning atmosphere within the university.

The following recommendations may help to improve similar projects that other universities may undertake.

1) Continued communications with the project participants is necessary throughout the year.

2) All communication to faculty needs to be clear and concise.

3) Be flexible so that some faculty not interested in working with colleagues can work individually with such a project.

4) Understand that there is not a common paradigm on campus about assessment, its definitions, purposes, etc.

5) Understand that all faculty do not have the same understanding of student learning and teaching methodology.

6) Remember that faculty have many activities throughout a school

year and that this project is just another professional activity that they are incorporating into their daily schedules.

7) Be sure that the project directors communicate effectively and meet on a regular basis.

8) Remember that effective communication is critical between the project directors and the consultants. The consultants need to clearly understand the goals of the project.

9) The survey for pre- and post-testing needs to be carefully and clearly developed.

10) When selecting departments for the project, try to get representation from across all colleges within the university.

Acknowledgments

The authors wish to thank Connie Stack and Joel Peterson for their work as faculty consultants and workshop presenters for this project and Laurel Malikowski for her assistance in conducting the project.

References

Angelo, T. A., & Cross, K. P. (1993). *Classroom assessment techniques: A handbook for college teachers* (2nd ed.). San Francisco, CA: Jossey-Bass.

Cross, K. P., & Steadman, M. H. (1996). *Classroom research: Implementing the scholarship of teaching.* San Francisco, CA: Jossey-Bass.

[This paper was initially presented in Fall 1997 at the Professional and Organizational Development Network in Higher Education Conference, at the MnSCU Center for Teaching and Learning Conference, and at a St. Cloud State University Faculty Forum.]

Contact:

Roseanna G. Ross
Faculty Center for Teaching Excellence
St. Cloud State University
720 Fourth Avenue South
St. Cloud, MN 56301-4498
(320) 654-5282
(320) 255-3217 (FAX)
teaching@StCloudState.edu

Roseanna G. Ross, is professor of, and internship director in, Speech Communication and has been Director of St. Cloud State University's Faculty Center for Teaching Excellence since 1995. Her research interests include experiential learning (co-author of the Internship as Partnership Handbook series published through the National Society for Experiential Education) and conflict management (co-author of the Ross-DeWine Conflict Management Message Style Instrument).

Anthony Schwaller is Professor and Chair of the Department of Environmental and Technological Studies at St. Cloud State University and was Assessment Director at St. Cloud State University from 1994 to 1998. His related research interests include teaching methodology. He co-authored the textbook entitled *Instructional Strategies for Technology Education*, and he has written numerous articles and chapters for other textbooks concerning teaching, learning, and delivery systems for technology teachers.

Jenine Helmin was the Graduate Assistant for the Teaching Excellence Center and Assessment Partnership Project. Helmin's master's thesis, *Classroom Assessment Techniques: Perceptions of Effectiveness for Teaching Diverse Student Populations in Higher Education*, combined her interests of teaching, assessment, and cultural diversity. She currently teaches in the Department of Women's Studies at St. Cloud State University.

APPENDIX 12.1

ST. CLOUD STATE
UNIVERSITY

720 Fourth Avenue South
St. Cloud, MN 56301-4498
Phone (320) 654-5282
(320) 202-0907

TEACHING EXCELLENCE AND ASSESSMENT PARTNERSHIP

Enhancing Student Learning Through Formative Assessment

December 9, 1996

Department Chairs and Program Directors:

Your department or program has a unique opportunity for enhancing teaching effectiveness and student learning! The Faculty Center for Teaching Excellence and the Assessment Office have developed a project called "the Teaching Excellence and Assessment Partnership: Enhancing Student Learning Through Formative Assessment," funded by a Q-7 grant. Your department/program is invited to join our efforts to encourage formative assessment (*a teaching technique used to monitor students' learning throughout the term*) to help improve the quality of teaching in your courses. We are requesting that your department/program select two to three faculty members, who are seriously committed to teaching effectiveness and student learning, to become involved in this project.

To enhance the quality of classroom teaching within your department/program, faculty representatives selected for the project will work with consultants and learn about and integrate formative assessment. During this project, the faculty representatives are expected to share the formative assessment techniques called CATs (Classroom Assessment Techniques) with other faculty in their department/program. The goal of this project is to integrate CATs into your department's/program's classrooms with the help of the chosen faculty representatives.

Participating departments/programs will be requested to complete a simple pre- and post-formative assessment profile survey. The survey is to provide evidence of project effectiveness and to assist consultants in working with individual faculty.

To launch this project, all faculty are invited to a university-wide address entitled, **Enriching Your Teaching: Classroom Research Through Classroom Assessment**, on **February 4**, from **10:00 to 11:30 a.m.**, Atwood Center. This address will focus on ways in which faculty can become involved in classroom research, and how classroom research is related to formative assessment and student learning. See enclosed materials for more detailed information.

This is an opportunity for departments/programs to utilize formative assessment and continue to create a culture of teaching excellence at SCSU. Your support is encouraged because, "assessment is most effective when undertaken in an environment that is receptive, supportive, and enabling" (Assessment in Practice, 1996).

Please find enclosed project and application materials.

Thank you,

Roseanna G. Ross and Tony Schwaller
The Teaching Excellence and Assessment Partnership

Jbh: enclosures

APPENDIX 12.2

CLASSROOM ASSESSMENT AND RESEARCH FACULTY SURVEY

This survey is designed to gather anonymous aggregate data from faculty in three areas:

1. Familiarity with the concepts of classroom assessment and classroom research.
2. Attitudes toward classroom assessment and research as a part of teaching practice.
3. Extent to which classroom assessment and research activities are used in regular teaching practice.

The survey begins with some demographic questions to be used to examine possible statistical correlations. Although the data will be aggregated, some of the analysis will be reported as related to departments or programs. Please record each answer on the line provided.

DEMOGRAPHICS

_____1. Did you submit an application to participate in the Q-7 grant funded project and workshop on Feb. 4 and April 14, 1997? (select one)

a. Yes
b. No

_____2. How many years have you been teaching in a university/college setting? (select one)

a. 1-2
b. 3-6
c. 7-10
d. 11-15
e. 16 or more

_____3. Which statement best reflects your background in learning theory? (select one)

a. I have a degree in a field involving rigorous study of learning theory and teaching practice.
b. I have taken some courses in learning theory and teaching practice.

c. I have taken no courses in learning theory, but I attend conferences and read books and articles focused on learning theory and teaching practice.
d. I have taken no courses in learning theory and have little interest in readings and workshops on improving teaching unless it is directly related to teaching in my own field.
e. My educational background and my current professional interests have been focused completely on research in my field, not on teaching.

_____4. Gender (optional)

a. Female
b. Male

FAMILIARITY WITH CLASSROOM ASSESSMENT AND RESEARCH

_____5. Which statement best describes your knowledge of classroom assessment and classroom research? (select one)

a. I am <u>not</u> familiar with any specialized sense of these terms. I can only infer what they refer to from my understand of the terms "classroom," "assessment," and "research."
b. I am familiar with some of the techniques included in classroom assessment (such as "The Muddiest Point" and "The Minute Paper"), but I've never read about or attended presentations on classroom assessment or research.
c. I have attended presentations and/or read some articles on classroom assessment or research.
d. I have read and used the book *Classroom Assessment Techniques*—by Thomas Angelo and Patricia Cross—extensively.
e. I have given presentations and/or written articles on classroom assessment and/or classroom research.

The remainder of questions will use the Likert Scale.
Please indicate the degree to which you agree or disagree with the following statements according to the following Likert Scale:

1 = Strongly disagree
2 = Somewhat disagree
3 = Neither agree nor disagree
4 = Somewhat agree
5 = Strongly agree

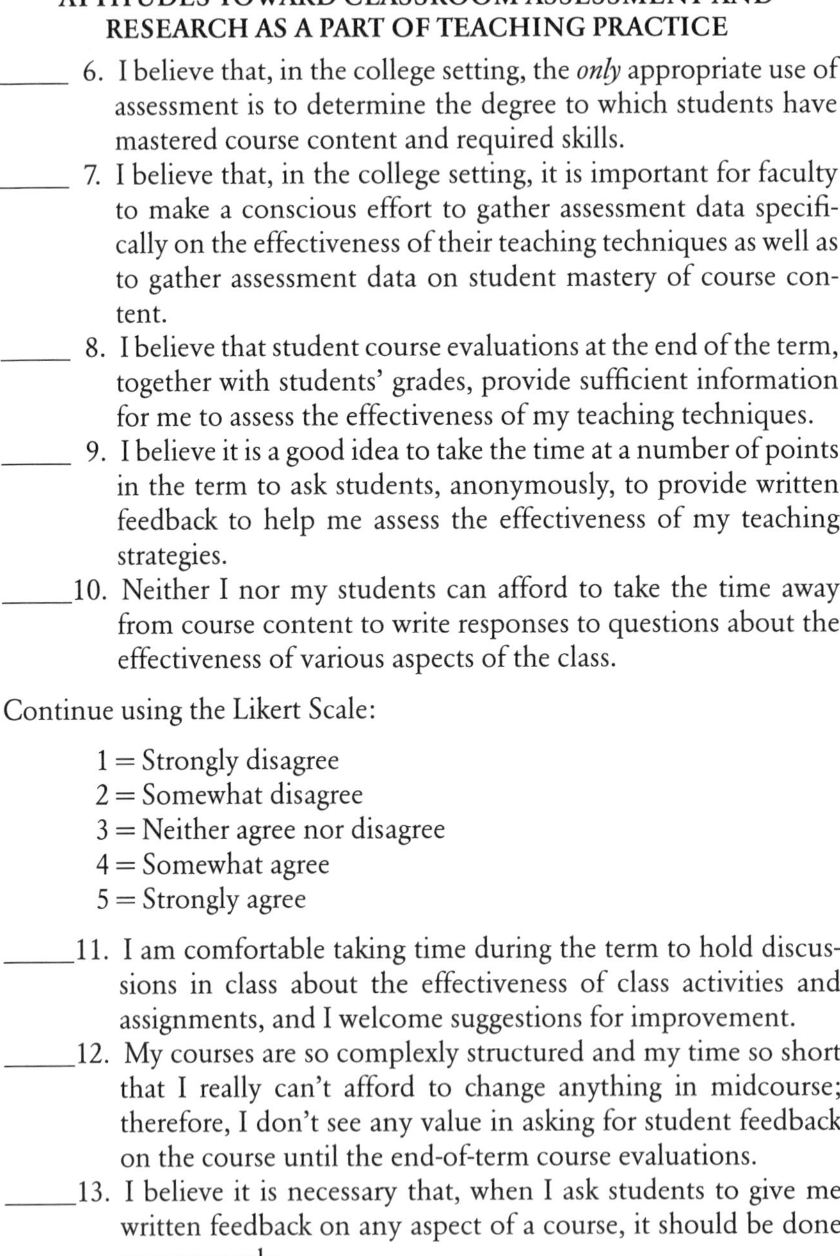

ATTITUDES TOWARD CLASSROOM ASSESSMENT AND RESEARCH AS A PART OF TEACHING PRACTICE

_____ 6. I believe that, in the college setting, the *only* appropriate use of assessment is to determine the degree to which students have mastered course content and required skills.

_____ 7. I believe that, in the college setting, it is important for faculty to make a conscious effort to gather assessment data specifically on the effectiveness of their teaching techniques as well as to gather assessment data on student mastery of course content.

_____ 8. I believe that student course evaluations at the end of the term, together with students' grades, provide sufficient information for me to assess the effectiveness of my teaching techniques.

_____ 9. I believe it is a good idea to take the time at a number of points in the term to ask students, anonymously, to provide written feedback to help me assess the effectiveness of my teaching strategies.

_____10. Neither I nor my students can afford to take the time away from course content to write responses to questions about the effectiveness of various aspects of the class.

Continue using the Likert Scale:

1 = Strongly disagree
2 = Somewhat disagree
3 = Neither agree nor disagree
4 = Somewhat agree
5 = Strongly agree

_____11. I am comfortable taking time during the term to hold discussions in class about the effectiveness of class activities and assignments, and I welcome suggestions for improvement.

_____12. My courses are so complexly structured and my time so short that I really can't afford to change anything in midcourse; therefore, I don't see any value in asking for student feedback on the course until the end-of-term course evaluations.

_____13. I believe it is necessary that, when I ask students to give me written feedback on any aspect of a course, it should be done anonymously.

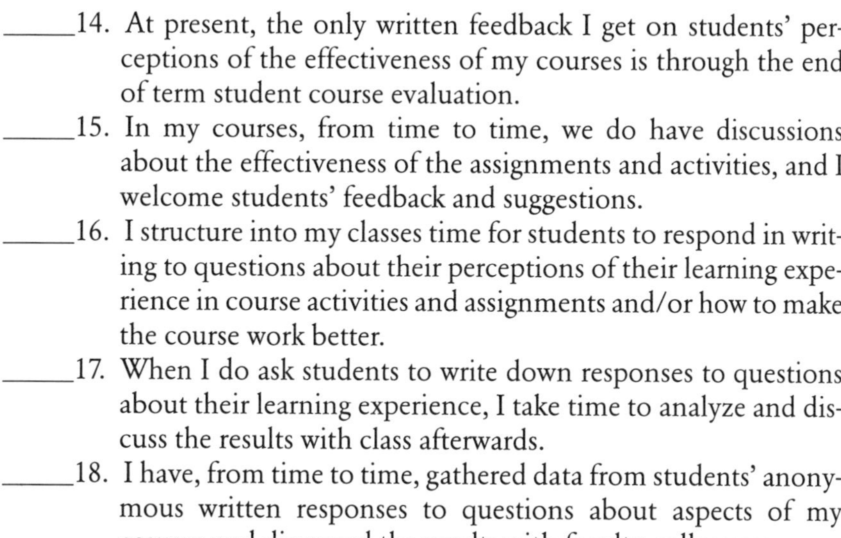

EXTENT TO WHICH CLASSROOM ASSESSMENT AND RESEARCH ACTIVITIES ARE USED IN REGULAR TEACHING PRACTICE

_____14. At present, the only written feedback I get on students' perceptions of the effectiveness of my courses is through the end of term student course evaluation.

_____15. In my courses, from time to time, we do have discussions about the effectiveness of the assignments and activities, and I welcome students' feedback and suggestions.

_____16. I structure into my classes time for students to respond in writing to questions about their perceptions of their learning experience in course activities and assignments and/or how to make the course work better.

_____17. When I do ask students to write down responses to questions about their learning experience, I take time to analyze and discuss the results with class afterwards.

_____18. I have, from time to time, gathered data from students' anonymous written responses to questions about aspects of my courses and discussed the results with faculty colleagues.

APPENDIX 12.3

TEACHING EXCELLENCE AND ASSESSMENT PARTNERSHIP

Enhancing Student Learning Through Formative Assessment

Pre- and Post-Test Survey Results

	Test 1	Test 2	Test 3	Test 4	
1	0.260				Participant in Q-7 Grant Funded Project (1=Yes, 2=No)
2	0.785	0.726	0.385	0.262	Years teaching in a university/college (1=1-2, 2=3-6, 3=7-10, 4=11-15. 5=16+)
3	0.230	0.290	0.536	0.795	Background in learning theory (1=degree in, 5=none)
4	0.364	0.935	0.205	0.482	Gender (1=female, 2=male)
5	**0.000	**0.000	0.109	*0.024	Knowledge of classroom assessment/ research (1=none, 5=much) (Remaining questions use scale: 1=strongly disagree, 2=somewhat disagree, 3=neither agree or disagree, 4=somewhat agree, 5=strongly agree)
6	0.340	0.190	0.168	**0.003	Only appropriate **use of assessment** is to determine mastery
7	0.180	0.950	0.105	*0.038	Important to make **conscious effort** to gather assessment data-effective & mastery
8	0.114	0.401	0.378	**0.000	Course **evaluation & grades** provide sufficient information to access effectiveness
9	0.099	0.624	.0137	**0.003	Good idea to ask for anonymous written feedback a **number of times** during term
10	0.164	0.536	0.344	**0.003	**Cannot afford the time** away from the course to get written responses
11	0.101	0.511	0.239	**0.003	**Comfortable taking time** for discussions about effectiveness & welcome feedback
12	0.134	0.450	0.238	**0.002	Courses complexly structured, see **no value in asking for feedback until end** of term
13	0.247	0.965	0.063	0.421	When written feedback is given, it should be done **anonymously**
14	*0.016	**0.004	0.687	**0.007	Only written feedback received is the **end of term** evaluations
15	0.089	0.051	0.674	0.434	**Hold discussions** & welcome students' feedback and suggestions about effectiveness
16	**0.008	**0.000	0.898	0.177	**Structure time for written feedback** into classes on their experience of the course
17	**0.000	**0.002	*0.021	*0.037	**Analyze and discuss results with class** after get written feedback, when I ask for it
18	0.067	*0.037	0.719	0.238	**Discuss results with colleagues** from students' anonymous written feedback

* = significant at the .05 level

** = significant at the .01 level

Test 1: a comparison of all respondent's (participants and members of their departments) pre-test (n=97) and post-test (n=73) survey responses.

Test 2: a comparison of the participants' pre-test (n=42) and post-test (n=39) survey responses.

Test 3: a comparison of the departmental colleagues' pre-test (n=55) and post-test (n=34) survey responses.

Test 4: a comparison of participants' responses (n=81) with department members' survey responses (n=89).

Section III:

Examining Assumptions About Teaching and Faculty Development

13

Fragmentation Versus Integration of Faculty Work

Carolin Kreber
University of Alberta

Patricia Cranton
Psychological Type Press, Inc.

Present faculty development practice encourages new faculty to integrate teaching, research, and other aspects of academic work early in their careers. By drawing on both the cognitive and the developmental psychology literature, we propose integration as an advanced stage of adult development that comes about as a result of extensive experience and expertise. We argue that faculty should be advised to focus on either research or teaching at different times during their early years and that integration of professorial roles should only be expected at a later stage. We discuss the implications of such an approach for faculty development.

The present culture of higher education, characterized by high demands for accountability in both research and teaching, leads administrators to encourage faculty to integrate research and teaching in the early stages of their career. Such integration occurs, according to the common understanding, if faculty are involved in all aspects of academic work and contribute to teaching, research, and service work. New faculty are expected to develop a program of research early while also sharing a heavy involvement in undergraduate teaching. A concern that present expectations of new faculty, particularly at research universities, might be excessive is articulated in a recent article by Bean (1998) who shared the following experience:

> An assistant professor coming up for tenure confided in me that her publications and teaching record were fine, but she didn't

> have a "big grant" and might not get tenure. It may not be enough to be a scholar and teacher, one also needs to be an "entrepreneur" (p. 509).

New faculty are not only expected to teach and publish but to also bring in external grant money.

Expectations change as faculty gain seniority and experience. Reaching the highest professorial rank, for many faculty, entails the privilege of teaching more graduate courses and focusing their career on either teaching or research. As faculty become more experienced, specialized, and expert in faculty work, the level of integration of all professorial roles ironically seems to decrease. This is an interesting phenomenon in light of the research from cognitive and developmental psychology that suggests a movement not from integration to specialization but from a stage of fragmentation to one of greater specialization *and* integration. In this conceptual article we propose a new model of thinking about faculty work with the goal of examining some of the assumptions about faculty development that we have come to take for granted. It is our intent to demonstrate that faculty careers might be more meaningfully conceptualized as a process of moving from fragmentation to integration, as professors, over time, develop work-related expertise, rather than, as is the case now, one of moving from integration of all professorial roles to greater specialization. Our four specific objectives are:

- To identify what we mean by the term integration
- To discuss how faculty development is presently conceptualized and practiced
- To present an alternative conceptualization derived from cognitive and developmental psychology
- To demonstrate the implications the model has for faculty development at the individual, departmental, and organizational level

Integration

For many years higher education scholars have struggled with the notion of integration of teaching and research as initiated in the German research university of the 19th century. Some have dismissed such integration as a *myth* (Weimer, 1997) given the realities under which late 20th-century American universities operate. Studies investigating the relationship between these two important strands of faculty work find little or no correlation between the two when the analyses are based on performance outcome measures such as numbers of refereed publications and student ratings of instruction (Braxton, 1996; Feldman, 1987; Hattie & Marsh, 1996). However, such studies have been criticized for ignoring the complex nature of research and teaching and the critical points where the two might intertwine.

Recently, scholars point to what they perceive as a natural synthesis or integration of teaching and research, which can be observed when university teaching is inquiry- or discovery-based (Clark, 1997; Colbeck, 1998; Rowland, 1996). Colbeck (1998) writes in this context that integration can be observed when "faculty occasionally engage in activities that accomplish teaching and research goals at the same time" (p. 648). While this symbiosis of research and teaching is found primarily in graduate seminars, the same authors also suggest that undergraduate teaching would be greatly enhanced by such a symbiosis.

But how do faculty themselves perceive the question of integration? On the basis of a study of 12 professors holding administrative positions as heads of their departments at a British university, Rowland (1996) summarizes his findings as follows: "All those interviewed expressed a view that active involvement in the research process directly improved the quality of teaching" (p. 13). Interestingly, though, all 12 informants of this study had extensive experience as members of the professoriate and had reached the highest professorial rank. In a study comparing administrators' and faculty's attitudes towards teaching and research, Li-Ping and Chamberlain (1997) report that administrators feel that research and teaching are mutually supportive, whereas faculty feel that research interferes with teaching and that they should be required to do either teaching or research but not both. While the two groups were compatible in terms of length of service, it should be noted that the study was based on a sample of 232 faculty at different career stages, with 142 faculty being at the ranks of assistant and associate professor. As the survey results were not broken down by length of service or professorial rank, it is difficult to tell whether more experienced faculty might have shared a view that mirrors more closely that of administration.

If it were indeed true that experienced faculty perceive a greater sense of integration than their less experienced colleagues, could this be the result of senior faculty having a greater opportunity to incorporate their research into their teaching? Often experienced senior faculty are in charge of small doctoral-level seminars in which there is plenty of opportunity to discuss and disseminate the results of their own work. Such seminars also offer the needed motivation and intellectual stimulation to further one's research. Junior faculty on the other hand are often expected to teach undergraduate courses unrelated to their doctoral studies, allowing little opportunity to incorporate their own research ideas. At the same time, new faculty are also encouraged to develop a program of research and to participate in community work. What appears to be integration on the surface may, considered at a deeper level, only be a mosaic or fragmentation of professorial work loosely held together by the pressures of institutional and individual accountability.

We do not argue with those of our colleagues who defend the traditional notion of "integration" of research and teaching and point to the pedagogical value such an orientation would have at the undergraduate level. To the contrary, we support an approach to teaching that is characterized by a pedagogy of helping students identify and solve problems and arrive at an understanding of how knowledge in the discipline is created. We do suggest though that it is the more experienced faculty, rather than the new faculty, who have the expertise to face the challenges that this type of integration requires. Expecting new faculty to carry out this important task might be grounded on a misconception of what such an integration entails.

Trends in Faculty Development

Since the mid-1970s, there has been a clear trend in higher education to expect new faculty not only to be productive in research but also to pay greater attention to teaching (Centra, 1993). Weimer (1990) writes in this context that "faculty development started out meaning the enhancement of teaching skill but soon became a more inclusive term connoting a broad range of professional activities, from support of scholarship to counseling on personal problems that impinge on professional effectiveness" (p. xv). By the mid-1970s, it was proposed that faculty development be more than the improvement of instruction alone and be a means of facilitating faculty renewal and vitality through changes on the personal or faculty level, on the departmental or instructional level, and on the organizational level (Berquist & Phillips, 1975; Gaff, 1975). Despite their intuitive appeal, the implementation of these comprehensive programs remained limited.

Since the early 1990s, as funding for higher education has been increasingly curtailed and demands for accountability have steadily increased, there is a renewed interest in comprehensive faculty development programs that assist faculty in developing the competencies needed not only for teaching but also for research and service (Bland & Schmitz, 1990; Boice, 1992; Hubbard, Atkins, & Brinko, 1998; Schuster & Wheeler, 1990; Sorcinelli & Austin, 1992). In this context, Gaff (1994) describes those programs that support the growth of faculty members in all aspects of their work as the most sophisticated. Boice (1992) suggests that programs to help new faculty resolve the tensions and stresses of competing work demands can result in more effective teaching and research. Johnston (1997) advocates holistic programs that introduce new faculty to teaching, research, and the interrelationships of both. Such programs assist faculty to understand their roles as *faculty,* not just their roles as teachers or researchers. The assumption underlying these models is that faculty's needs are best met by programs that assist them in performing all their professorial roles at once. In many ways such models should be applauded as they are a direct response to new faculty who are often expected to teach courses nobody else wishes to teach (usually at the undergraduate level), to make themselves available as supervisors to students working on topics outside their area of expertise, to serve on committees, and above all to develop a program of research. However, while integration of academic work is the desired outcome of these expectations, it is in fact a sense of fragmentation of work that is maintained.

An interesting alternative to such a comprehensive program is envisioned by Candy (1996) as well as Brew and Boud (1996). Candy draws on two ideas from Boyer (1990): his four-faceted model of a scholarship of discovery, application, teaching, and integration, and his notion of seasons or cycles of faculty concentrating on, or specializing in, different aspects of scholarship for certain periods of time. Candy (1996) proposes that an effective faculty development program would take into account these seasons and hence "[need] to be comprehensive and not fixated on one aspect of academic work, nor offered just once and then set aside" (p. 12). Brew and Boud (1996) echo such a view when they argue that faculty development programs need to be holistic and, as such, "acknowledge diverse roles and work patterns"; "recognize that roles and responsibilities will shift throughout careers"; "prepare staff at each stage of their career as they take on new roles and responsibilities" (p. 20); and "incorporate a staged approach which corresponds to different needs at different times" (p. 21). Candy's (1996) and Brew and Boud's (1996) models differ from the others discussed earlier in that they challenge the assumption that faculty need to learn to integrate all their professorial roles at once. The following model draws on their framework and adds to it the notion of fostering integration in later career stages.

An Alternative Model

It stands to reason that as faculty gain seniority and move through the academic ranks they also become more expert in academic work. But do all faculty automatically become experts at professorial work? Cognitive science research on the development and nature of expertise shows that expertise is acquired through active engagement with experience or, as Bereiter and Scardamalia (1993) suggest, through "progressive problem-solving" (p. 120). According to this view, people who engage in progressive problem-solving continually reinvest the mental resources that have been set free by the process of pattern learning and automatization in problems that are typical for their practice or work domain. In other words, progressive problem-solvers are not satisfied with following certain routines and algorithms when dealing with tasks but do so only to the extent that existing algorithms allow them to concentrate their energy on exploring the problem in greater depth. As a result, they approach problems at increasingly higher levels of complexity, which, in turn, leads them to develop more sophisticated skills and knowledge. Put differently, as the job gets easier with experience, time, and repetition, one gets a better sense of the broader picture, is more likely to take risks, and takes more and more variables into account when defining and solving the problem. This leads to a more integrated body of knowledge. Interestingly, while the role of experience in developing professional knowledge has repeatedly been highlighted for the teaching profession (Calderhead, 1988; Russell & Munby, 1991; Schön, 1995; Tiberius, Smith, & Waisman, 1998), it has not been similarly highlighted for the academic one.

What might be some of the tasks or problems that typically engage faculty? Braskamp and Ory (1994) provide a fairly comprehensive list of the tasks that constitute faculty work. The authors list 75 different activities or tasks that faculty do, 39 of which pertain to faculty's teaching and research roles. To provide just a few examples, we have selected ten tasks from their list, five each for teaching and research.

Teaching

- Advising students on their senior research projects, theses, and dissertations
- Developing, reviewing, and redesigning courses

- Instructing students in courses, laboratories, clinics, and studio classes
- Developing teaching materials, manuals, and software
- Managing a course (grading, maintaining student records, and planning learning experiences)

Research

- Writing proposals to funding agencies
- Writing books, monographs, and textbooks
- Writing papers in refereed journals and conference proceedings
- Editing journals or other learned publications
- Managing and serving as consultants of exhibitions, performances, and displays (Braskamp & Ory, 1994, p. 43).

Clearly, as this short list of examples of academic tasks shows, the work faculty do is multi-faceted and challenging. From a cognitive psychological perspective (Bereiter & Scardamalia, 1993; Tennant & Pogson, 1995), each of these tasks or activities can be considered a potential problem to be solved. Repeated engagement, or simply *experience*, with these tasks results in more advanced ways of conceptualizing and solving the problem or, in other words, in more sophisticated cognitive structures and patterns of thinking about academic work. These patterns of thinking are characterized by greater levels of complexity as well as integration (Bereiter & Scardamalia, 1993; Glaser & Chi, 1988; Ericsson & Smith, 1991). Cognitive psychologists consider integration a function of experience and an important feature of expertise.

Considering the complex nature of academic work, is it meaningful to expect faculty to demonstrate high levels of performance in all of the tasks associated with professorial work? In line with the literature discussed earlier, this makes sense only to the extent that faculty have the opportunity to gradually increase their specialized knowledge and expertise first in one domain (either teaching or research), then in the other, and, as a result of having acquired expertise in each, to develop the ability to integrate the two. Whether or not faculty will learn to integrate their roles is likely connected to the level of motivation or effort they commit to this process. In a recent article Garrison (1997) discusses the links between motivation and self-direction in learning, arguing that motivation is greatest when people perceive a sense of gratification and satisfaction as a result of assuming control and responsibility over their learning. It would seem that one critical factor in the development of expertise in academic work is the self-direction by which faculty approach their development. When faculty resist the temptation to continuously draw on already existing routines and algorithms and instead engage in progressive problem-solving when dealing with work-related tasks they demonstrate a high degree of self-direction (Kreber, in press).

The notion of integration has also been of interest to developmental psychologists. Research in developmental psychology focusing on adult thought patterns has consistently shown a movement from a more fragmented to a more synthesized or integrated conceptualization of issues and worldviews (Basseches, 1984; King & Kitchener, 1994; Kramer, 1983, 1989; Labouvie-Vief, 1982; Loevinger, 1976; Perry, 1970). The same notion of integration or wholeness seen as an advanced stage of development can also be observed in the work of Jung (1971) and Kolb (1984). The key to this development is once again seen in the nature of the adult learner's experience. According to Kramer (1983), most models of development and adult thinking suggest that individuals at the highest stage of development integrate or synthesize contradictions into an "overriding, more inclusive whole made up of two or more formally consistent systems" (cited in King & Kitchener, 1993, p. 39). When faculty integrate teaching and research (and other aspects of professorial work), they synthesize the contradictions between the two into a holistic, all-encompassing, and integrated domain of experience: academic work.

In the present culture of higher education, new faculty are expected to demonstrate high levels of performance in all areas of professorial work. As a result, faculty development programs are geared towards what on the surface appears to be an integration of academic work at the early stages of a faculty member's career. However, in light of the research discussed above, it seems likely that such practice ignores the natural process of adult development, learning, and the nature of work-related expertise. A more meaningful approach might be to allow inexperienced faculty to specialize in one area, teaching or research, in the early years and to foster greater integration of professorial responsibilities once they have had opportunity to develop expertise. Once faculty have acquired expertise, cognitive as well as developmental psychology research suggest that they would develop a greater propensity for integration. Therefore, it would seem a more plausible expectation for these faculty to also teach undergraduate courses, be involved in teaching as well as research, serve on university committees, and supervise students. The nature of faculty careers thus conceived has important implications for the practice of faculty development on three levels.

Implications for Faculty Development

Historically, faculty development dealt primarily with the technical improvement of classroom teaching skills and was therefore often referred to as instructional development. In early projects such as the University of Massachusetts's Clinic to Improve Teaching, teaching was not only separated from the rest of academic work, but it was treated in a laboratory-like fashion. Faculty repeated specific teaching skills under close observation or under the scrutiny of a video camera. Fragmentation was indeed the goal. Following a behavioral model, teaching was broken down into small bits, rehearsed, and reinforced. By and large, movements toward faculty development in the more general sense of considering the faculty member as a whole person were viewed with skepticism though they provoked debate and controversy in the field.

To some extent, we still live under the shadow of that past. Most faculty developers focus primarily on teaching skills. Recent discussions of development in terms of academic work as a whole are the exception rather than the norm, especially in practice. Yet, we simultaneously expect faculty to be able to integrate miraculously all aspects of academic work—teaching, research, and service—and the quicker the better.

If we view integration of academic work as a goal of faculty development, and if we recognize that integration is a developmental process that comes along with the acquisition of experience and expertise, then we need to think of our practice as faculty developers in a different way. In our work with individual faculty members, we need to foster development and integration *over time* rather than provide skills training. At the departmental level, we need to help chairs and program directors find ways to allow some new faculty to specialize in teaching while others focus on research. And we need to work toward changing the role of senior faculty so that their integrated expertise is fully utilized. In our role within the institution, we need to promote an understanding of the process of faculty *development* over time, leading to a full integration of the fragments of academic work.

In our consultations with individual faculty, we would:

- Learn about the entire scope of the faculty member's work, her research as well as her teaching

- Pay attention to the stage of the person's career
- Work with new faculty so as to develop their expertise in either teaching or research, according to their choice
- Foster integration of research and teaching by encouraging faculty to search for and nurture areas of overlap between them
- Help faculty develop courses or become involved in programs related to their research interests
- Use developmental activities to support integrative approaches to academic work, including critical incidents, simulations, discussion groups, and debates
- Work to promote self-directed faculty development
- Encourage later-career stage faculty to work with new faculty and act as models of integrated academic work

At the departmental level, we need to support the structure of a new approach to faculty development. More specifically, we can:

- Help chairs design ways to allow some faculty to focus on teaching and others on research without incurring any further costs or jeopardizing the quality of teaching
- Assist with program review and revision with a view to encouraging integration of academic work (for example, ensuring that courses in a program reflect faculty research interests)
- Help program directors find ways for new faculty to teach specialized and upper-level courses related to their research expertise
- Where appropriate, help departments recruit graduate students who are interested in studying in the areas in which faculty are currently doing research, thereby encouraging a good match between faculty's and students' research interests, which in turn helps to increase the integration of supervision, graduate courses, and research
- Help departments find ways to fully utilize the integrative experience and expertise of their senior faculty, especially in undergraduate teaching

In our role within the institution, we need to work to develop an atmosphere that values the integration of teaching and research while recognizing that this integration takes place over time. We should:

- Ensure that promotion and tenure committees understand the developmental process of integration and the acquisition of expertise over time
- Initiate a reward system for new faculty who are specializing in either teaching or research
- Review merit pay or point systems with a view to encouraging first the development of expertise in teaching or research then the integration of the two
- Prepare jargon-free summaries of the literature on expertise and adult development to assist administrators as well as faculty to understand the process of professional development
- Encourage discourse among faculty and between faculty and administrators on the integration of academic work

Summary

Cutbacks in government funding for postsecondary education and an increasingly diverse student population render the roles of faculty more and more complex. As a result of these developments, recent years have witnessed a call for more holistic or comprehensive faculty development programs that do not focus on faculty's teaching role but encompass all aspects of professorial work. The assumption underlying these models is that new faculty need to integrate their academic roles. While integration is indeed a worthwhile goal, it is also an advanced stage of development that should be expected not in the early but in the later stages of faculty careers. Present faculty development practice, despite its laudable intentions to foster integration, may instead lead to a fragmentation of work. Faculty might be better advised to seek concentration in one area of scholarship so that they develop greater specialization before they are expected to integrate. The proposed model addresses some of the most intriguing challenges of faculty in the year 2000.

References

Basseches, M. (1984). *Dialectical thinking and adult development.* Norwood, NJ: Ablex.

Bean, J. P. (1998). Alternative models of professorial roles: New languages to reimagine faculty work. *Journal of Higher Education*, *69* (5), 496-513.

Bereiter, C., & Scardamalia, M. (1993). *Surpassing ourselves.* Chicago, IL: Open Court.

Berquist, W. H., & Phillips, S. R. (1975). Components of an effective faculty development program. *Journal of Higher Education, 46* (2), 177-211.

Bland, C. J., & Schmitz, C. C. (1990). An overview of research on faculty and institutional vitality. In H. J. Schuster & D. W. Wheeler (Eds.), *Enhancing faculty careers* (pp. 41-61). San Francisco, CA: Jossey-Bass.

Boice, R. (1992). *The new faculty member.* San Francisco, CA: Jossey-Bass.

Boyer, E. L. (1990). *Scholarship reconsidered: Priorities of the professoriate.* Princeton, NJ: The Carnegie Foundation for the Advancement of Teaching.

Braskamp, L. A., & Ory, J. C. (1994). *Assessing faculty work.* San Francisco, CA: Jossey-Bass.

Braxton, J. M. (1996). Contrasting perspectives on the relationships between teaching and research. In J. M. Braxton (Ed.), *Faculty teaching and research: Is there a conflict?* (pp. 5-14). New Directions for Institutional Research, No. 90. San Francisco, CA: Jossey-Bass.

Brew, A., & Boud, D. (1996). Preparing for new academic roles. *The International Journal for Academic Development, 1* (2), 17-26.

Calderhead, J. (1988). The development of knowledge structures in learning to teach. In J. Calderhead (Ed.), *Teachers' professional learning* (pp. 51-64). London, UK: The Falmer Press.

Candy, P. (1996). Promoting lifelong learning: Academic development and the university as a learning organization. *The International Journal of Academic Development, 1* (1), 7-20.

Centra, J. A. (1993). *Reflective faculty evaluation.* San Francisco, CA: Jossey-Bass.

Chi, M., Glaser, R., & Farr. M. (Eds.). (1988). *The nature of expertise.* Hillsdale, NJ: Erlbaum.

Clark, B. (1997). The modern integration of research activities with teaching and learning. *Journal of Higher Education, 68* (3), 241-256.

Colbeck, C. (1998). Merging in a seamless blend: How faculty integrate research and teaching. *Journal of Higher Education, 96* (6), 647-672.

Ericsson, K. A., & Smith, J. (Eds.). (1991). *Toward a general theory of expertise.* Cambridge, UK: Cambridge University Press.

Feldman, K. A. (1987). Research productivity and scholarly accomplishments of college teachers as related to their instructional effectiveness: A review and exploration. *Research in Higher Education, 26* (3), 227-298.

Gaff, J. (1975). *Toward faculty renewal.* San Francisco, CA: Jossey-Bass, CA.

Gaff, J. (1994). Faculty development: The new frontier. *Liberal Education, 80* (4), 16-21.

Garrison, D. R. (1997). Self-directed learning: Toward a comprehensive model. *Adult Education Quarterly, 48* (1), 18-33.

Glaser, R., & Chi, M. T. (1988). Overview. In M. T. Chi, R. Glaser, & M. Farr (Eds.), *The nature of expertise* (pp. xv-xxxvi). Hillsdale, NJ: Erlbaum.

Hattie, J., & Marsh, H. M. (1996). The relationship between research and teaching: A meta-analysis. *Review of Educational Research, 66*, 507-542.

Hubbard, G. L., Atkins, S., & Brinko, K. T. (1998). Supporting personal, professional, and organizational well-being. *To Improve the Academy, 17*, 135-150.

Johnston, S. (1997). Preparation for the role of teacher as part of induction into faculty life and work. In P. Cranton (Ed.), *Universal challenges in faculty work: Fresh perspectives from around the world* (pp. 31-39). New Directions for Teaching and Learning, No. 72. San Francisco, CA: Jossey-Bass.

Jung, C. G. (1971). *Psychological types.* Princeton, NJ: Princeton University Press.

King, P. M., & Kitchener, K. S. (1994). *Developing reflective judgment.* San Francisco, CA: Jossey-Bass.

Kolb, D. (1984). *Experiential learning.* Englewood Cliffs, NJ: Prentice Hall.

Kramer, D. A. (1983). Post-formal operations? A need for further conceptualizations. *Human Development, 26* (2), 91-105.

Kramer, D. A. (1989). The development of an awareness of contradiction across the lifespan and the question of postformal operations. In M. L. Commons, J. D. Sinott, F. A. Richards, & C. Armons (Eds.), *Adult development, vol. 1: Comparisons and applications of developmental models* (pp. 133-159). New York, NY: Praeger Publishing.

Kreber, C. (2000). Becoming an expert university teacher: A self-directed process. In H. Long (Ed.), *New ideas about self-directed learning.* Norman, OK: Oklahoma Research Center for Continuing Professional and Higher Education.

Labouvie-Vief, G. (1982). Dynamic development and mature autonomy: A theoretical prologue. *Human Development, 25* (3), 161-191.

Li-Ping, T., & Chamberlain, M. (1997). Attitudes towards research and teaching: Differences between administrators and faculty members. *Journal of Higher Education, 68* (2), 212-228.

Loevinger, J. (1976). *Ego development: Conceptions and theories.* San Francisco, CA: Jossey-Bass.

Perry, W. G. (1970). *Forms of intellectual and ethical development in the college years: A scheme.* Troy, MO: Holt, Rinehart, & Winston.

Rowland, S. (1996). Relationships between teaching and research. *Teaching in Higher Education, 1* (1), 7-21.

Russell, T., & Munby, H. (1991). Reframing the role of experience in developing teachers' professional knowledge. In D. Schön (Ed.), *The reflective turn* (pp. 164-188). New York, NY: Teachers College Press.

Schön, D. (1995, November/December). The new scholarship requires a new epistemology. *Change, 27* (6), 27-34.

Schuster, J. H., & Wheeler, D. W. (Eds.). (1990). *Enhancing faculty careers.* San Francisco, CA: Jossey-Bass.

Sorcinelli, M. D., & Austin, A. E. (Eds.). (1992). *Developing new and junior faculty.* New Directions for Teaching and Learning, No. 50. San Francisco, CA: Jossey-Bass.

Tennant, M., & Pogson, P. (1995). *Learning and change in the adult years.* San Francisco, CA: Jossey-Bass.

Tiberius, R., Smith, R., & Waisman, Z. (1998). Implications of the nature of expertise for teaching and faculty development. *To Improve the Academy, 17,* 123-138.

Weimer, M. (1990). *Improving college teaching.* San Francisco, CA: Jossey-Bass.

Weimer, M. (1997). Integration of teaching and research: Myth, reality, and possibility. In P. Cranton (Ed.), *Universal challenges in faculty work: Fresh perspectives from around the world* (pp. 53-62). New Directions for Teaching and Learning, No. 72. San Francisco, CA: Jossey-Bass.

Contacts:

Carolin Kreber
Adult and Higher Education
Educational Policy Studies
7-152 Education North
University of Alberta
Edmonton, AB T6G 2G5
(780) 492-7623
(780) 492-2024 (FAX)
carolin.kreber@ualberta.ca

Patricia Cranton
Psychological Type Press Inc.
One Gregory Road
Route 2, Box 199
Sneedville, TN 37869
(423) 733-2025
(423) 733-4392 (FAX)
typepress@naxs.net

Carolin Kreber has been a faculty member in the department of Educational Policy Studies at the University of Alberta since 1997. She obtained her Ph.D. in higher education from the University of Toronto. She teaches undergraduate and graduate courses on the psychology of adult learning, adult development, and instructional design. From 1993 to 1997, she worked as an educational development consultant at the Instructional Development Office at Brock University in Southern Ontario. Her present research focuses on faculty's integration of their professorial roles and the conceptualization and implementation of the scholarship of teaching in universities.

Patricia Cranton is a professor of adult education and is presently an independent consultant. She was the founding Director of the Instructional Development Office at Brock University. From 1977-1987, she was a faculty member at the University Centre for Teaching and Learning at McGill University in Montreal, where she was cross-appointed with the Department of Educational Psychology. She is the author of five books, including *Promoting and Understanding Transformative Learning* and *Professional Development as Transformative Learning,* both published with Jossey-Bass.

14

Getting Lecturers to Take Discussion Seriously

Stephen Brookfield
University of St. Thomas

Stephen Preskill
University of New Mexico

In this chapter we examine how faculty resistant to experimenting with discussion methods can be encouraged to take them seriously. We begin by acknowledging and addressing publicly the objections to using discussion most frequently raised by skeptical faculty. We then turn to proposing what we believe are the most common reasons why attempts to use discussion sometimes fail: that teachers have unrealistic expectations of the method, that students are unprepared, that reward systems in the classroom are askew, and that teachers have not modeled their own participation in, and commitment to, discussion methods. For each of these reasons we suggest a number of responses and strategies.

One of the most fervently cherished hopes of POD members, indeed of faculty developers everywhere, is that of persuading faculty to drop their instinctive reliance on didactic lecturing and turn instead towards active, participatory learning approaches. Central to the success of this effort is getting uninterested faculty to take the discussion method seriously. In this paper we want to explore ways this effort might be accomplished through three complementary strategies: (1) acknowledging and addressing publicly the objections to using discussion most frequently raised by skeptical faculty; (2) warning faculty about the most common reasons why attempted discussions sometimes fail (thereby helping them set up discussions that might be successful); and (3) suggesting some things faculty can do before discussion begins that increase the likelihood of avoiding student silence and that increase faculty's confidence that their use of the method can be successful.

Acknowledging and Addressing Common Objections to Discussion

Faculty developers like the two of us usually have an activist bent that impels them to light a fire under colleagues that they are often too quick to stereotype as recalcitrant Neanderthals clinging to outmoded pedagogies. Consequently, when quite legitimate objections are raised by faculty regarding the extent to which the discussion method is realistic or appropriate in a particular situation, faculty developers (ourselves included) can easily fail to address them. We shake our heads sadly and conclude that the objections raised by colleagues demonstrate nothing so much as their evident reluctance to give up power and authority in their classrooms. However, an important early conversation faculty developers need to have with colleagues is one in which legitimate objections to discussion can be acknowledged and addressed. In our experience, the two objections examined below are those that are most frequently raised.

1) Spending time in discussion will allow me less time to cover necessary content through lectures. The concern about having insufficient time to cover content is felt by teachers who believe that the material they want students to learn is too important to be left to chance. If they lecture, so their argument goes, at least this ensures that the material is aired in students' presence.

We share this same concern. We acknowledge that there are times when lecturing is an efficient way of sketching out the intellectual topography of an area of knowledge for students. In a lecture you can present contrasting schools of thought, group a confusing variety of opinions into general interpretive categories, model intellectual approaches you want your students to emulate, and nurture enthusiasm for a topic by demonstrating your own passionate interest and animated engagement in learning. As Freire acknowledged, "The questions is not banking lectures or no lectures . . . the question is the content and dynamism of the lecture, the approach to the object to be known. Does it critically re-orient students to society? Does it animate their critical thinking or not?" (Shor & Freire, 1987, p. 40).

We have found that in building an argument as to why discussions should be interspersed with lectures (we would never advocate that the one replace the other), it is best to concentrate on the theme of engaging and animating students' attention. We stress that we want our students to engage seriously with ideas and information we think important enough for us to lecture about. We argue that it is risky to expect lectures on their own to do this. We point out that building connections—personal and intellectual—is at the heart of discussion. Ideas that seems disconnected when heard in a lecture come alive when explored in speech. We stress that there is no point in covering content for content's sake—the point is to cover content in a way that ensures that students engage with it. It is because we take content so seriously, and we want students to understand certain key ideas accurately and thoroughly, that we feel discussion is indispensable.

One of the traps that advocates of discussion methods often fall into is that of setting up a false dichotomy between lecturing and discussion. As POD members and other skilled faculty developers know, this pedagogic bifurcation is too simplistic. Lectures are not, in and of themselves, oppressive and authoritarian. And lecturers are not, by definition, demagogues. Similarly, discussions are not, in and of themselves, liberating and spontaneous. And discussion leaders are not, by definition, democratic. We have both been participants in discussion sessions where leaders manipulate the group to reach certain predefined conclusions (and we have no doubt done this ourselves). Through their power to control the flow of talk, to summarize and reframe students' comments, and to respond favorably to some contributions and unfavorably to others, discussion leaders can act in extremely authoritarian ways.

Instead of reducing questions of pedagogic method to a simplistic dichotomy—discussion good, lecture bad—we see these two methods as symbiotic. Again, we quote Paulo Freire's observation that "a liberating teacher will illuminate reality even if he or she lectures" (Shor and Freire, 1987, p. 40). Both of us use lectures, simulations, independent study, video, intensive reading, and any other method that works to engage students in learning. For example, both of us love to lecture, and both of us believe that lecturing is often necessary to introduce difficult ideas and to model critical inquiry. Therefore, we have no difficulty in honoring our colleagues' commitment to, and belief in, lecturing. But we do believe that discussion can serve many important purposes and that teachers sometimes abandon discussion too early simply for lack of some creative ideas for implementation.

2) Discussion is fine for "soft" subjects like the humanities and social sciences where disagreement and divergence is possible, even endemic, to the content. But it has no place in "hard" subjects like mathematics, statistics, and the natural sciences. We agree that discussion should be used only when appropriate. In the teaching of unambiguous factual information (for example the population of Baltimore in 1850, the chemical composition of sodium chloride, or Boyle's law) or the inculcation of specific skills (how to open email software or how to give an injection) there seems to be little scope for using the discussion method. However, things are not always as simple as they seem. The exact figure given for Baltimore's 1850 population is actually a human construct, dependent on the data gathering techniques and modes of classification statisticians decide to use, as well as on the learned behaviors of the data gatherers themselves. The hypothetico-deductive method that lies at the heart of intellectual inquiry in the natural sciences is actually a human system of thought developed at a particular moment and place by a particular person (Francis Bacon) and refined over time by philosophical advances in the logic of the scientific method (for example, Karl Popper's principle of falsifiability). What seem to be standardized, objective, and unambiguous skills of computer usage or nursing care are actually protocols developed by particular groups and individuals. Which program or protocol becomes accepted as professionally dominant, as representing commonsense or the norm, depends on which group has the power to promote their way of interpreting good practice over other contenders.

We would argue there is no knowledge that is unambiguous or reified (that is, that exists in a dimension beyond human intervention). The seemingly immutable laws of physics are always applied within a certain range, and the boundaries of that range shift according to research and according to who has the power to define standards for acceptable scientific inquiry. It is also possible to organize discussion around the analysis and interpretation of data from an experiment, allowing students to generate competing hypotheses and discuss how these might be tested. Or, students could discuss the merits of different approaches that they could take toward investigating a mathematical or natural sciences problem.

However, we would also acknowledge that there are times when discussion is not the best way to help students learn something. When we attend workshops to learn how to use the World Wide Web, we don't want to spend the first hour problematizing computer technology. Rather than consider how access to this technology is stratified by class, gender, and race, and how it reproduces existing economic inequities, we want to know which search engine to use. Instead of questioning whether or not this technology privatizes life and thus prevents new social movements that challenge the status quo from forming, we want to know which button to press to display graphics. Of course, we would argue that the best teachers start with learners' needs (such as which search engine to use and which button to press) and then nudge students to question the social organization of the very technology they are using.

We would also point to the example of McMaster University in Hamilton, Ontario, where medical students spend three years working in small groups and where Schools of Nursing and Rehabilitation Science organize their whole curriculum around the exploration of clinical cases, problems, and dilemmas in small groups. Ferrier, Marrin, and Seidman (1988) report that, according to their supervisors, graduates of the program perform better in their first years of practice than graduates from other universities. The first attempt pass rate of McMaster students when taking the exams of the Royal College of Physicians and Surgeons of Canada is higher than the national average. Palmer (1998) visited an unnamed large research university where medical students (under the guidance of a mentor) work in small circles to diagnose and treat real patients. In the words of the Medical School dean, "not only did the test scores not decline, but they actually started going up, and during the time we have been teaching this way, they have continued, slowly, to rise. In this approach to medical education, our students not only become more caring but also seem to be getting smarter, faster" (p. 127).

Acknowledging That Discussions Can Fail and Examining Why This Happens

We need to recognize that teachers new to discussion methods can easily lose heart at their first experiments with the method. Given the complexity of the process this is hardly surprising. It would be almost miraculous if one's early attempts at teaching through discussion were not accompanied by moments of failure and the accompanying temptation to return to tried and trusted methods such as lecturing. In this section we want to examine the most common reasons why teachers jump to the mistaken conclusion that their experiments with discussion are failing. A conversation on these issues with teachers can help them prepare for discussion with a grounded sense of its possibilities.

Teachers' Unrealistic Expectations

One reason teachers feel their discussion sessions are not working is because they have hopelessly inflated images of what a "successful" discussion looks like. In these visions of "good" discussion there is little silence in the room. What conversation takes place focuses only on relevant issues with a suitably sophisticated level of discourse. Talk flows scintillatingly and seamlessly from topic to topic. Everyone listens attentively and respectfully to everyone else's contributions. People make their comments in a way that is informed, thoughtful, insightful, and unfailingly courteous. Wildean epigrams dart impishly across the room interspersed with haiku of great profundity. The Algonquin roundtable or a Bloomsbury dinner party begin to pale in comparison to our febrile imaginings.

The reality is that discussions like this rarely, if ever, happen. Learning to participate in discussion is a lifelong project and most of us go to our graves feeling we still have a lot to learn. Compounding the problem is the fact that two of the most common models of public discourse we have available to us—political debate and TV or radio talk shows—foster an image of conversation as loud, dichotomous, oppositional, and inflammatory. Students who are introverts, or those who need time for reflective analysis, may find the pace and tone of conversation intimidating. If students have suffered public humiliation in previous discussions, or if teachers mandate participation with no case being built as to why students should take the process seriously, then discussion will not work. If students don't know what the teacher's image of a good discussion looks like, or if teachers haven't first modeled their participation in critical, respectful discussions in front of students, then teachers can't blame students for not acting the way they are supposed to.

As teachers we need to justify to students why we believe so strongly in using discussion. Many students will likely have had experiences in classes where teachers manipulated the discussion's outcome and even humiliated their students. Being clear about what we hope to achieve through discussion helps combat students' understandable cynicism and raises our chances of drawing them into conversation. We can clarify our expectations and purposes in a number of ways. For example, a strong statement as to why discussion will be used so much in class can be inserted into the syllabus. One of us includes in his course syllabus a section titled What You Need to Know About this Course. This section is a kind of truth in advertising statement that makes explicit the non-negotiable elements of the course (see Appendix 1).

You can also involve former students in communicating your expectations and purposes to new students. We like to use panels of former students as contributors to the first or second class. These former students come to class and talk about their previous experiences in the course. They are asked to pass on to new students whatever advice they have as alumni on how to survive and flourish in the class. Frequently they end up making the case for discussion that you would have made and elaborating on the benefits that you would have stressed. But their testimony is far more powerful. If former students talk about the value of discussion, their comments have far more credibility in the eyes of new students than anything that you as the teacher could say or do.

A variant on this approach is the "letter to successors" technique. In this exercise, current students are asked to compose a letter that will be sent to new students who are entering the same course the next time it is offered. The letter puts into print the departing students' insights about how to survive the experience. After these letters have been written privately, students form small discussion groups to read each other's letters. Group members look for common themes that are then reported back in a whole class plenary session. Because responses are given by a group reporter, anonymity is preserved, and no one is required to say anything about a particular concern of theirs unless they wish to do so. If one or more of these letters contain passages that urge skeptical students to prepare for discussions and to take them seriously, then we try to obtain permission from the students concerned to let us reproduce these comments in the syllabus for the next version of the course.

Students Are Unprepared

At the beginning of a course teachers often issue unilateral declarations to the effect that "in this class we're going to use discussion." They do this in the confident belief that students will sigh in appreciative relief that finally they have met a teacher who believes in active learning and democratic process.

In reality many students are suspicious, and quite rightly so, of these kinds of unilateral pedagogic fiats. Sometimes they sense the teacher has a covert agenda for the discussion that the students are supposed to guess. Sometimes students just fear looking stupid in front of their peers because they think they don't know enough about something to be able to discuss it intelligently. Often they have no idea what kinds of contributions the teacher values. When discussion becomes a game in which students try to guess what kinds of comments will earn the teacher's approval, the conversation is stilted and hesitant. What looks on the surface like a participatory, democratic experience only serves to reinforce the existing power dynamic. Preparing students for the moral culture and intellectual arena discussion represents is, therefore, crucial to discussion's success. This is where ground rules can help.

Students learn quickly how to gain the teacher's attention in a discussion. Get in quickly and say something, anything, so that your participation is noted and logged. In students' minds participation becomes equated with speaking, and not saying anything becomes an indication of one's mental inertia or idiocy. Students' perceptions in this regard are often pretty accurate. Teachers often have an implicit sense that the "best" kinds of discussions are those in which everyone speaks for roughly the same amount of time, with no awkward silences. For students, the pressure they feel to "participate," to say something intelligent, means they devote a great deal of energy to thinking of a point, silently rehearsing what they will say and how they will say it, and then interjecting when they've got their contribution word perfect. The purpose of this careful rehearsal is to make them look smart. Of course, in a perverse, catch-22 manner, by the time they intervene with their perfectly rehearsed contribution the discussion will probably have moved on so they end up feeling ridiculous anyway.

Students know too that discussion groups can quickly become emotional battlegrounds, arenas in which only the strongest egos survive relatively intact. We've all been in discussion groups where a small minority of participants accounted for the greater part of the conversation. We've all seen one forceful individual's personality shut down any meaningful discourse. We've all seen people disagree with another's point in a way that seems personally abusive. And we've all watched while factors of race, gender, and class played themselves out in our discussion groups, reproducing the unequal patterns of communication found in the wider society.

Without clearly defined ground rules that try to ensure an equal chance for everyone to participate, there is little hedge against the dominant few setting the agenda and claiming the air space. Without ground rules that work to help people understand how disagreement can be respectfully expressed, attempts at critical discussion soon descend into abuse or disengagement. Without ground rules that stress how periods of silence are as integral to conversational rhythms as is the most garrulous speech, students think that good discussion participation involves making as many comments as they can fit into the time available.

Evolving Ground Rules for Discussions

As we argue above, faculty skeptical of discussion are likely to enter into it in a tentative or half-hearted manner. Not surprisingly, a skepticism concerning the possibility of the method's success usually turns into a self-fulfilling prophecy. Students sense the instructor's uncertainty and lack of commitment and, in the absence of a clear signal from the instructor concerning the importance of participation, decide that it's not worth the risk or effort to venture into speech. One way to reduce the chances that a cautious approach by instructors will lead to student silence is for teachers to begin by involving the class in setting ground rules for discourse. Rules of conduct and codes of behavior play a crucial role in determining whether or not students take discussion seriously. Although we emphasize that discussions should be completely open regarding the possible directions the conversation could take, and although we're skeptical about the concept of guided discussion, this doesn't mean we're opposed to structuring the process of democratic conversation. There is no contradiction between guiding the *ways* in which people talk to each other but refusing the guide *what* they talk about. Our experience is that when students know that there are fair and democratic ground rules that frame how people speak, there is a much better chance that they will get involved.

We advocate to faculty ready to consider experimenting with discussion that they spend some time at the start of a discussion-based course talking with students about the ground rules for conversation that they would like to see in operation. How would students like to be addressed by their peers? What are students' feelings about good manners, respect, or courtesy in discussion and what do these things look like? Do they want discussions to be nothing but talk, or would they like some periods of silence? How do students want to indicate that they're ready to speak? Should we call on people by a show of hands, deciding on the order of contributions by the order in which people raise their hands? Or, should we allow the same few people to have two or three contributions in short order if this leads to a deeper analysis of a particular theme or idea? Before bringing a new person into a discussion should the leader check whether the comment applies to the current theme or if it instead takes the discussion on a new track? How does the group feel about the leader calling directly on individuals to speak (because these students are known to possess particular knowledge or experience that's relevant to the theme being discussed) even if they have not indicated that they wish to do so? One way faculty can generate ground rules is to work from students' most vivid recollections of their experiences as discussion participants. For a description of such an approach, see Appendix 2.

The role of the teacher in this exercise is not to suggest images of how they think good discussants behave. That's the business of group members. However, when it comes to translating these images into specific rules of conduct, students do need some help. If the class agrees that good discussions involve lots of people talking, then teachers should work with them to suggest ways to make this more likely. They could suggest some specific possibilities, such as putting a time limit on individual contributions or regularly calling for a circle of voices in which each person in turn is given the floor.

Another approach to evolving ground rules is to ask participants to focus on the "golden rule"; that is, ask them how they would like to be addressed in a discussion and use their responses to frame a code of conduct for how they will speak to others. Again, the instructor's role is to help students move from general declarations such as "I want people to listen carefully to what I'm saying" to specific behaviors (such as suggesting a weekly, circular-response discussion period in which students take turns listening carefully, paraphrasing, and then responding to each other's contributions).

In their work on cooperative learning, Johnson, Johnson, and Smith (1991) emphasize that we cannot assume that students possess the social and communicative skills necessary for collaboration—these need to be taught. The T-Chart they propose is a technique that can be adapted well to help students develop ground rules for discussion. The characteristic of discussion that students desire is written on the top of a large piece of newsprint. Imagine that students say they want their discussions to be respectful. Under the heading "Respectful," the instructor divides the sheet in two, labeling one side "Sounds Like" and the other side "Looks Like." Students and the instructor then suggest items that would fall under each column so that after a few minutes a list is available of how students think respectful discussions look and sound.

Finally, teachers can use videos of discussion vignettes as a useful way to focus students' attention on how they want their discussions to look. The instructions for such an exercise that teachers might give to students can be found in Appendix 3, along with a list of ground rules our students have generated in the past.

Reward Systems Are Askew

Asking students to invest time and energy in discussion and then grading them on how well they do on mid-terms and finals is akin to telling faculty that teaching is important and then giving tenure only to those with good publishing records. In both situations people know what the real rules of the game are and what behaviors get rewarded. If students know that their final grade depends on the quality of their written work in term papers or examinations, then that is where they're going to put their effort.

If teachers are going to ask students to take discussion activities seriously, they need to underscore their intentions by adjusting the rewards system for the course. There need to be clear statements at the outset of the course—both verbally and in the syllabus—of the ways in which serious discussion participation will be expected, recognized, and affirmed. This is why the establishment of unequivocal criteria for participation is so important. Bland, generalized declarations that students will be graded partly on their "participation" ignores the subtleties and complications of race, class, gender, and personality and serves chiefly to induce panic and suspicion in those who don't feel comfortable in the culture of academe. Unfortunately, the situation described by Bean and Peterson (1998) is typical. In studying core curriculum syllabi at their university they note that "93% of courses included class participation as a component of course grades. Our informal discussions with professors, however, suggest that most professors determine participation grades impressionistically, using class participation largely as a fudge factor in computing final course grades" (p. 33).

One problem in assessing discussion is that most evaluative systems work in a positivist way. First, an ideal type or exemplar of how an educational process should look is established. The standard of what counts as a proper demonstration of the process is usually determined by polling experts in the field and then translating theoretical tenets into practical terms. Then, whether or not an activity is judged to be done well or poorly is determined by how closely it reproduces these exemplary characteristics. But a discussion cannot be judged by how closely it approximates a decontextualized ideal. Discussions are like marriages—no two are alike and no one on the outside can ever really understand what's happening inside them. Because discussions are always contextual—always shaped by the cultural backgrounds, social classes, genders, experiences, and personalities of their participants—they can only be evaluated from the inside. Therefore, in regard to the evaluation of discussion we generally advocate that teachers work from students' own testimony regarding the nature of their discussion experience.

However, we do acknowledge that even the most phenomenologically inclined teachers have to survive in a system that often puts them through positivist paces. Few of us have the luxury of rejecting standardized evaluative formats, no matter how misconceived we might judge them to be. So we need to use an evaluative approach that at least gives the appearance of being grounded in clear and unequivocal criteria. One approach is to assess how well students have observed the rules of conduct that they have evolved to govern the discussion process. If the class has created guidelines for democratic discussion in which several specific behaviors are proposed, then evaluating students' participation becomes a matter of working with them to assess how often these were exhibited. Students could keep a weekly audit of their participation in class discussions and then present a summary and analysis of their entries in an end-of-semester learning portfolio. See Appendix 4 for an example of a discussion audit used in a course in which getting students to think critically was a prime objective.

Teachers Have Not Modeled Effective Participation in Discussion
One of the mistakes we have both made is to walk into a classroom on the first day of a new course, announce to students that we believe in discussion, and tell them why the experience will be good for them. Then we assign topics to students and put them into small discussion groups. The trouble with this scenario is that it omits a crucial element. We have neglected to model in front of the students an engagement in the very activity—participating in group discussion with peers—we are urging on them. As teachers we have to earn the right to ask students to engage seriously in discussion by first modeling our own serious commitment to it. If we want students to believe us when we say discussion is good for them, we have to show them how it's good for us too. So, in any course in which teachers are intending to use discussion methods it's a good idea for them to invite a group of colleagues into the classroom at an early stage in the course. They can then hold a discussion about some aspect of the course's content in which they try to show the kinds of behaviors they'd like students to exhibit in their own subsequent discussions.

As hooks (1994, p. 21) forcefully writes: "in my classrooms, I do not expect students to take any risks that I would not take, to share in any way that I would not share . . . it is often productive if professors take the first risk, linking confessional narratives to academic discussions so as to show how experience can illuminate and enhance our understanding of academic material." If instructors are prepared to take this risky, but essential, step of modeling discussion participation in front of their learners, we give some specific guidance. We ask that they make sure to introduce new perspectives by showing how these have been prompted by, or are intended to illuminate, earlier contributions from others. If possible we tell them to clarify in the midst of the discussion how others' comments are helpful in getting them to recognize, and examine critically, some familiar assumptions they hold. We suggest they thank colleagues for suggesting radically new interpretations or perspectives they had not previously considered. But they should also feel free to reject these and show that they don't feel duty bound to change their views because of colleagues' comments. We want to show students that it is quite permissible to be the only one holding a dissenting view in a discussion and that groups should avoid trying to convert the lone holdout to majority opinion. We also stress that teachers don't finish by giving a set of conclusions. Instead, they should finish by listing all the unresolved issues and areas for future inquiry that the discussion has prompted.

This modeling can also be used to show students that silence is a necessary and desirable part of conversation. If one colleague asks another a question that she or he has no ready response for, the person asked should feel comfortable saying, "I'm not sure, I'll need a minute or two to think about that" and then take that time before responding. During this period everyone else waits silently. It's been interesting for us to observe how shocked and uncomfortable students are when they see their teachers just sitting quietly as a group while one of us thinks about what we want to say next.

Finally, we urge that faculty try to avoid talking in a rarefied, overly academic manner. They should use specialized terminology when they feel it's warranted but try to mix in plenty of colloquial speech and familiar metaphors. We tell them to be comfortable starting a sentence, then hesitating in mid-sentence, stumbling to find the right words to express their meaning, starting the sentence again, pausing, re-grouping, and then finishing by letting their words trail off. Better to do this than to strive to make ringing, grammatically impeccable, eloquent, and unequivocal declarations of truth. Our concern is that faculty avoid putting on a beautifully articulated, seamless, exemplary display of dazzlingly erudite, high status, academic discourse. We want students to see that hesitations, pauses, and colloquial language are all a normal and valued part of discussion. If we model discussion participation for students, the last thing we want to do is act as if we're characters in a play by Noel Coward or Tom Stoppard.

Although we're advocating modeling the discussion process with colleagues, we want to admit that we have done this far less than we would like. Partly this is because of time. We often worry that we've sacrificed too much time working on process that should be spent studying content. To add a role play of discussion to a course already full of participatory learning activities can seem like overkill. But mostly our problem is that it's difficult to convince colleagues that it's worth their while to spend time modeling the discussion process with us. At the very least we can offer to return the favor by helping out our colleagues in whatever way they think is useful.

Conclusion

One final thought. In our experience, there is no point in proselytizing discussion or trying to convert skeptics into becoming enthusiastic advocates for discussion. Teachers who resolutely dismiss discussion as time-wasting, touchy-feely, experiential mush usually only come to take it seriously when they are so dissatisfied with what they're doing that they'll try something new, or when they are irresistibly intrigued by the sense of joyful engagement they witness in their own colleagues' experiments with the method. But we do think there is a category of college teachers out there who are willing to contemplate introducing discussion activities into their classrooms provided they are reassured that this doesn't mean they have to abandon lecturing entirely and provided a good case is built as to the benefits of the method.

References

Bean, J. C., & Peterson, D. (1998). Grading classroom participation. In R. S. Anderson & B. W. Speck (Eds.), *Changing the way we grade student performance: Classroom assessment and the new learning paradigm* (pp. 33-40). New Directions for Teaching and Learning, No. 74. San Francisco, CA: Jossey-Bass.

Ferrier, B., Marrin, M., & Seidman, J. (1998). Student autonomy in learning medicine: Some participants' experiences. In D. Boud (Ed.), *Developing student autonomy in learning*. New York, NY: Nichols Publishing.

hooks, b. (1994). *Teaching to transgress: Education as the practice of freedom*. New York, NY: Routledge.

Johnson, D. W., Johnson, R. T., & Smith, K. (1991). *Active learning: Cooperation in the college classroom*. Edina, MN: Interaction Book Company.

Palmer, P. (1993). *To know as we are known*. San Francisco, CA: Harper Collins.

Palmer, P. (1998). *The courage to teach: Exploring the inner landscape of a teacher's life*. San Francisco, CA: Jossey-Bass.

Shor, I., & Freire, P. (1987). *A pedagogy for liberation: Dialogues on transforming education*. South Hadley, MA: Bergin and Garvey.

Contacts:

Stephen Brookfield
Mail #MOH 217
University of St. Thomas
1000 La Salle Avenue
Minneapolis, MN 55403-2009
(651) 962-4982 or (651) 227-6904
(651) 227 6904 (FAX)
sdbrookfield@stthomas.edu

Stephen Preskill
College of Education
University of New Mexico
Albuquerque, NM 87131
(505) 277-7784
(505) 277-5553 (FAX)
preskill@unm.edu

Stephen Brookfield is Distinguished Professor at the University of St. Thomas in St. Paul, Minnesota. He is a three-time winner of the World Award for Literature in Adult Education and holds an honorary doctor of letters degree from the University System of New Hampshire for his contributions to understanding adult learning.

Stephen Preskill is Associate Professor of Education and Director of the Division of Educational Leadership and Organizational Learning in the College of Education, University of New Mexico. Together with Stephen Brookfield he is the co-author of *Discussion as a Way of Teaching: Tools and Techniques for Democratic Classrooms* (San Francisco, CA: Jossey-Bass, 1999).

APPENDIX 14.1

What You Need to Know About This Course

As a student, I very much appreciate the chance to make informed decisions about the courses I take. I want to know who the educator is, what her assumptions are, and what she stands for before I make a commitment to spend my time, money, and energy attending the class. So, let me tell you some things about me, and how I work as an educator, that will allow you to make an informed decision as to whether or not you wish to be involved in this course.

I have framed this course on the following assumptions:

1. That participating in discussion brings with it the following benefits:

    - It helps students explore a diversity of perspectives
    - It increases students awareness of, and tolerance for, ambiguity or complexity
    - It helps students recognize and investigate their assumptions
    - It encourages attentive, respectful listening
    - It develops new appreciation for continuing differences
    - It increases intellectual ability
    - It helps students become connected to a topic
    - It shows respect for students' voices and experiences
    - It helps students learn the processes and habits of democratic discourse
    - It affirms students as co-creators of knowledge
    - It develops the capacity for the clear communication of ideas and meaning
    - It develops habits of collaborative learning
    - It increases breadth and makes students more empathetic
    - It helps students develop skills of synthesis and integration
    - It leads to transformation.

2. That students attending will have experiences that they can reflect on and analyze in discussion.
3. That the course will focus on the analysis of students' experiences and ideas as much as on analysis of academic theories.
4. That the chief, regular class activity will be a small group discussion of experiences and ideas.

5. That I, as teacher, have a dual role as catalyst to your critical conversation and as a model of democratic talk.

So, please take note of the following product warnings!

- If you don't feel comfortable talking with others about yourself and your experiences in small groups, you should probably drop this course a.s.a.p.
- If you don't feel comfortable with small group discussion—you think it's a touchy-feely waste of valuable time—you should probably drop this course a.s.a.p.
- If you are not prepared to analyze critically your own and other people's experiences, you probably should drop this course a.s.a.p.

APPENDIX 14.2

Generating Ground Rules for Discussion

As a first step in setting up this discussion group, I suggest that we spend some time trying to create ground rules for our participation. Ground rules are the rules we follow to ensure that the discussion is a useful, respectful, and worthwhile experience for everyone. To help us decide on some rules I would like each of you to do the following:

1. Think of the best group discussions you've ever been involved in. What things happened that made these conversations so satisfying? Make a few notes on this by yourself.
2. Think of the worst group discussions you've ever been involved in. What things happened that made these conversation so unsatisfactory? Made a few notes on this by yourself.
3. Now form a group with 3 other people. Take turns in talking about what made discussion groups work well for you. Listen for common themes, shared experiences, and features of conversation that a majority of you would like to see present in this course.
4. Take turns in talking about what made discussion group work awful for you. Listen for common themes, shared experiences, and features of group conversation that a majority of you would like to see avoided in this course.
5. For each of the agreed-upon characteristics of good discussion, try to suggest three things a group could do to ensure that these characteristics are present. Be as specific and concrete as you can. For example, if you feel good conversation is developmental, with later themes building on and referring back to earlier ones, then you could propose a rule that every new comment made by a participant is prefaced with an explanation as to how it relates to an earlier comment.
6. For each of the agreed-upon characteristics of bad discussion, try to suggest three things a group could do to ensure that these characteristics are avoided. Be as specific and concrete as you can. For example, if you feel that bad conversation happens when one person's voice dominates, then you could propose a rule whereby once someone has spoken they are not allowed to make a second comment until at least three other people have spoken (unless another group member explicitly invites the participant to say something else).
7. Try to finish this exercise by drafting a charter for discussion that comprises the specific, agreed-upon ground rules. We will make each group's rules public and see if we can develop a charter for discussion to guide us in the coming weeks.

APPENDIX 14.3

Video Vignettes of Discussion

You're going to see two 5-minute excerpts of different discussions. Please watch for the kinds of comments, contributions, and actions that you think are good and bad discussion behaviors. Note these down by yourself. Don't discuss your reactions with others at this stage. You might find it helpful to watch the video with the following questions in mind.

1. In your view, which participants made the best, most helpful, or most useful contributions to the discussion? Why were these contributions so worthwhile?
2. In your view, which participants made the worst, least helpful, or least useful contributions to the discussion? Why were these contributions so irrelevant or unproductive?
3. What changes would you introduce to improve either of these discussions?

Now, compare your responses with the reactions of others in your group. Look particularly for areas of agreement. Based on these, could you suggest any guidelines that would ensure that helpful discussion behaviors are encouraged?

When we reconvene we will see if your notes can help us decide on the discussion guidelines we want to follow in this course.

The following are some examples of ground rules generated by different groups with whom we have worked.

- Faculty are not to call on students by name to speak, though students may call upon each other.
- Students designate an umpire for each discussion to ensure rules for respectful discourse are followed.
- Students are not to interrupt each other.
- Students are to show their desire to intervene in a conversation by raising their hands and the umpire or facilitator will keep track of the order.
- Students do not have to raise their hands to intervene—just jump in when they're ready.
- To build connections and show appreciation we must strive to preface our comments with a declaration of how it builds on, adds to, contradicts, or departs from an earlier contribution.

- In deciding who gets to speak next, the chair, umpire, or facilitator always gives preference to those who wish to speak but have not yet spoken.
- Every 15 minutes or so we are to pause for a reflective interlude.
- Every 15 minutes or so we are to run a circle of voices in which all those who have not spoken in the previous period have the floor if they wish to say something.

APPENDIX 14.4

Discussion Audit Instructions

Please write down anything that occurs to you about your contributions to, and learning within, the discussions we've had in class this week. If you want, you can record your thoughts in a free-flowing way. For those of you who like more structure, it might be helpful to consider the following questions. Don't feel you have to answer every one, or even any of them—they're just here to help your reflections.

- List the assumptions that you held about the topic of the discussions this week that were uncovered or clarified for you.
- Of all these assumptions, which did you feel were accurate and valid? Try to write down what was said during the discussion that confirmed the accuracy of your assumptions.
- Of all these assumptions, which did you feel were most challenged by the discussion? Try to write down what was said during the discussion that challenged the accuracy of your assumptions.
- What different perspectives on the topics were suggested for you by our discussions?
- What's the most important learning you've taken from this week's discussions?
- What's the most pressing question(s) you're left with about the topic as a result of this week's discussions?
- In what ways did you, and other group members, observe and implement the class rules for discussion?
- In what ways did you, and other group members, contradict the class rules for discussion?
- After your experience this week, which of these class rules should be amended or abandoned? And what new rules would you like to propose?

Midway through the semester, and then again at the end, you will be asked to read what you've written each week about your discussion experiences. You will be expected to prepare a summary in which you identify patterns, similarities, contradictions, discrepancies, and surprises. This summary (not individual weekly entries) will be a part of your learning portfolio for the course.

An option that is less time consuming than the audit is to ask students to keep a short discussion log. A discussion log is a set of brief responses to three questions.

1. What do you know as a result of participating in this discussion that you didn't know this time last week?
2. What can you do as a result of participating in this discussion that you couldn't do this time last week?
3. What could you teach someone as a result of participating in this discussion that you couldn't teach them this time last week?

The information in this log can then be used in two possible ways. Students can submit their responses to you once a week and you can start the next class by summarizing their responses. Used this way it is crucial that students know their anonymity is assured. No names are allowed on the logs that students submit. Or, taking a more longitudinal approach, students can use these logs as primary data for a report on their discussion learning that they will include in their portfolios.

15

"It's Hard Work!": Faculty Development in a Program for First-Year Students

Martha L. A. Stassen
University of Massachusetts, Amherst

Academic programs designed specifically for first-year students provide an important opportunity for faculty growth. This chapter contributes to the limited literature on this topic through a qualitative analysis of interviews with faculty members who taught in an experimental living-learning community for first-year students at a Research I Public University. The analysis suggests at least four dimensions of faculty growth as a result of their involvement in first-year programs. In addition to outlining the types of impact this experience has on the faculty involved, the article suggests the implications of these findings for faculty development.

Introduction

In an effort to improve the experience of their undergraduates, many colleges and universities are developing special living-learning communities or other focused academic experiences to help first-year students adjust to college life. There is a growing literature on the benefits of these types of programs for improving student academic and social integration and, ultimately, student retention (Upcraft, Gardner, & Associates, 1989). When these programs include seminars or other types of academic experiences taught by faculty, increased opportunities for student-faculty contact also exist.

Except for these opportunities for increased faculty-student contact, little is known about the effect of first-year programs on the faculty members who teach in them. The literature on faculty involvement in these programs focuses almost exclusively on the "how-to's" of engaging and preparing faculty for their involvement (Evenbeck, Jackson, & McGrew, 1999; Gordon, 1989). Much less is known, or at least documented, about the effect these experiences have on the instructor. There are some impressionistic pieces which assert that participation has a positive effect on faculty. For example, in her article "A President's Perspective on the Value of Freshman Seminars," Siegel (1989) suggests that participation in her college's freshman seminar program improved faculty morale, made it possible for faculty to enjoy new mentoring relationships with students, and provided a new opportunity for faculty collegiality. As she puts it, "I believe the faculty came to enjoy and take pride in a new dimension of their professional role" (p. 255). More recently, Evenbeck et al. (1999) suggest that involvement in first-year learning communities leads faculty to pedagogical improvements and increased awareness of university resources. However, no direct evidence to support these conclusions is provided.

Information drawn directly from the faculty themselves, and analyzed in a systematic manner, is hard to find. In a survey of faculty who taught in a freshmen seminar at a mid-sized university, almost three-quarters of the faculty reported they had learned more about freshmen, had used new pedagogical techniques, and tried these techniques in their other courses as a result of the seminar experience (Barefoot, 1993). Others have found that participation in learning communities contributes to faculty vitality and renewal (Matthews, Smith, McGregor, & Gebelnick, 1997). And, in a study of faculty involvement in another learning-centered innovation (assessment), faculty report increased knowledge of students' abilities and improved collegiality around teaching (Sutherland & Guffey, 1997). While these studies provide some initial insights into how involvement in first-year programs affects faculty, the evidence provided in this literature is limited. Faculty members' own reflections on the issue are, for the most part, not provided.

This chapter is designed to contribute to this literature by analyzing faculty members' reflections on teaching in a pilot living-learning community for first-semester students at a Research I Public University. In addition to outlining the types of impact this experience had on the faculty involved, this paper suggests the implications of these findings for faculty development.

The First-Year Seminar

In 1996, a new first-year living-learning program (called the "Patterson Program" for the residence hall in which it is housed) was developed to improve retention of students without declared majors. The program was designed to help these traditional college-age, first-year students adjust to the university and to socialize them into the demands of college-level work.

In addition to assigning these students to the same residential hall and providing on-site services specific to their needs, a central feature of this program is a three-credit seminar designed to introduce them to methods of inquiry in a variety of academic disciplines. The seminar begins with an overview of university culture and then exposes the students to inquiry in the physical/natural sciences, social sciences, and the humanities. One of the underlying purposes of the course is to help students develop a clearer understanding of the similarities and differences across disciplines and, as a result, clarify their academic interests. The seminar is taught in small sections of 20-24 students, primarily by tenured faculty. These instructors are recruited based on their interest in the program, their reputations as teachers, and their personal relationships with seminar organizers. All of them have substantial teaching experience, although their primary type of teaching experience (upper-level vs. first-year students, large classes vs. small) varies. They are provided with a stipend to be used for travel and other discretionary needs. In the first two years, 10 full-time faculty participated. It should be noted that because the program requires faculty members to teach a course outside of their own disciplines and presents a number of pedagogical challenges to be discussed later, recruitment of faculty to teach in the program has not been easy. This is a challenge documented by others as well (see, for example, Evenbeck et al., 1999).

The path toward successfully implementing the seminar has not been smooth. Faculty did not share a common understanding of the purpose of the seminar from the start, and the lack of consistency across sections has been an ongoing source of confusion to students. In addition, various elements of the course, as well as characteristics of the students themselves, have created a host of challenges for faculty. Finally, the original design was for faculty to work together in teams, meeting on a regular basis to develop and adapt the syllabus and course objectives while sharing teaching strategies with each other. However, this has not always occurred in the systematic manner originally intended.

Students' responses to the course, collected as a part of the larger program evaluation, also show mixed results. Survey data suggest that the seminar has a positive effect on the amount of contact first-year students have with faculty. Patterson students report much more informal, out-of-class contact with faculty than do other undeclared students (both those students enrolled in other residential academic programs and those not enrolled in any program). These findings are supported by student course evaluation results: Most of the instructors received high marks on their willingness to take a personal interest in helping students learn and on their overall teaching effectiveness.

As these results suggest, students generally seem to like their teacher and report receiving the personalized attention and support the program was designed to provide. Students' ratings of the course itself, however, show substantial variation by course section. For example, in the second year of the program just over half (55%) of the Patterson students agreed that they would recommend the course to other, undeclared first-year students. However, when student responses to this question are compared across sections, the percentage agreeing ranges from 0 to 83% depending upon the course section. Similarly dramatic differences across section are found in other course-related items. This variability across sections highlights the different degrees to which the instructors were able to make the course "work" for their students during the first two years of the program. For a host of reasons, teaching this course presented a number of challenges for instructors. These reasons will be discussed throughout this paper.

Perhaps exacerbating some of these difficulties is the fact that the seminar was implemented without any structured efforts to help faculty members prepare for the challenges of this type of instruction. This contradicts the recommendations of the first-year experience literature, which strongly encourages programs to include specific preparations for faculty participants particularly because this type of instruction can be so challenging (Evenbeck et al., 1999; Gardner, 1989; Matthews, et al., 1997; Middendorf, 1998). While the university has a well-regarded Center for Teaching that works closely with a variety of departments and individual faculty, those who developed the seminar did not include a faculty development component into its design.[1] As a result, this experience became a kind of "baptism by fire" for faculty.

Research Design

Even as the program was being developed, those involved knew that evidence of success would be a central factor in achieving permanent funding. As a result, a campus evaluation office was asked to develop and implement a systematic evaluation plan for the program. As a part of this plan, all available faculty who had taught the seminar during its first two years (8 of 10 faculty) were interviewed in spring 1998. Seven of the eight faculty respondents were tenured, and as a group they represented various stages of the academic career (4 full professors, 3 associates, and 1 assistant). They also varied in academic discipline (half in the humanities and half in the sciences) and in gender (3 females and 5 males).

The interview protocol developed had nine sections, reflecting various areas of interest to the program evaluation purpose. These included the participant's reason for involvement in the program, their understanding of course purpose and goals, their description of the experience, and the impact of the experience on their role as teachers as well as their faculty role more broadly. Interviews lasted approximately one hour each and were taped and transcribed. Data analysis was conducted using the content analysis method outlined by Patton (1987). As he describes it, the method is designed to identify "coherent and important examples, themes, and patterns in the data" through an iterative process of reading the responses, developing emerging patterns of similarities, and using these patterns to identify major themes in the data (p. 149).

Many of the themes that emerged from this analysis suggest that changes occurred in faculty members' knowledge, attitudes, and behaviors as a result of their experiences teaching in the program. These faculty stories form the substance of this article. To ensure respondent anonymity with the small discrete population included in this study, extra effort is made to mask faculty identity. References to faculty members' discipline and gender in the text are limited, and references to other identifying information are edited to protect respondent identity.

The willingness of these individuals to open up themselves and their teaching to formative evaluation is particularly laudable. The early stage of any innovation is rife with difficulties. As a result, it is a particularly vulnerable time to have your work evaluated. However, as these instructors understood, the early stages of a new project are also when systematic information on the successes and failures is most needed. That these faculty members were willing to have their difficulties scrutinized by others illustrates their dedication to improving the first-year experience for students at their university. Their cooperation also suggests they have enough confidence and security in their own teaching abilities to talk openly about the particular challenges the program made them face.

The Faculty Experience

As was indicated earlier, faculty members teaching the seminar came to the project from different disciplines and at different stages in their academic careers. In addition, faculty had varying teaching experiences and style preferences. What they had in common was an openness to participate in this new program and a general concern for first-year students.

This section outlines faculty members' overall assessment of the experience by sharing their responses to the question, "What was it like to teach in the program?" From the opportunity to develop a greater range of instructional tools to being confronted with one's limits as a teacher, these instructors' stories provide a sense of the range of experiences associated with involvement in the program. These excerpts also illustrate some of the drawbacks that emerge from the course design (e.g., an interdisciplinary approach unfamiliar to students, unclear course goals, no upper-division students to help socialize first-year students).

This first faculty response illustrates the difficulty of teaching the seminar as well as the opportunity it provided for re-tooling one's instructional methods.

> Well, as I mentioned in the beginning it was very frightening to me, because all of a sudden I realized that I could not stand up and lecture. I had to generate some discussions. I had assigned some readings and then we had to discuss the readings. And then I realized half the class had not done the readings, and so what do you do to encourage [a] class that hasn't done the readings to do the readings? [I had] to threaten them [in a sense] that if they didn't contribute to the discussion that it would hurt in the final analysis of the grade. So I really had to grasp, for the first month, how do you generate discussion? . . . So I think [I] was basically relearning some of my techniques [from] years ago when I had small classes. But it was scary. I never ever looked at the clock when I lecture[d]. I looked at the clock constantly during these times. "Oh my God! What am I supposed to do? I've hit a lull here, and I don't know where to go."

Without specific preparation for the experience, this professor had some fairly difficult moments in adapting to this new learning environment and had to figure out how to adjust his teaching methods accordingly.

Another professor was more prepared to teach a small class but was unaccustomed to the type of faculty-student engagement the program seemed to require.

> I never like it while it's going on. . . . As problems develop, they become consuming. And if you have a few students who aren't

> attending class, you begin to worry about how to deal with that. It's kind of like being at a restaurant and you're waiting for the food for a half-hour, and you're not sure whether they've forgotten about you or what. You know you're the one who's got to speak to the waiter and you start thinking about what you're going to say and so on. Even if the food then comes, you've still psychologically gotten involved in this confrontation. And this course intensifies all of that, because in a regular course, we let students attend or not attend as they see fit. It doesn't have the same goals as this class. Because this class deals with students who are just beginning and we're trying to mold them more . . . we invest more and we expect more. We have more disappointments.

The course, within the context of the living-learning program, required "humanitarian efforts" (as this professor later referred to them) of the instructor that were more complex and demanding than are required in other teaching environments. Again, in these comments one can sense the anxiety related to teaching in this context.

The following professor had little trouble working with young students, although he acknowledges the particular challenges associated with trying to bridge the apparent generation gap. A major source of difficulty, however, was the lack of clarity surrounding course goals and purpose.

> Well, first of all, I liked it both semesters. It was not easy either semester. . . . But I like people that age, you know, kids. It takes—being my age—it takes a little while to kind of set up a rapport with students before they kind of let their guard down and realize that you're there for no other reason than that one. And I like the whole process of discussing something with a bunch of students. . . . But it was hard in the sense that . . . it was difficult to communicate to the students why the class was the way it was. And we all, I think, pretty much do a bad job at that, and I think that's been a mixed message from the organization of the course from the very beginning.

For many of the instructors, the vague course goals and students' resistance to a course not directly related to a specific major or discipline created instructional difficulties. The structure and content of the course itself also presented challenges for this professor.

> How was the experience for me? Well, you know, it's a great deal of work. . . . We don't have other courses—at least I've never taught in other courses—that are reserved for first-semester students. So . . . there's always been—even if you're teaching a 100-level course, which I have repeatedly done—there's leavening, and so you have . . . a third of the class that's farther along. And some of them even are majors or they have some declared interest in the subject, even if it's a gen. ed. course. This course is specifically designed to eliminate any of those buffers. So you're in there teaching kids who are basically eight weeks out of high school. And for many of us . . . again, the older you get, the farther away you get from that age group, so you really have to teach. I mean, it teaches you a lot . . . you can make no assumptions. I mean, the only assumption that you make is anything you want the students to learn, you have to teach. And for most of us, we're not used to doing that.

Teaching this seminar made this professor keenly aware of the particular demands of helping young college students learn, particularly in the context of a non-discipline based course.

The combination of student characteristics and the course design made the teaching experience particularly unpleasant for the following professor. The course required a type of teaching that the instructor did not think was appropriate at the university level.

> Most of the students basically were not interested in most of the topics. For a given topic, there might have been a couple of students that were interested. That's an awful way to teach a course, as you go from topic to topic. There [are] a few people that actually want to be there, and the rest of the students don't want to be there, because they're not interested or they think that they're not interested enough so [they] just shut their ears, which comes to the same thing. I mean, I'm sure that . . . I'm not . . . God's gift to the students when it comes to teachers. I think I do a good job [of] teaching [in my discipline] and also some non-majors, so maybe there [are] other teachers who are . . . much more skilled, and they can somehow manage to find ways to enter people's minds that are really closed. . . . I would agree that it was a hard semester, but not so much because of the teaching. I think it was hard in the same way that I . . . think of the great amount of

> respect I have for high school or junior high school teachers. . . . What you are is a disciplinarian. And that so much of your energy . . . teaching pre-college is spent trying to get the kids to pay attention. [Teaching the class] was an experience that demanded a lot of hard work, but I think for reasons that are not appropriate at a university.

While this instructor is very concerned about issues of retention and student success, this course was not a good fit. At another point in the interview, this individual said, "I realize[d] that I'm probably not good for teaching that kind of class."

Out of the struggles illustrated in these narratives, however, came a number of positive learning experiences for instructors. The specific dimensions of faculty growth are outlined in the following section.

Opportunities for Development: Emerging Themes

None of the faculty members interviewed came away from their teaching experience unchanged. While the specific type of effect varies by instructor, four broad categories of growth occurred: (1) better understanding of the first-year student; (2) rethinking of the teaching-learning process; (3) increased collegiality around teaching; and (4) changes in other aspects of the faculty role. These four faculty development outcomes also suggest areas where instructors might have benefited from additional information and support.

Outcome One: Better Understanding of the First-Year Student

Whether or not their other teaching experiences had put them in small classes before, all the instructors came away with a clearer understanding of first-year students. The ways in which this clarity manifested itself varies from instructor to instructor, although they can be clustered into four broad categories.

1) Sensitivity to the first-year experience. In working closely with 24 first-year students over the course of the semester, faculty learned a lot about the challenges and complexities of the first-year experience. Many instructors expressed surprise at the stories their students told them about residential hall life (the drinking, the noise, how difficult it is to study in the halls, etc.) and the ways students used their time. For most of these faculty members, this was new, and eye-opening, information.

Other instructors articulated a broader empathy for first-year students and their struggles. This professor was struck by the type of development students experience in the first semester.

> I mean, so much happens within the course of that first semester. And when they first come in, they are so completely agog, bewildered, utterly unformed, and by the end, those who remain are . . . already starting to be acculturated and they're starting to be aware [of who] they're becoming. . . . [W]e had this fascinating discussion, which didn't really have much to do with the class, right after Thanksgiving, which is the first time a lot of them had gone home. And they realized that you can't go home again. And it was just fascinating.

Another instructor was particularly struck by how difficult the first year can be.

> [Teaching this course has] strengthened my belief that we've got to do more for the first year. We really have to, because they are so vulnerable. They are so vulnerable. Whether they're good or bad, whether they're the brighter students that we brought in for honors scholarships or what have you, or whether they're at-risk students. They're all in the same kettle of fish in terms of, How are they going to adapt to this? . . . It certainly made me more aware of what these kids are up against. And it's not just here. It's back home. Many of them have become the parents. I mean, a couple of the students who I don't think came back, basically were the mother and the father. And eventually I found that out.

2) Awareness of the "generation gap." Related to this deepening understanding of the realities of the first-year experience, faculty members also express a greater awareness of the differences between themselves and their students.

> By the time you're 55, as I am, and you're dealing with students who are 18, as most of them are, the most that you can say is that we're humans on the planet. That gives us something in common. But even where we have encountered the same historical or cultural phenomenon, our relationship to it is so different. So you're translating all the time. You have to describe everything and make sure that your understanding of what we're doing and their understanding of what we're doing is as close to the same as it can be. And it often requires intense negotiation to get to that

> point. So you can't take anything for granted. . . . And because the course is one that's [intended] . . . to get the students to a position where they can reflect on what they're doing, you can't do what you might be tempted to do in other classes, which is to simply, as it were, "teach the material." . . . You know: teach the material, there will be a test, you'll pass, you'll fail, I don't care. You know, you're engaged in trying to get them to engage with the material and engage with their own engagement, which means that you've got to hear from them all the time. At the beginning, particularly, what you hear from them is mass confusion.

A deepening awareness of this chasm between student and professor led this instructor to make significant changes in approaching students and helping them learn. The following instructor had a similar, and perhaps more dramatic, reaction.

> I'm glad I did it. It taught me that there's such a generation gap that I have to sort of throw out of my head what I've gone through, what I am, and my own standards, and sort of listen to them, study them, find out where they're at. And although you hear them, I mean, they're so young and inexperienced, you sort of have to take, again, [what they say] with a grain of salt because they . . . I don't know. I don't think they're able to judge what they're getting. They're sort of like your own children. If you're hard on them, in 20 years they'll come back and say, "God, I'm glad you did that. Now that I have my own children, I realize what you're going through." It may take a long time! . . . You know, I wouldn't teach it again, but [I] know that I have to learn to compromise. The students change so quickly . . . it's amazing to me. It's almost like a generation gap every three years.

3) Awareness of students' difficulties in engaging with course material. The structure and size of the course provided an opportunity for faculty to observe weaknesses in students' preparation for college. Faculty were struck by students' difficulty in writing, discriminating between types of information, becoming engaged in the topic at hand, and making inferences from readings. Students' difficulties in participating in meaningful classroom discussions were mentioned by a number of instructors.

> Once I got into the class, I sort of pretty quickly—within the first week or two—came to the belief that the biggest limitation for

> this class was the ability to have discussions with each other. . . . I was very, very surprised by what I perceived as a real inability to have basic discussions, to be able to sit and listen to the flow of the conversation and then think, well, I have a point, and add it in and not to sort of get lost in all this. I even started watching them in [the] conversations that they were having amongst themselves on other things. I still saw that, it seemed to me. So that was a skill that I then decided to try to make permeate the whole course, because it seemed to me like that was going to be really critical for students' ability to do well and to really derive something from the next four years of experience.

For a number of the instructors, like this one, the awareness of the students' weaknesses served as an impetus for developing new teaching or instructional design strategies.

4) Exposure to the Realities of Student Learning. For those instructors whose primary exposure to first-year students had been in large classes, this teaching experience provided an opportunity to observe student ability and performance in another context. For these two instructors, this exposure led them to reconceptualize student learning.

> [I'd like to teach a small class again] just to get to know the students in a much better way. I really don't get to know the students [in my large classes], other than, yeah, they got an A. And yes, they came to every class. But how well do they understand the material? Did they memorize the material? Could they explain it? Because it's a multiple-choice exam. So I miss that with the large lecture. The small [class] . . . really gives you an opportunity to . . . pinpoint a student who doesn't have a great deal of academic self-confidence to help them develop that, whereas if a student doesn't do well in my [large] class now, my gut reactions is, "You don't study."

> I hadn't seen the students in the same way [before]. In fact, it's very ironic, because I was teaching [the introductory course in my discipline] and [the Patterson] course at the same time. I had one student who was in both courses. So . . . I would say, how do I look at this person as a student in [my discipline-based course] and how do I look at her as a student in [the Patterson] course? And it was like they were two completely different people.

> Because she was a pretty good student—I think she probably got a B in [my discipline-based course]. In [the Patterson] course, she sort of brought all [of] what I perceived as all the shortcomings that all the other students had. She brought them. So what I was thinking there [in the discipline-based course], oh this is a pretty good student . . . I'd give her the content; she gives it back to me. She seemed to be doing pretty good. . . . Here [in the Patterson course], when I was . . . asking for something different, I was like, wow! So that was frustrating.

For both of these professors, the experience of teaching the seminar showed them aspects of student comprehension they had not seen before and, as a result, made them question their assumptions about student learning in their other classes as well.

Outcome Two: Rethinking the Teaching-Learning Process

Teaching the Patterson course, as has been suggested earlier, required instructors to teach and interact with students in ways that were new to most of them. Many admitted that the course was "hard work" and that it forced them to step out of comfortable means of interacting with students. As one instructor said, who called the experience "rejuvenating": "[in my other classes] after a while you get into a routine, . . . you can do it in your sleep. In this class, I couldn't do it in my sleep. Everything was new."

As faculty gained a greater awareness of the realities of the first-year experience and the abilities of the students in their class, many adapted their course and their behaviors to better meet the needs of their students. A number of individuals talked about implementing instructional techniques that were new to them including small group work, guest speakers, and innovative reading and writing assignments. For many, this opportunity to "try something new" was an important benefit of the program.

> I think the best justification for . . . this course, too, is the stimulation that it provides for the faculty. I think the best outcome so far is that I tried to do some things differently in my course, and I got all excited about it, and I wasn't just running through the same thing I was running through. . . . That was a good outcome.

Changes in faculty members' understanding of the teaching-learning process went beyond the implementation of new techniques for a number of instructors. These instructors' comments suggest that the experience fundamentally changed the way they conceptualize teaching.

> It's done for me what I've asked . . . the students [to do]. But much more. I mean, it has made me go back to the fundamentals about teaching and engaging with students in a way that I haven't had to do . . . in a way, ever. And that's been very interesting.

> But all this other stuff that's going on [for students], I just . . . I was just not seeing it. And I recognize that now, and I realize the impact that that actually has on the students and what they're getting out of the course. . . . I think it also makes me question a little bit what I was sort of giving the students credit for. I'm saying to myself, "Now, wait a second. . . . Is it really possible that when we're talking about just maybe general approaches to life and the students seem that unsophisticated about that, could they really be as sophisticated on these [discipline-based] concepts as I think? Or are they just very good . . . have they just really been well-trained at appearing to be sophisticated by taking in the right information and giving it back in sort of the right form?" So it made me sort of think about that quite a bit.

> If we can teach them how to learn, [then we have really accomplished something]. . . . The course helped me to understand learning styles and learning, in general, in a much different way than I had in previous teaching experiences here. . . . I didn't have the opportunity before to [interact] with incoming, first-year students that really are lost. Some of them have study habits; some of them have none. But many of them confuse study habits with learning. And I think that in my mind, that was a real important distinction. . . . I mean, we have been emphasizing for years here teaching—and I think that is real important—you have to be competent teachers. But you cannot become a better teacher unless you understand how students learn. It doesn't matter how many props that I bring to my class. I'm jumping around like a clown and making them laugh and whatever. I may not be teaching them anything. I may be teaching, but they're not really learning. The important thing is to make sure that they have the tools to learn, and even if they don't learn in the class, that they have the tools to learn the material that I cover when they read it.

Taken together, these professors identify an array of changes in how they think about teaching. From going back to the "fundamentals" of teaching to reconsidering one's beliefs about student learning and academic performance, these instructors report new understanding and changing behavior related to the teaching-learning process.

Outcome Three: Developing Collegiality Around Teaching

One of the original intents of the program was for faculty members to work in teams to develop and implement the course. In this design, instructors were to meet throughout the course of the semester to share ideas, observations, and adapt the course accordingly. This aspect of the program was never fully implemented, in large measure because no one was appointed to coordinate the group, and faculty availability waned as the semester progressed.

However, there were periods when a small group of instructors would get together. This was particularly true in the early stages of the program when faculty were first confronting the unanticipated challenges of the students and the course design itself. Most of those who attended the meetings identified a number of ways in which those meetings helped them. Faculty helped each other by confirming each other's observations of the difficulties of teaching the course, sharing specific techniques for addressing problems, and sharing assignments.

> Well . . . basically [we talked about] what's working and what isn't working. What are some good articles . . . they fed off of me for science articles. I fed off them for humanities articles, for poems, for good readings, short stories. I think we basically served as resources. . . . Without that, I would have been lost, because . . . what I thought would be exciting . . . didn't work. But then I remember [another instructor] gave me an idea for something . . . that worked much better. . . . None of us was doing exactly the same thing at the same time, which was good, because then we could feed off each other.

Even those instructors who did not find the group meetings helpful, found ways to develop collegial relationships around teaching.

> After this [teaching technique] didn't work, I went to this meeting and I didn't find any useful hints or suggestions. . . . So I called [another seminar instructor] whom I knew tangentially

> and I knew was an experienced teacher. . . . [This instructor] did cue me in to a lot of basic teaching things that were things I wouldn't have thought of. For example, stressing these are people just out of the high school door, and they don't have these kind of skills. And even if you are teaching second-semester freshmen, it makes a big difference. . . . [This instructor] understood the problems I was outlining and was able to give some useful teaching feedback. So that was useful. And that did help a bit. The classroom experience got a little bit better after that.

One of the most consistent recommendations of the group of faculty who were interviewed was that the opportunity to meet as a group should have been more systematic and better organized. In their view, this feature of the program was underutilized.

> Ideally, the piece that's . . . the complementary piece to the teaching is the sitting around in a group of teachers and talking about teaching. Now that . . . piece of the program was never really built into the program. I'm not sure how much everybody else is interested in that. . . . For this moment in my life, I'm not sure how much time I have in my life to devote to this, but . . . if you're asking a question about what does it do to one, you know, it can ideally put one into a relationship again—or for the first time—of really a community of teachers. And I think that's very interesting, personally.
>
> But I really think in the long run for there to be institutional development, there has to be more institutional coordination. . . .There ought to be a parallel faculty seminar where faculty . . . get together and have their discussions about whatever issues are being raised in those 11 sections for this particular two-week period or whatever. That's the kind of stuff that would lead to institutional development, I think, that level of organization. I think as it is now, one guy, you know . . . in my case, one guy—me—got stimulated and learned a few things and I'll try to use them in other places. . . .

Clearly, for all participants interviewed, the opportunity to meet with colleagues to discuss teaching these first-year students was an important developmental experience—one most wish they could have engaged in more systematically.

Outcome Four: Changes in Other Aspects of the Faculty Role
While the experience of teaching this first-year seminar primarily affected instructors' roles as teachers, for a subset of faculty the experience had other effects as well. For some of these individuals, it simply provided a broader view of the institution (e.g., meeting students not affiliated with their discipline or meeting university staff and faculty they hadn't known before). One instructor, who was also a department chair, expressed a desire to take some of what he had learned to his department. A couple of individuals, however, identified broader effects that influenced their identities as scholars.

For this instructor, teaching the course provided the opportunity to explore discipline-based ideas in a broader context.

> [Teaching the course] gave me a chance to kind of develop . . . or to put into words something that I've been playing with all along—that relationship [between message intended and message received]. And when I was asked to give the [campus] lecture a year ago, that was really the center of it. And the teaching in the Patterson program is basically what I was talking about [in the lecture] and . . . people describe that as my triumph. Here I was talking to five hundred people, and it was just very successful. And I wouldn't have done it . . . I don't think I would have been able to do it [otherwise]. Speaking about a perception in my own field . . . wouldn't have had the marvel. . . . I mean, my context is usually much smaller. So it's really allowed me to kind of articulate things in a much larger context that I normally wouldn't have been able to. Actually, some of the perceptions that I've had while teaching it I've passed on to my graduate classes. We've talked at length about some of this stuff, so it really kind of informs other classes I teach.

The following individual found a particularly unique connection between the program and other aspects of the faculty role.

> [Participating in the program has] put me in a situation that I didn't anticipate when I first became an academic, because I was basically a pure academic. I mean, the teacher who influenced me the most I remember once said, in class, that if you were interested in social service or something for humanitarian reasons, you'd never become an academic. You become an aca-

> demic because you were interested in the field. But I found that I do have the capacity to do . . . different things at once. While I find the course psychologically consuming, like I said before, I don't find it very time-consuming, so it's not like a great imposition to my research schedule. . . . So I feel like it's sort of given me a broader academic identity. . . . I'm not referring to teaching now, but writing and research. . . . I take a very critical look at [some of the scholarship in the discipline]. And I think that teaching a course like this helps me to do that without guilt. . . . For example, when I go to a conference, and someone gives a paper, I may be the first person to raise my hand and I'll devastate the presentation. People might think, well, there's something wrong with him. And I'll do that without guilt, because I'm nice to students. And when you're nice to students . . . you don't have to be nice to everyone. There are situations where you're supposed to be nice to people and situations where it's not that relevant to be nice to people. . . . I see academic life in pretty competitive terms. Not so much competitive, but people should say what they think, and it's certainly not going to help someone who died in the industrial revolution and has been dead for two hundred years that I show sympathy for his life. It will make a difference for someone who's alive and in my classroom. So I see [my discipline] as much more theoretical, detached, critical terms. But I see teaching as the place where any residual humanitarianism can be played out.

Discussion

As the faculty members' comments suggest, the seminar presented the instructors with a number of pedagogical challenges: The students were less prepared, less engaged, and more like high school students than they had anticipated. In addition, specific aspects of the course created instructional design difficulties for faculty members more used to teaching in their own disciplines.

Despite these factors, which virtually all the faculty admitted made the teaching of the course "hard work," faculty members' comments identify a number of areas in which they grew or developed as a result of the experience. The most common change in faculty was a deeper and more empathic understanding of the needs and abilities of first-year students. For most, this understanding went beyond basic awareness to changes in their own teaching behaviors. From making a first attempt at small group work to developing ways to bridge the overwhelming "generation gap," these instructors worked hard to identify means for helping students both learn and adjust to college life.

In addition to learning more about first-year students and how to help them succeed, these faculty members also developed new collegial relationships around teaching. Despite the fact that the group meetings didn't occur in the systematic and consistent manner in which they were intended, faculty did meet together to talk about teaching. While a few did not find the group discussions helpful, they still sought out trusted colleagues in the group for guidance and commiseration. At a Research I University, these types of opportunities are rare—except for faculty who participate in the activities of the Center for Teaching—and many in this group were clearly hungry for the opportunity to work together more closely on the course and its development.

To varying degrees, these findings echo the conclusions drawn in the other studies of faculty members' involvement in first-year programs and other innovations. The results of this study also suggest another, more transformative outcome for faculty (an outcome also suggested by Evenbeck et al., 1999). Two instructors spoke specifically and directly about the ways the course helped shape their broader academic identity. Four others suggested that the experience caused them to question some of their fundamental assumptions about who they are in relation to the students and the course. As Palmer (1997) suggests, this type of effect can be particularly powerful: "As important as methodology might be, the most practical thing we [as teachers] can achieve is insight into what is happening inside us as we [teach]" (pp. 20-21).

Implications for Faculty Development

What lessons does the faculty experience in this project provide to faculty developers? Given the difficulties these faculty members experienced, it seems clear that they could have used additional support and assistance. As Palmer (1997) suggests, "teaching is a daily exercise in vulnerability" (p. 18). Despite their substantial teaching experiences, these instructors were made particularly vulnerable by the unexpected challenges of teaching these first-semester, first-year students in a course so different from what students are used to in high school. By openly sharing their frustrations, these faculty members provide valuable insights into the kind of support the university should have provided in order to help the seminar meet its full potential.

Based on faculty members' comments, three specific areas of possible support emerge. First, despite their teaching experience and concern for students, these faculty members were, to varying degrees, unprepared for the realities of teaching this particular student population. Information on the demographics of the freshman population at the university as well as data on national trends in student attitudes and orientations would provide a broader context for understanding the students in their classes. In addition, clueing faculty into the complexity of the transition from high school to college—and the pressures and disorientation that occurs as a result—would also be helpful. Having made these suggestions, however, it is important to point out that at least one faculty member didn't think *anything* could prepare him for the students he faced.

> I mean, it was a big shock in the beginning. And everybody was telling me, you know, "This is going to be a big shock." . . . I talked to [a colleague in the program] a lot, before I decided to do this and after I decided to do it, so he had a very similar experience, and he was telling me, "Boy, you're not going to believe this . . . and this is what it's going to be." And I'd listen to him. I'd say, "Yeah, you're probably right." So I was expecting all those things, but I just . . . you could not have been prepared for what I ran into.

For this instructor, it is not clear that an orientation to "who are our students" would be enough.

What would probably be of even more use would be support in developing effective pedagogical and instructional design techniques for teaching these students. Faculty were often nonplussed by students' general lack of engagement as well as their lack of preparation in important college skills (specifically, class discussion, writing, time management, discernment, and application). In addition, some faculty were unaccustomed to teaching small classes; guidance in managing this type of format would also be useful. Indeed, the faculty members who did meet together shared ideas on how to teach these students, and many found the input of their colleagues particularly useful.

Finally, it appears as though faculty would have benefited from a more organized and systematic structure for sharing ideas with each other. Clearly, for this group of faculty the most powerful lever for improving their instruction in the seminar was the help of their colleagues. However, many expressed a wish that someone had taken administrative responsibility for scheduling regular meetings at times when everyone could attend. While not said directly, some faculty comments also suggest that assistance with facilitating group discussions would also have been helpful.

These three themes (information about the student population, specific pedagogical and instructional design techniques, and structured opportunities for collegial sharing) are not new to the faculty development field, but it is confirming to see them emerge in yet another instructional context. What is ironic, however, is that despite the fact that these three areas of emphasis are centerpieces of its work, the campus's Center for Teaching was not invited to be a part of this project at its inception. The steering committee did ask the Center to get involved when problems surfaced during the first semester of implementation. However, because the Center had not been included in the program planning stages, Center activities were not imbedded into initial plans or faculty expectations, and no resources were set aside for Center support. As a result, by the time the Center became involved, faculty patterns of interaction and inclusion were fairly well ingrained, and including new activities in their schedules was difficult. In addition, the Center was already over-committed in its many other programs. Therefore, the Center's input was limited, as was faculty participation in the services offered by the Center.

If faculty development activities had been integrated into the program from the initial planning stages, the outcome may have been quite different. As a contrasting example, program evaluation (another area of intervention that can meet with resistance) was imbedded in the project from the beginning. For example, a campus evaluation office designed the evaluation and oversaw its implementation. This office was also represented on the steering committee and Patterson project funds supported a research assistant. Finally, faculty members cooperated in various data collection and assessment activities at a number of stages in the project.

The difference between the experience of faculty development and evaluation in this project provides an important lesson for the early stages of implementing campus innovations. It highlights the importance of integrating relevant (and perhaps controversial) activities into the fabric of the project from the outset.[2] When this is not done, it is often difficult to introduce the component later—regardless of how helpful the service might be to the success of the innovation.

Limitations

Because of the small sample and the nature of the data collection, these results cannot be considered generalizable. In addition, because they reflect faculty members' self-reports, it is not possible to determine the extent to which these self-reported changes have actually led to changes in faculty behavior. Nor can we know whether these new perspectives will maintain when the faculty members are no longer teaching the seminar. However, the findings do suggest the promising nature of first-year programs for giving faculty members a teaching experience that provides new and stimulating challenges and important opportunities for professional growth.

Conclusion

Clearly faculty participants were affected by the experience of teaching in this first-year program. While teaching the seminar was "difficult" and "hard work" for the faculty members, each of them came away reporting some type of growth or development. Being thrown into a difficult situation and having to cope is not always the best way to learn. However, it sometimes has its merits. Brookfield (1996) suggests that, in order to understand what students go through as they try to learn something new, teachers should:

> deliberately put ourselves in the position of being a student who "just doesn't get it." This means that we will volunteer to learn something that we find intimidating or threatening, in the sure knowledge that what awaits us is a sustained experience of private shaming and public humiliation (p. 8).

While what Brookfield describes may be a more dramatic and traumatic episode than what faculty in this project experienced, there is a sense in faculty members' comments that teaching this seminar was a significant learning experience for many of them. As a result, a number became students themselves (as this instructor's comments illustrate):

> For all of us, we're teaching outside of our subject matter, and for all of us, we're teaching outside of our chosen audience of students, our majors or potential majors—because there's no way that anybody's going to major in this course. So you're attempting to sort of seduce the student into the life of the mind,

> and in order to do that, you have to engage yourself with material you don't ordinarily engage. . . . you have to admit ignorance and vulnerability, and you have to master material yourself so that you can teach it.

ENDNOTES

[1]While a full analysis of the reasons for this goes beyond the purview of this study, clearly a significant aspect of this lack of inclusion was the fact that those designing the course felt adequately prepared to design and deliver the new seminar. However, as the instructors' comments will illustrate, the combination of a non-discipline based course taught to a classroom full of first-year, first-semester students created a situation full of challenges for which the instructors were not entirely prepared.

[2]Of course, this is sometimes better said than done, and the factors that affect inclusion will differ by institutional context, innovation, and the leaders of the innovation. These data also suggest the need to be persistent, because people don't always see the benefit of support during the initial stages of program development.

REFERENCES

Barefoot, B. (1993). *Exploring the evidence: Reporting outcomes of freshman seminars.* (Monograph No. 11). Columbia, SC: National Resource Center for the Freshman Year Experience.

Brookfield, S. (1996). Through the lens of learning: How experiencing difficult learning challenges and changes assumptions about teaching. *To Improve the Academy*, *15*, 3-16.

Evenbeck, S. E., Jackson, B., & McGrew, J. (1999). Faculty development in learning communities: The role of reflection and reframing. In J. H. Levine (Ed.), *Learning communities: New structures, new partnerships for learning* (Monograph No. 26) (pp. 51-58). Columbia, SC: University of South Carolina, National Resource Center for the First-Year Experience and Students in Transition.

Gardner, J. N. (1989). Starting a freshman seminar program. In M. L. Upcraft, J. N. Gardner, & Associates (Eds.), *The freshman year experience* (pp. 238-249). San Francisco, CA: Jossey-Bass.

Gordon, V. P. (1989). Origins and purposes of the freshman seminar. In Upcraft, M. L., Gardner, J. N., & Associates (Eds.), *The freshman year experience* (pp. 183-197). San Francisco, CA: Jossey-Bass.

Matthews, R. S., Smith, B. L., McGregor, J., & Gebelnick, F. (1997). Creating learning communities. In J. Graff, J. Ratcliff, & Associates (Eds.), *The handbook of the undergraduate curriculum* (pp. 457-475). San Francisco, CA: Jossey-Bass.

Middendorf, J. K. (1998). A case study in getting faculty to change. *To Improve the Academy*, *17*, 203-224.

Palmer, P. J. (1997, November/December). The heart of a teacher: Identity and integrity in teaching. *Change, 29* (6), 15-21.

Patton, M. Q. (1987). *How to use qualitative methods in evaluation*. Newbury Park, CA: Sage Publications.

Siegel, B. L. (1989). A president's perspective on the value of freshman seminars. In M. L. Upcraft, J. N. Gardner, & Associates (Eds.), *The freshman year experience* (pp. 250-257). San Francisco, CA: Jossey-Bass.

Sutherland, T., & Guffey, J. (1997). The impact of comprehensive institutional assessment on faculty. *To Improve the Academy*, *16*, 151-164.

Upcraft, M. L., Gardner, J. N., & Associates. (1989). *The freshman year experience*. San Francisco, CA: Jossey-Bass.

Contact:

Martha L. A. Stassen
Director of Assessment
Office of Academic Planning and Assessment
237 Whitmore Administration Building
University of Massachusetts, Amherst
Amherst, MA 01003
(413) 545-5146
(413) 545-3010 (FAX)
mstassen@acad.umass.edu

Martha L. A. Stassen is Director of Assessment and Adjunct Assistant Professor of Higher Education at the University of Massachusetts, Amherst. In her position she conducts program evaluation, directs a variety of studies on the student experience, and works with academic departments and individual faculty on developing appropriate methods for assessing student learning. In all her work she has a strong interest in developing better linkages between assessment, evaluation, and development. She holds a Ph.D. in Higher Education Administration from the University of Michigan.

16

The Influence of Disciplinary Differences on Consultations with Faculty

Virginia S. Lee
University of North Carolina, Chapel Hill

In recent years researchers have begun to investigate the nature of disciplinary differences in higher education and their implications for teaching and learning. While researchers have studied several aspects of disciplinary differences, they have given comparatively little attention to the significance of these differences for faculty development. After reviewing selective, representative studies from the literature on disciplinary differences, this paper develops a general framework for determining how the characteristics of a discipline influence the dynamics of the consulting relationship using the example of the hard sciences. It explores what kinds of discipline-specific knowledge will be important for consultants and under what circumstances and the implications for effective consulting strategies. The paper concludes with recommendations for future research in this area.

In recent years researchers have begun to investigate the nature of disciplinary differences in higher education and their implications for teaching and learning. While researchers have studied several aspects of disciplinary differences, they have given comparatively little attention to the significance of these differences for faculty development. In fact, the concepts, knowledge structures, methods of inquiry, and habits of mind learned in disciplines play a critical, mediating role in consultations. They shape fundamental assumptions about teaching and learning, influence problem representation in the classroom, and affect receptivity to, and interpretation of, pedagogical innovation. Educational consultants need a better understanding of the influence of disciplinary differences on their interactions with clients and the mechanisms by which that influence occurs.

After reviewing selective, representative studies from the literature on disciplinary differences, I use the example of the hard sciences to develop a general framework for determining how the characteristics of disciplines may influence the dynamics of the consulting relationship and under what circumstances these influences will be most salient. I describe certain characteristics of the sciences and the types of challenges these characteristics will pose for consultants. Subsequently, I highlight features of the consulting situation that may heighten or lessen the impact of these characteristics on the consulting relationship. The section concludes with a set of consulting strategies that may be particularly effective in working with science faculty in light of the previous discussion. In the summary section, I suggest that the framework developed with reference to the hard sciences may apply equally well in all consulting relationships regardless of the faculty member's discipline, and I recommend future areas of research in this area.

Review of the Literature

Existing research on disciplinary differences falls broadly into four areas: subject matter and knowledge structure, teaching practices, student learning, and the characteristics of departments. In his early work, Biglan (1973a) identified a model of disciplinary differences based on the distinguishing characteristics of subject matter: degree of paradigm development ("hard" or "soft"), orientation to practical application ("pure" or "applied"), and concern with life systems ("non-living" or "living"). Subsequently, Donald (1983, 1995), exploring the distinctive knowledge structures of disciplines, found four areas of difference: characteristics of concepts, logical structure, the processes of knowledge validation, and the validation criteria themselves. After a period when much educational research focused on certain generic teaching behaviors as the fundamental ingredients of effective teaching, Shulman (1986, 1987) reinstated the importance of subject matter or content knowledge in teachers' professional repertoire. Advancing the construct of pedagogical content knowledge, he claimed that teachers needed to know both "the structures of subject matter, the principles of conceptual organization, and the principles of inquiry" (1986, p. 9) of their discipline as well as how to transform these aspects of their disciplines to facilitate the understanding of their students. Murray and Renaud (1995) noted disciplinary differences in the frequency of occurrence of specific low inference teaching behaviors related to organization, pacing, interaction, rapport, and the use of mannerisms. Braxton (1995) suggested differences in teaching goals, teaching practices, and the balance of teaching and research in hard and soft disciplines, using Biglan's terminology. Kolb (1994) noted the correspondence between two of Biglan's dimensions, degree of paradigmatic development ("hard," "soft") and orientation to practical application ("pure," "applied") and the dimensions of his learning styles model—abstractness-concreteness and reflective-active, respectively. Donald (1995) also explored the comparative challenges of different disciplines' knowledge structures on student learning. And Entwistle and Tait (1995) developed various ways of typifying student styles of learning and approaches to study: deep, surface, and strategic approaches to study; serialistic and holistic styles of learning; and differences in breadth, depth, and structure of their understandings of subject matter. While finding some disciplinary differences in student learning, they identified more general principles to guide effective teaching and learning. Finally, using his model of subject matter differences, Biglan (1973b) noted differences in various aspects of the structure and output of departments: social connectedness, productivity, types of scholarly production, and relative commitments to research, teaching, and service.

Disciplinary Differences and Faculty Development

While this literature is certainly suggestive for faculty developers, researchers need to investigate more explicitly how the characteristics of a particular discipline influence the dynamics of the consulting relationship, what discipline-specific knowledge consultants need, and under what circumstances. Certainly not all consulting situations require discipline-specific knowledge. In many cases, application of general principles of teaching and learning, imagination, and intuition may be sufficient to resolve a client's problem. But at times, discipline-specific knowledge may be helpful and even necessary:

- To enhance consultants' credibility with the client
- To diagnose the underlying problem in a consultation accurately and to identify the appropriate strategies for addressing it
- To assess faculty members' expectations of the consulting relationship properly, including how they define the teaching and learning issue and the consultant's role in resolving it

- To understand possible areas of resistance such as prior knowledge and beliefs about teaching and learning, or how previous academic training influences how faculty assess new information
- To enhance consultants' understanding of the influence of their own academic training on their perception of teaching and learning issues
- To determine faculty members' position and status within their departments and the extent of their influence over teaching and learning processes

Research suggests subject areas for which discipline-specific knowledge may be most essential for the success of the consulting relationship. Using Biglan's model, most faculty developers should work with comparative ease in soft disciplines (e.g., English, psychology, social work) due to their own academic training in these disciplines (Graf & Wheeler, 1996) and the nature of the client disciplines themselves. These are "affinity" disciplines (Braxton, 1995) whose teaching practices are most consistent with those associated with effective teaching and enhanced student learning. Among the soft disciplines, consultants may work with greater ease in applied-life subject areas. This is due ultimately to the fundamental object of attention of these disciplines—human beings and human processes, interaction, development, and change—and their paradigmatic and methodological flexibility. Conversely, the need for discipline-specific knowledge will be more urgent when working in the hard disciplines (e.g., chemistry, engineering, statistics), both because of their relative paradigmatic and methodological rigidity and because the majority of faculty developers lack advanced training in these areas (Graf & Wheeler, 1996).

The following section examines specific characteristics of the hard disciplines (e.g., chemistry, physics, astronomy, biology) and their influence on the dynamics of the consulting relationship. By examining a category of consulting relationships where the influence of the discipline is clear and dramatic, I hope to illuminate features of this influence that exist in interactions with all clients but that are often subtler and thus harder to recognize.

The Case of the Hard Disciplines

The Nature of the Hard Disciplines

In his classic essay, *The Structure of Scientific Revolutions* (1962/1996), Thomas Kuhn portrayed the inherent conservatism of science and the overwhelming power of the prevailing paradigm in scientific inquiry in the following description of normal science, the type of science practiced by most scientists most of the time:

> Closely examined, whether historically or in the contemporary laboratory, that enterprise seems an attempt to force nature into the preformed and relatively inflexible box that the paradigm supplies. No part of the aim of normal science is to call forth new sorts of phenomena; indeed those that will not fit the box are often not seen at all. Nor do scientists normally aim to invent new theories, and they are often intolerant of those invented by others. Instead normal-scientific research is directed to the articulation of those phenomena and theories that the paradigm supplies (p. 24).

He further describes the necessary restrictions, "born from confidence in a paradigm," that "[force] scientists to investigate some part of nature in a detail and depth that would otherwise be unimaginable" (p. 24). In periods when paradigms are well-established, fact-gathering in two forms—determination of significant fact and matching of facts with theory—characterizes the vast majority of scientific research.

Kuhn also discusses the influence of the dominant paradigm on the education of future scientists:

> The study of paradigms is what mainly prepares the student for membership in the particular scientific community with which he will later practice. Because he there joins men who learned the bases of their field from the same concrete models, his subsequent practice will seldom evoke overt disagreement over fundamentals. Men whose research is based on shared paradigms are committed to the same rules and standards for scientific practice. That commitment and the apparent consensus it produces are prerequisites for normal science (p. 11).

In post-secondary science education, students typically first learn the dominant paradigm through textbooks, then by replicating experiments, and finally, in graduate or post-doctoral study, by conducting original, but still highly circumscribed research of the sort described above.

In other words, there is a high degree of interdependence between the characteristics of the dominant paradigm—its subject matter, knowledge structures, and methods of inquiry on the one hand—and characteristic teaching practices and qualities of student learning on the other. The dominant paradigm in a given field often comprises many concepts with highly technical meanings that may be represented symbolically and at a high level of abstractness. Further, concepts have a high degree of salience, leading to hierarchical knowledge structures with high concept interdependence. The understanding of subordinate concepts depends upon mastery of superordinate concepts. And as discussed above, accepted methods of inquiry in these disciplines are relatively circumscribed, restricted almost exclusively to the scientific method using quantitative analytical tools and focused on very narrow, specialized research questions.

Methods (e.g., experiment, reproducibility, the use of conflicting evidence, counterexamples) and standards (e.g., consistency, precision, accuracy) of knowledge validation are rigorous (Donald, 1995).

Given the sheer density of subject matter and the often unquestioned pedagogical assumption of paradigm mastery, teaching goals often emphasize mastery of technical subject matter, knowledge acquisition, and, in some disciplines, direct application. Curricula have a tendency to become quite rigid, and courses, most with a strong emphasis on content coverage, often highly interdependent. Because of the importance of content acquisition, most instructors employ a very restricted set of teaching practices that focus on delivery of content, primarily in the lecture mode. Effective teaching practices emphasize organization of content, appropriate pacing in the delivery of content, and clarity in its presentation. Emphasizing mastery of the dominant paradigm, assessment practices typically favor traditional in-class testing with a reliance on multiple-choice and short-answer formats that test low-level outcomes at the knowledge and comprehension levels and problem sets that test application.

The structural characteristics of departments and the organization of inquiry are additional influences on teaching practices in the hard disciplines. Given the overwhelming influence of the dominant paradigm, research frequently takes place in teams, minimizing the contribution of individual researchers. Correspondingly the individual instructor plays a far less important role than the paradigm itself and the collective effort to first master and then modify and test it. Finally, the reward structure in the hard disciplines often favors research overwhelmingly over teaching.

Implications for the Educational Consultant

The density of the dominant paradigm alone—the nature of concepts, their number, and their high interdependence—presents real challenges in transforming its subject matter in ways that facilitate student understanding (Shulman, 1986). In addition, the interdependence between the dominant paradigm, the organization of inquiry, and teaching practices can create formidable barriers to implementation of effective principles of teaching and learning. The resulting culture of teaching and learning in the hard disciplines will affect the frequency with which instructors in these disciplines seek the advice of consultants as well as the dynamics of the consulting relationship itself. Because the sciences have traditionally placed less emphasis on teaching per se and more emphasis on mastery of content, instructors in these fields are less likely to solicit the expertise of educational consultants. When consulting relationships are formed, the subject matter and habits of thought shaped by the dominant paradigm and their effect on teaching practices will strongly influence client expectations, the facility with which consultants will work in these fields, and ultimately, the types of consulting strategies that will be most effective. Consultants working in these fields will face several challenges:

Credibility. Traditionally, the hard-pure disciplines have held a privileged position in the hierarchy of universities by virtue of the technicality, abstractness, and symbolic representation of their concepts and the refinement and rigor of their methods of inquiry and standards of validation. As a soft-applied discipline, education occupies a substantially lower position in the hierarchy, and the disparity in status between the hard-pure and soft-applied disciplines is large. This discrepancy may influence the frequency with which instructors in the hard disciplines seek the advice of educational consultants and their degree of skepticism concerning its value. Educational consultants may have particular difficulty establishing their credibility with instructors in the hard disciplines.

The nature of the subject matter. As paradigms develop and mature, their concepts proliferate, acquire increasingly technical meanings, and become highly interdependent. As a result the field becomes more and more impenetrable to those outside the discipline. Even for those inside the discipline, decisions concerning selection and representation of content to facilitate student learning will be difficult. Unless they have advanced scientific training, consultants may have particular difficulty working in these fields. They will naturally have less confidence working in fields they themselves do not understand. Further, they may have difficulty interpreting and evaluating teaching practices that emphasize content delivery. Finally, they may simply be less interested in fields so far outside their own training. Their inability to "talk the language" may further undermine their credibility with faculty in the sciences.

Accustomed patterns of thought and methods of inquiry. As described above, patterns of thought and methods of inquiry in the sciences are far more circumscribed than in other academic disciplines. These habits and methods influence a number of areas: how scientists frame problems; the types of questions they ask; the kinds of evidence they will accept; the methods they will use to examine it; the types of inferences they will be willing to make; and the methods and rigor with which they accept knowledge claims in their fields, and the value they assign to them. These characteristics of scientific inquiry may affect how readily science instructors accept methodologies from other fields like education and the knowledge claims that result from them, and how willing they would be to apply the implications of these claims to their own classrooms.

Classroom practices and implied assumptions about teaching and learning. The most common classroom practices in the sciences as described above emanate from a number of assumptions, both implicit and explicit, about teaching and learning. These include the following: instructors dispense and students receive knowledge; until students have mastered a large portion of the dominant paradigm, they are unable to engage in real scientific inquiry; in undergraduate science courses we are training future scientists who will conduct independent research in their fields; the way the field practices science and how students learn are different; and learning is mastery of content. At the same time, most of these assumptions contradict what we know about teaching practices that facilitate student learning. These assumptions are held tenaciously and are largely unexamined, making them all the more recalcitrant. Changing teaching practices without first unearthing these assumptions and bringing them to light is very difficult.

Features of the Consulting Relationship

The impact of these challenges on the relationship between consultants and instructors in these disciplines will depend upon certain features of the consulting situation:

Nature of the consulting problem. Educational consultants encounter a wide range of issues and problems as defined by their clients. Some problems may lend themselves to "quick fixes" and may require comparatively little discipline-specific knowledge (e.g., handling a difficult student), while others will be more extensive and require more knowledge (e.g., curricular design). Certain factors also determine whether the consultant chooses to define the problem differently in a manner that recognizes the need for more discipline-specific knowledge and then makes this known to the client. In part, a proper diagnosis of the client's problem may depend upon discipline-specific knowledge. But the consultant's options about problem-definition must be based on an assessment of the client, his or her readiness to accept alternative representations of the problem, and the consultant's ultimate investment and interest in the consulting problem. For purely pragmatic considerations (e.g., current workload), the consultant may choose to resolve a problem satisfactorily, but not optimally, using general principles of teaching and learning, intuition, and imagination, and move on to other assignments.

Likely impact of the consultant's intervention. At the outset of the consulting relationship, consultants may wish to assess the likely impact of their intervention based on factors such as the interest and motivation of the client and the instructor's status within the department. A single instructor can be a powerful change agent in a given department, depending upon his/her interest, status, and influence. If this is the case, it may be well worth a consultant's time to develop discipline-specific knowledge to help effect a deep and long-lasting impact on teaching practices in the department.

Length of the consulting relationship. The length of a consulting relationship can vary from a single session to several years, depending upon a variety of factors. The instructor's dedication to teaching, the expertise and interest of the consultant, the personal chemistry between consultant and client, and the tangible results of consultations can all be important. As the relationship matures, discipline-specific knowledge may play an increasingly important role as the consultant gradually becomes more familiar with the field and is able to advise at deeper and deeper levels.

Client expectations and the role of the consultant. Clients enter consulting relationships with different expectations concerning the role of the consultant and the purpose of the consultation, which will in turn affect the role discipline-specific knowledge plays in the interaction. Some instructors may define the consultant's role quite narrowly in ways that touch the nature of the discipline only tangentially, while others will define the role far more comprehensively. Other clients will assume that the consultant brings expertise primarily in teaching and learning, while they themselves will supply subject matter expertise. Still another group of instructors may expect the consultant to provide both content and pedagogical expertise. Depending upon their assessment of the consulting relationship, consultants may try to alter client expectations to coincide more closely with their own.

Effective Consulting Strategies

The culture of the discipline may also determine the most effective consultation strategies in working with clients. Given the characteristics of the hard disciplines described above, the following strategies may be particularly effective in working with instructors in the hard disciplines:

1) During the first interaction with the client, speak openly about the powerful influence discipline culture plays in our assumptions about teaching and learning, the roles instructors and students typically play, content representation, and teaching and assessment practices.

2) Support suggested revisions in classroom teaching practice and claims concerning teaching and learning with evidence from the educational research literature.

3) Ask clients about the major concepts in their fields, their interrelationships, and how the field constructs knowledge including methods of inquiry and validation criteria. The use of concept maps to represent course content and vee diagrams (Novak & Gowin, 1984) to clarify the relationship between course content and methods of inquiry may be particularly effective consultation tools in working with clients in the hard disciplines.

4) Utilize a variety of techniques to gather empirical evidence about teaching and learning in the classroom including classroom observations, videotaping, peer and student evaluations, student assessment results, and small group instructional diagnoses (SGIDs).

5) Apply a consulting model that mimics the research process itself. By using a classroom research approach, the consultant may assist the client in defining a teaching and learning problem arising in the classroom, gather relevant data to investigate it, analyze the data, and, based on the analysis, decide upon an appropriate revision of classroom practice (Nyquist & Wulff, 1988). Similarly classroom assessment techniques, designed by instructors to obtain localized evidence of learning, provide an empirical basis for evaluating the effectiveness of teaching and may appeal to instructors in the hard disciplines (Angelo & Cross, 1993).

6) Identify key individuals in the hard disciplines who have an interest and commitment to teaching, and work with and support them intensively. Grounded both in the language and logic of the dominant paradigm as well as principles of effective teaching and learning, such individuals may have greater credibility than educational consultants themselves and become highly effective change agents within their disciplines.

Summary

The specific characteristics of a discipline—the nature of the subject matter and its knowledge structure, methods of inquiry, typical teaching practices, the quality of student learning, and the structure of departments—all influence the dynamics of the consulting relationship. The previous discussion utilized the robust case of the hard disciplines to illuminate the mechanisms of this influence as well as the role played by certain parameters of the consulting situation (e.g., nature of the problem, likely impact, length, client expectations, consultant role). However, this framework should be helpful in assessing the influence of disciplinary differences in consultations with instructors from any discipline area. It also suggests a number of areas for future research, including more rigorous, empirical examination of selected features of the framework itself; the effectiveness of specific consulting strategies in dissipating faculty resistance in different disciplines; the relationship between the knowledge structure of a particular discipline and its teaching practices; and the influence on the consulting relationship of differences in academic training between consultants and faculty members.

References

Angelo, T. A., & Cross, K. P. (1993). *Classroom assessment techniques: A handbook for college teachers* (2nd ed.). San Francisco, CA: Jossey-Bass.

Biglan, A. (1973a). The characteristics of subject matter in different academic areas. *Journal of Applied Psychology, 57*, 195-203.

Biglan, A. (1973b). Relationships between subject matter characteristics and the structure and output of university departments. *Journal of Applied Psychology, 57*, 204-213.

Braxton, J. M. (1995). Disciplines with an affinity for the improvement of undergraduate education. In N. Hativa & M. Marincovich (Eds.), *Disciplinary differences in teaching and learning: Implications for practice* (pp. 7-17). San Francisco, CA: Jossey-Bass.

Donald, J. G. (1983). Knowledge structures: Methods for exploring course content. *Journal of Higher Education, 54* (1), 31-41.

Donald, J. G. (1995). Disciplinary differences in knowledge validation. In N. Hativa & M. Marincovich (Eds.), *Disciplinary differences in teaching and learning: Implications for practice* (pp. 7-17). San Francisco, CA: Jossey-Bass.

Entwistle, N., & Tait, H. (1995). Approaches to studying and perceptions of the learning environment across disciplines. In N. Hativa & M. Marincovich

(Eds.), *Disciplinary differences in teaching and learning: Implications for practice* (pp. 93-104). San Francisco, CA: Jossey-Bass.

Graf, D., & Wheeler, D. (1996). *Defining the field: The POD membership survey*. Valdosta, GA: POD Network.

Kolb, D. A. (1994). Learning styles and disciplinary differences. In K. A. Feldman & M. B. Paulsen (Eds.), *Teaching and learning in the college classroom* (pp. 151-164). Needham Heights, MA: Ginn Press.

Kuhn, T. (1996). *The structure of scientific revolutions* (3rd ed.). Chicago, IL: University of Chicago Press. (Original work published 1962.)

Murray, H. G., & Renaud, R. D. (1995). Disciplinary differences in classroom teaching behaviors. In N. Hativa & M. Marincovich (Eds.), *Disciplinary differences in teaching and learning: Implications for practice* (pp. 31-40). San Francisco, CA: Jossey-Bass.

Novak, J. D., & Gowin, D. B. (1984). *Learning how to learn*. Cambridge, UK: Cambridge University Press.

Nyquist, J. D., & Wulff, D. H. (1988). Consultation using a research perspective. In Lewis, K. G. (Ed.), *Face to face: A sourcebook of individual consultation techniques for faculty/instructional developers* (pp. 33-50). Stillwater, OK: New Forums Press.

Shulman, L. S. (1986). Those who understand: Knowledge growth in teaching. *Educational Researcher, 15*, 4-14.

Shulman, L. S. (1987). Knowledge and teaching: Foundations of the new reform. *Harvard Educational Review, 57* (1), 1-22.

Contact:

Virginia Lee
Center for Teaching and Learning
University of North Carolina, Chapel Hill
CB #3470, 316 Wilson Library
Chapel Hill, NC 27599-3470
(919) 966-1289
(919) 962-5236 (FAX)
vslee@email.unc.edu

Virginia Lee has been the Director of Teaching Assistant Development and a consultant at UNC-Chapel Hill's Center for Teaching and Learning since 1995. She is also a Clinical Assistant Professor in the University's School of Education. A relative newcomer to the academy, she has over 20 years of professional and administrative experience in corporate, non-profit, and academic settings. She earned an MBA with a concentration in organizational management and strategic planning in 1982 and a Ph.D. in educational psychology in 1995. She has published articles on postsecondary teaching and learning and has presented nationally on a variety of topics.

17

Faculty Development Centers in Research Universities: A Study of Resources and Programs

Delivee L. Wright
University of Nebraska, Lincoln

The purpose of this study was to compile updated information on resources and programs of faculty/instructional development centers in Carnegie classification Research I and Research II universities. It allows centers across the country to see where they stand in regard to a number of specific aspects of center operation. Size of institution, mission, resources, budgets, and staffing vary greatly, while activities and services have a greater degree of similarity. The data reveal a number of questions for further study and discussion.

Introduction

Each time directors of faculty/instructional development centers are asked how their program compares to what other universities are doing, they must respond on the basis of estimates from personal contacts, or perhaps quick communication with other directors to get some information to share with those who make decisions about the future. The need for data that are representative of the resources and programs such centers provide prompted this survey.

Faculty development literature has only a few studies describing the kinds of resources and services that are characteristic of the field. Centra (1976) reported survey results of faculty development practices in US colleges and universities. Erickson (1986) replicated that study with a survey of 1,588 four-year institutions, concluding that "probably half or more . . . offer some formal faculty development, instructional development, and/or teaching improvement services." A survey by Gullatt and Weaver

(1997) studied faculty development activities used in 116 institutions. After identifying the topics covered, they concluded that centers were in existence and able to offer the greatest number of faculty development activities at campuses with larger institutional operating budgets. Chambers (1998) reported results of a survey of 1,350 two-year and four-year institutions finding similarity of services regardless of size or mission of the institution. He concluded that professional support is a need in higher education.

This study responds to the need to examine the resources and programs of faculty/instructional development centers in US research universities and to compile information into a single source that would allow centers in research universities across the country to see where they stand in regard to a number of specific aspects related to center administration. Crawley (1995) surveyed research universities to study their senior faculty renewal programs, but a broader examination of these centers has not been done.

Procedures

In the fall of 1997, senior academic officers at 125 Carnegie classification Research I and Research II universities were sent letters requesting center director's names. Fifty-five centers were identified and each was invited to participate in this study; thirty-three completed the survey (60% response rate; see Appendix 1 for a list of institutions). The survey instrument was reviewed by 10 directors of centers in October 1997, and the surveys were revised and mailed in November 1997, followed by an additional mailing. Results are reported in raw numbers and percentages for the total of 33 responding campuses.

Results

The size of the audiences served by these centers varied greatly. Figure 17.1 represents the range and mode for faculty, part-time faculty, graduate teaching assistants, and international graduate teaching assistants. It also provides estimates of undergraduate and graduate student numbers.

Line of Report and Funding

Considerable commonality exists in the lines of reporting and funding sources, with 27 (81.8 %) centers reporting to the senior academic offices

FIGURE 17.1
Estimates of Raw Numbers of Various Population Sizes on Responding Campuses

Group	Range	Mode
Full-time faculty	413-3,500	750
Part-time faculty	11-2500	200
Graduate teaching assistants	150-3,000	197
International teaching assistants	50-800	200
Undergraduate students	6,000-42,000	17,000
Graduate students	700-15,000	7,000

of the institution. Other lines of report included deans, university librarians, associate deans, or directors. In two cases, report is both to the senior academic office and to a dean.

All centers receive general funds, instructional funds, or administrative funds, and 21 centers (63.6%) are entirely funded from one of these sources. The other 12 (36.4%) reported additional funding from external revenues (5); grants or contracts (4); student fees (3); endowment or gifts (5); or earned income (1).

Center Directors

The administrative officers of 27 centers (81.8%) are designated as a directors; for 3 others, the title of director is combined with associate provost, associate dean of undergraduate studies, or associate vice-provost; 1 reported the title of assistant vice-chancellor; 1 was a coordinator; and 1 center had co-directors. These leaders have served in their roles for a range of 0-16+ years, with 15 (45.5%) having served for 5 or fewer years and 16 (48.5%) for over 5 years.

Twelve directors (36.4%) were tenured faculty members at the same institutions before becoming center directors. A number of directors (8 or 24.2%) reported previous positions on the staff of the same center or were untenured faculty from the same institution (4 or 12.1%). Typically the director was promoted from "the inside" (27 or 81.8%), with only 3 (9.1%) reporting that they came from a different institution. Other prior positions included 1 (3%) each as a faculty developer at this institution but different school, a teacher abroad, and a full-time graduate student (1 did not respond).

Respondents did not always answer the question on whether salaries represented an academic (nine month) or fiscal (twelve month) appointment, so it is difficult to know how this omission affects the salary data. Twenty-two directors indicated fiscal-year appointments, and four indicated academic-year appointments. Of the latter, two directors were also on half-time appointments in their academic departments. One center has three co-directors who were on quarter-time appointments with three-quarter time as departmental faculty. Other variables including the cost of living, tenure-status, and years of experience need to be considered in salary data. See Figure 17.2 for salary levels reported for directors.

Center Staff

Most common titles for employees in centers (other than the director) include tenured faculty, faculty on tenure track, faculty on non-tenure track, non-tenured faculty plus courtesy appointment, academic administrative, professional classified, consultant, lecturer, administrative assistant, graduate assistant, clerical/secretarial. Technical staff were included if centers were combined with media/technology production services. See Figure 17.2 for salary levels reported for a total of 92 individuals. Of these, 90 had fiscal-year appointments, while 17.2 had academic-year appointments.

Staff promotion mechanisms vary: 10 centers (30.3%) reported no opportunity for promotion; 6 (18.2%) reported merit salary or raises; 3 (9.1%) reported changing to administrative titles; 7 (21.2%) said staff

FIGURE 17.2
Salary Ranges for Directors and Staff of Faculty Development Centers

Salary Range	No. of Directors	No. of Staff
$80,000-100,000	9.0	2
$70,000-79,999	9.0	2
$60,000-69,999	3.5	8
$50,000-59,999	6.0	16
$40,000-49,999	2.0	25
$30,000-39,999	1.0	29*
$20,000-29,999	0.0	10
Total Reporting	0.5	92

*The only two academic appointments reported were in this salary range.

could be reclassified; and 7 (21.2%) did not respond to this question. When staff did not hold faculty positions, promotions or raises tended to be determined by the campus personnel office. One campus reported having an academic professional track that paralleled the tenure-track ranks.

Center Functions, Budgets, and Facilities

All centers that were surveyed engaged in faculty/instructional development; however, many have additional functions. These included instructional technology skills development (19 or 57.6%), media production (9 or 27.3%), examinations services (7 or 21.2%), grant programs (3 or 9.1%), student learning skills (2 or 6.1%), supplemental instruction learning skills (1 or 3%), teaching awards (1 or 3%), and multicultural teaching and learning services (1 or 3%). Very little staff time was allocated to *basic* instructional research (a range of 0.1-0.6 FTE was reported by 7 centers that did this activity). A greater number of centers (20 or 60.1%) reported doing some *applied* instructional development research, with 15 (45.5%) allocating a range of 0.1-0.5 FTE to such research. Five (15.2%) of these indicated no time was allocated even though they do it.

Operating budgets for center programs (excluding salaries) varied greatly depending upon, at least in part, whether the budgets included technology/media production or grants programs. Other variables affecting these figures were the size of the institution and the range of services provided. Overall, 7 programs reported budgets over $300,000; 6 were in the range of $150,000-$299,999; 4 were between $75,000-$149,999; 4 were in the range of $50,000-$74,999; 5 were between $25,000-$49,999; 6 were below $24,999; and one did not report this data. During the past five years, financial resources have increased for 17 (51.5%) of the centers; 8 (24.2%) stayed the same; 6 (18.2%) reported a decrease; and 2 (6.1%) did not report.

Travel funds allocated to centers also varied widely and were affected by the number of staff. The allocations in descending amounts were in the ranges of $15,000-$29,999 (2 or 6.1%), $7,500-$14,999 (7 or 21.2%), $3,500-$7,499 (7 or 21.25%), $1,500-$3,499 (12 or 36.3%), less than $1,499 (1 or 3%), and none (4 or 12.1%).

Facilities for most centers include a reception area, director's office, staff office(s), conference room, and resource room. Classrooms and storage rooms are also common. These units tend to be centrally located (17 or 51.5%), with 4 (12.1%) located at the edge of campus. While 2 (6.1%) had their own buildings, most (17 or 51.5%) were housed with other units or in classroom buildings (4 or 12.1%). Five (15.2%) were in administration buildings, and 7 (21.1%) were in libraries.

Center Services for Faculty

All 33 (100.0%) reporting centers provide consultation services. Most indicated that individual consultation included such activities as conferencing, observations, videotaping, gathering student feedback, and providing self-help materials. Consultation to campus groups was a service of 26 (78.8%) of the programs.

Workshops were provided to faculty by both "in-house" and "campus" experts on 32 (97.0%) campuses, while 1 (3.0%) expects to provide workshops in the future. Eighteen centers (54.5%) also used external experts for workshops. Other group activities sponsored by centers included general-interest discussion groups on teaching (29 or 87.9%); special-interest groups (27 or 81.8%); breakfast/luncheon groups (20 or 60.6%); and book groups (3 or 9.1%).

Another frequently provided service was a newsletter on teaching or faculty development, distributed by 21 (63.6%) centers. Ten centers (30.3%) used an assigned editor, while 10 (30.3%) others rotated the responsibility among staff. One campus (3%) reported using the POD Network's *Teaching Excellence* as their newsletter.

Resource rooms provided materials for faculty as well as developers on pertinent topics, and 28 (84.8%) centers reported having resource rooms. Some were relatively small while others had extensive collections. Figure 17.3 shows the estimated numbers of materials and usage rates.

FIGURE 17.3

Estimated Quantity of Resource Room Materials and Usage in Raw Numbers

Material	Range	Mode
Book titles	10-2000	100
Subscriptions	5-25	10
Videotapes	10-141	20
Self-instructional material	10-4000	10
CD-ROMs	8	1
Usages/year	20-200	no mode

Awards and Grants for Faculty

Centers engage in the selection process for campus teaching awards on 17 campuses (51.5%): 12 (36.4%) reported that they supervise or assist in the development of criteria for these awards; 13 (39.4%) review award nominations; 10 (30.3%) sponsor recognition of the awardees; and three (9.1%) prepare external award nominations.

Grant programs are administered by centers on 17 (51.5%) campuses. The range of funds for small grants for teaching development were as follows: $150,000-$299,999 (1); $50,000-$149,999 (2); $25,000-$49,999 (4); $10,000-$24,999; (9); less than $5,000 (1). Requests for proposals were issued once a year (9); 2-3 times per year (7); accepted any time (6).

Center Services for Graduate Teaching Assistants

Centers on 27 (81.8%) campuses offer individual consultation for graduate teaching assistants (GTAs) similar to those offered to faculty. In addition, 3 campuses provide mentoring services. Most respondents (28 or 84.8%) also consult with departments on GTA programs, and 13 (39.4%) offer training for departmental GTA supervisors.

Organized, campus-wide programs for GTAs are provided by 28 campuses (84.8%). These are taught by center staff, campus faculty, administrators, and other GTAs. Frequency of programs vary, with 18 campuses (54.5%) holding them annually; 14 (42.4%) holding them each semester; 4 (12.1%) holding them each quarter; and 1 (3%) holding them monthly. Collaboration with other units to provide GTA workshops was reported by 12 centers (36.4%). Collaborators included the English as a Second Language (ESL) program (10 or 30.3%), the graduate college (9 or 27.3%), international affairs (5 or 15.2%), the library (2 or 6.1%), and 1 (3.0%) each with the writing center, judicial affairs, computing, the higher education center, the center for women, the College of Arts and Sciences, the provost, instructional technology, freshman seminar, and academic departments.

Twenty-six centers (78.8%) provide materials for GTA training. These include teaching handouts (24 or 72.7%); teaching handbooks (21 or 63.6%); videotapes (19 or 57.6%); and published books (12 or 36.4%).

Courses on college teaching are taught by 17 centers (51.5%): 6 (18.2%) teach them once a year, while 3 (9.1%) provide them each term, and 3 (9.1%) provide them 2-4 times per year. One center (3%) even teaches these courses 5 or more times per year. The least frequent was a center that taught the course every 2-5 years.

International Teaching Assistants

Special needs of international graduate teaching assistants (ITAs) are served by 12 centers (36.4%); 18 campuses (54.5%) report that ITAs are taught elsewhere. Topics include: English as a second language, inter-cultural communications, videotaped microteaching, and individual consultation.

Collaborators in ITA workshops included the ESL program (9 or 27.3%), the graduate college (6 or 18.2%), and international affairs (7 or 21.2%). The average number of ITA participants in each workshop is: 10-24 ITAs (5 or 15.2%); 25-40 (6 or 18.2%); 41-60 (6 or 18.2%); and 60 (4 or 12.1%). The largest number reported was 400 for the fall term.

Handouts provided to ITAs by 18 centers included in-house workbooks and materials (15 or 45.5%) or published books and workbooks (4 or 12.1%). Only 3 centers (9.1%) had representative ITA advisory groups that assist in designing the programs.

Classroom consultation is provided for ITAs during their teaching assignments by 17 centers (51.5%). Fourteen centers (42.4%) respond to requests, 3 (9.1%) routinely observe all ITAs, and 1 (3%) observes for science and engineering ITAs only.

Evaluation and Assessment Services

Instructionally related evaluation and assessment work occurs in some centers in several ways. Consultation on student evaluation of teaching instruments was reported by 22 centers (66.7%), while only 5 (15.2%) actually manage student evaluation of the teaching process. In addition, 8 centers (24.2%) provide computerized examination services including examination scoring, test analysis statistics, consultation on test construction, scoring of student evaluations of teaching, and scoring surveys or questionnaires.

At 11 institutions (33.3%), centers are involved in activities to assess learning outcomes in the following ways: individual consultation (11 or 33.3%), serving on committees (10 or 30.3%), providing materials (9 or 27.3%), consulting with departments on ways to assess learning (8 or 24.2%), synthesizing literature (7 or 21.2%), providing workshops (6 or 18.2%), and managing programs of outcomes assessment (2 or 6.1%).

Technology and Distance Learning Services

Respondents from 27 centers (81.8%) indicate that they support instructional technology (IT) development in a variety ways, including IT application workshops (23 or 69.7%), individual consultations on IT (18 or

54.5%), workshops on distance learning (17 or 51.5%), consultations with distance learning units (15 or 45.5%), consultations with departments on IT (14 or 42.2%), software workshops (14 or 42.2%), technical instruction on software (8 or 24.2%), technical equipment assistance (7 or 21.2%), serving on a local Teaching, Learning, and Technology Roundtable (TLTR) (7 or 21.2%), or sponsoring a local TLTR (5 or 15.2%).

Directions in the Next Five Years

When asked what new initiatives centers expected to pursue in the next five years, the most frequent response involved increasing services related to instructional technology (7 or 21.2%) or the enhancement of graduate student programs (7 or 21.2%). Other directions mentioned more than once were assessment services (3 or 9.1%), peer review (3 or 9.1%), and preparing future faculty or a formal professional development program (3 or 9.1%). The following responses occurred only once: grants, research, classroom research support, pre-tenure support, post-tenure review support, diversity, examinations services, book groups, departmental chair program, center staff enhancement, and center facilities improvement.

Implications for the POD Network

1) Professional Staff Development. This study raises significant concerns about professional development opportunities for, and the appointment of, staff at teaching centers. Directors of centers come from a variety of backgrounds, some tenured and some not, but generally they were identified in some way as faculty or academic-administrative appointments. On the other hand, staff members of centers are not necessarily faculty and are occasionally hired through the personnel offices as "professional staff." Inconsistencies in selection processes, promotion issues, merit salary increases, evaluation of performance, and collegial status of faculty members are issues that the professional association should at least examine. Such examination could lead to recommendations that would ensure some support for non-traditional academics who are interested in improving their career status on campus. The inconsistencies in appointments of faculty development staff members may simply reflect the local culture of the campus, but they merit consideration by the field.

2) Travel. The limitations on travel budget funds also should be a consideration for the POD Network in planning costs associated with its annual conference. The amount of money allocated to a center's travel fund may range from $1,500-$3,500, allowing only one to four trips per center per year.

3) Center Directors. It is worth noting that almost half of all center directors have been in their positions for five years or less. This may indicate a professional development need that the POD Network could respond to by offering additional programs designed for new center directors.

4) Growth in the Future. Future directions identified by many centers include instructional technology or graduate student development programs. Secondary directions include learning outcomes assessment and peer review. These are areas that the POD Network members may be interested in as future conference topics.

5) Diversity. Finally, it is interesting to note that only one center reported diversity as a future area of new development. It would be useful to consider why this issue has been identified by a great many institutional missions but is not cited as a growth area for many programs. It may be that centers currently address diversity and, therefore, do not define this as a *new* direction. It may also be that other units on campus address diversity issues, in which case members of the POD Network may want to consider the role faculty/instructional developers might play in collaborating with these units. Additionally, if the need for mentoring diverse faculty is currently being addressed at some institutions, POD members may be interested in exploring the methods being used in such programs.

REFERENCES

Centra, J. A. (1976). *Faculty development practices in US colleges and universities.* Project Report, 76-30. Princeton, NJ: Educational Testing Service.

Chambers, J. (1998). *Teaching and learning centers in US higher education: Current and projected roles and services.* Unpublished report, Florida Community College, Jacksonville.

Crawley, A. L. (1995). Faculty development programs at research universities: Implications for senior faculty renewal. *To Improve the Academy, 14,* 65-90.

Erickson, G. (1986). A survey of faculty development practices. *To Improve the Academy, 5,* 182-196.

Gullatt, D. E., & Weaver, S. W. (1997, October). *Use of faculty development activities to improve the effectiveness of US institutions of higher education.* Paper presented at the meeting of the Professional and Organizational Development Network in Higher Education, Hines City, FL.

Contact:

Delivee L. Wright
121 Benton Hall
University of Nebraska, Lincoln
Lincoln, NE 68588-0623
(402) 472-3079
(402) 472-4932 (FAX)
dwright@unlinfo.unl.edu

Delivee L. Wright is Director of the Teaching and Learning Center and Associate Professor of Educational Administration at the University of Nebraska, Lincoln. She has worked in faculty development for 31 years and with the TLC for 25 years and taught a graduate seminar in college teaching. She has received a Kudo Award from the University of Nebraska Board of Regents for meritorious service and dedication to improving the quality of the university. She served as "Co-Executive Director" (President) of the POD Network in 1989-1991, was on the CORE Committee for 7 years, and has served on numerous committees. She is a frequent contributor to POD programs.

APPENDIX 17.1

INSTITUTIONS PARTICIPATING IN THIS SURVEY

Brigham Young University
Carnegie Mellon University
Case Western University
George Washington University
Indiana University
Kansas State University
Massachusetts Institute of Technology
Stanford University
Temple University
Texas Tech University
The Ohio State University
The University of Texas at Austin
University of Arkansas
University of California, Berkeley, GSI Teaching Resource Center
University of California, Berkeley, Educational Development
University of California, Davis
University of California, Los Angeles
University of California, Santa Cruz
University of Colorado, Boulder, Graduate Teacher Program
University of Delaware
University of Georgia
University of Illinois, Champaign-Urbana
University of Iowa
University of Kentucky
University of Massachusetts, Amherst
University of Michigan
Virginia Polytechnic Institute and State University
University of Nebraska, Lincoln
University of North Carolina, Chapel Hill
University of Oklahoma
University of Rhode Island
University of Wyoming
Vanderbilt University